Natural Encounters

Natural Encounters

Biking, Hiking, and Birding Through the Seasons

BRUCE M. BEEHLER

With Illustrations by John C. Anderton

Yale

UNIVERSITY PRESS

New Haven and London

Yale University Press books may be purchased in quantity for
educational, business, or promotional use. For information, please
e-mail sales.press@yale.edu (US office) or sales@yaleup.co.uk
(UK office).

Designed by Sonia Shannon.
Set in Bulmer type by IDS Infotech, Ltd.
Printed in the United States of America.

Library of Congress Control Number: 2018961776
ISBN 978-0-300-24348-2 (hardcover : alk. paper)
A catalogue record for this book is available from the British
Library.
This paper meets the requirements of ANSI/NISO Z39.48-1992
(Permanence of Paper).

10 9 8 7 6 5 4 3 2 1

To my wife, Carol, and our children,
Grace, Andrew, and Cary,
for joining me in embracing nature

Contents

List of Illustrations | ix

Preface | xi

Introduction | 1

Illustrations

Preface

In November 1981, I returned from doing ecological research in Papua New Guinea to start my first paying job—as scientific assistant to the secretary of the Smithsonian Institution, S. Dillon Ripley, a fellow ornithologist with a shared interest in the birds of the Asia-Pacific region. That was the start, for me, of more than three decades working in our nation's capital. I held positions at the Smithsonian Institution, Wildlife Conservation Society, US Department of State, Counterpart International, Conservation International, and National Fish and Wildlife Foundation before I retired to a tiny office in the back of the bird collection of the National Museum of Natural History, which sits on the National Mall across from the red sandstone Smithsonian castle.

The geographic focus of my work over the years spanned the globe, but my office remained in the DC area. I designed and supported science and conservation projects in places ranging from Papua New Guinea and Indonesia to Bosnia-Herzegovina, the Philippines, Sri Lanka, India, Zimbabwe, and Mexico. For my work, I traveled to more than thirty-five countries and attended world conservation congresses, scientific symposia, and intergovernmental treaty negotiations in such varied cities as

Paris, Bonn, Abu Dhabi, Brisbane, and Auckland. In spite of all the travels, home was the DC area, and while at home, I pursued my interest in natural history in and around Washington and up and down the East Coast.

During those decades of serving as a Washington-based scientist and conservationist, I never stopped being a *naturalist*. And even though most of my professional research focused on the study and conservation of forests and biodiversity of the developing world, I never stopped seeing wonder in the wildlife and the natural places of the Mid-Atlantic. I was able to practice my avocation as a local naturalist in three ways. First, five days a week, year-round, rain or shine, I biked to and from work through DC's greenways and parklands, keeping my eyes open for nature and recording what I observed. Second, I spent many weekends on nature outings with my family—collecting fossils, canoeing, hiking, birding, doing nature photography, and the like. And, third, I periodically made longer natural history field trips to various of the natural green spaces in the East, again keeping notes on the highlights of those travels farther afield.

This book is a synthesis of those encounters with nature, consolidated into the calendar year, beginning in summer, ranging through fall and winter, and finishing with the glories of spring. I offer up the best of nature across these twelve months, showing what each can offer nature lovers willing to head outside and be curious about their surroundings.

As well as a nature-oriented journey through the seasons, this book is something of a travel guide, describing where and when to tap the joys of nature in eastern North America. I describe locales worth visiting from central Maine to southern Florida and from southern New Jersey to northern Ohio. I hope that these examples will inspire readers to head off on natural adventures of their own over the calendar year.

And last, my story is an argument for what nature can give each of us if we allow it to enter our daily lives. Nature's restorative powers can enrich our lives with treasured moments of joy, peace, and celebration.

Map numbers (all on bottom map)

1 Anne Arundel County
2 Calvert County
3 South Mountain
4 Oakland
5 Swallow Falls State Park
6 Silver Lake
7 Backbone Mountain
8 Fairfax Stone
9 Bethany Beach
10 Rehoboth Beach
11 Burton's Island
12 Indian River Inlet
13 Huntley Meadows Park
14 Violette's Lock
15 McKee-Beshers Wildlife Management Area
16 Pennyfield Lock
17 Cape Henlopen
18 Randle Cliff
19 Chesapeake Beach
20 Mount Vernon
21 Little Bennett Regional Park

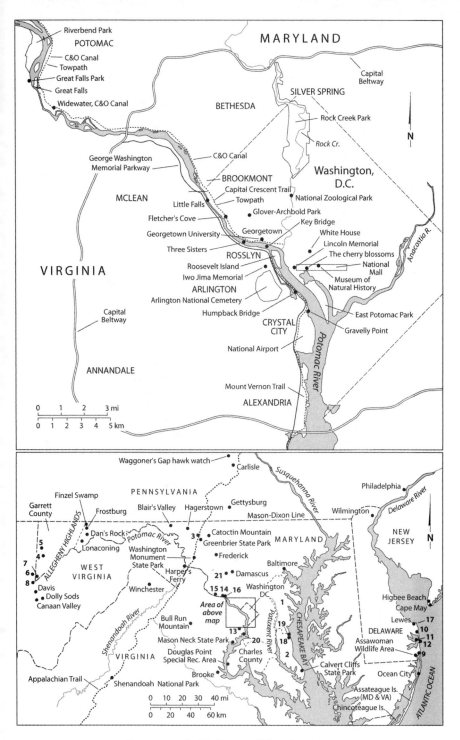

Locator map for Washington, DC, and environs

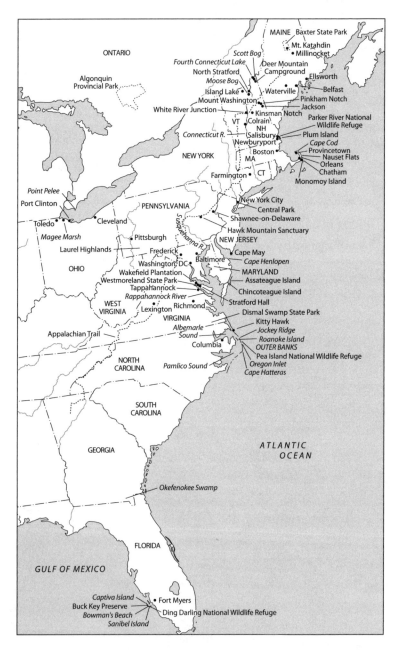

Locator map for East Coast sites visited

Natural Encounters

Introduction

Therefore I undertook to be monitor of the Washington seasons, when the government was not looking.

—LOUIS HALLE, *Spring in Washington*

One day it might be two adult Bald Eagles circling each other in the sky above Key Bridge in Georgetown, their heads and tails gleaming white in the sunlight. Another day it might be a ten-point buck White-tailed Deer on the towpath of the C&O Canal, letting me approach within a few feet as he forages quietly on the greenery beside the path. Or a Gray Fox that has, by some strange happenstance, found itself in morning traffic at a busy downtown intersection. It could be the doglike barks of a Barred Owl heard from our back porch or a young Five-lined Skink as it creeps up the slate steps to explore our front porch. Every day of the year brings some gift from nature that gives me private pleasure in the environs of the nation's capital.

Nature is all around us—to be detected and savored by anyone willing to pause and make the effort. When you are caught in snarled traffic on the Capital Beltway, isn't it nice to look up and see a big and burly Red-tailed Hawk circling in the blue? Wouldn't it be wonderful to be high above with that soaring raptor rather than stuck in traffic? We can't

1

float up into the blue, of course, but contemplating the sight of this graceful raptor overhead happily distracts us from the earthly travails of automotive gridlock.

By gathering these enjoyable natural encounters and recording them in a diary, it is possible, over time, to cobble together a record of the seasons—the annual comings and goings of nature and the natural phenomena that enrich our lives. And by following nature through its annual cycle, we develop relationships with all sorts of creatures that make their lives around us. The first time you encounter a Red Fox near its den along a woodsy path it is just a stranger. After encountering the same fox a number of times, this animal becomes an acquaintance. I have spoken quietly to these individual creatures when I have encountered them, and often, instead of dashing off, they have stood their ground and looked at me with limpid eyes. What were they thinking? I'll never know. But to stare, eye to eye, at a sentient wild being such as a Red Fox is a special experience, not to be forgotten. Most of urban society, in its rush to get to work or do its pressing errands, ignores and overlooks this recondite bonanza that awaits us, forgoing the satisfaction to be had from communing with the wild.

This book, then, is my personal encyclopedia of the joys of nature's seasons, based on daily experiences with nature and wildlife over the thirty-six years I have lived in the Washington, DC, area. Favorite diary entries have inspired launching points for short discursions built on particular observations in nature. My purpose is to paint a picture of wild nature over the calendar year to demonstrate how bountiful our seasons are when we include all of nature in the mix. From my experience, I can report that nature's treasures have enriched my life and made my days happier. Nature is a lifeline to a refuge of peace, filled with simple pleasures.

The seasons in the eastern United States are nature's annual pageant. Year after year the changing seasons are an ever-shifting backdrop to our lives. Our own experiences are like the written narrative that gets laid atop the colors, images, and sounds of nature—the video background—that together constitute the movie clips that make up life's memories. For instance, when I proposed marriage to my wife-to-be, Carol, in Lexington, Virginia, in late May 1982, I remember it as a hot day in late spring that gave the first intimations of a torrid Virginia summer. That little town in the Appalachian foothills was bursting with life—colored by banks of flowers and the deep green canopy of oaks and maples. Mockingbirds saluted us.

The memories of those special moments get deeply burned into our gray matter in large part because of the captivating sounds and scenery supplied by nature at that particular point on the astronomical calendar. Our memories are made whole by their earthly and heavenly contexts.

The varied seasons in the Mid-Atlantic region are the product of geography and physics. Because of our north temperate location and our positioning between the Appalachians to the west and the Chesapeake Bay and Atlantic Ocean to the east, seasons here are pronounced yet suffer substantial year-to-year uncertainty. And the location of Washington, DC, is such that it is neither northern nor southern: depending on the year, we might see a hot summer matched with a cold winter or a mild winter allied with a cool summer.

Spring is nature's most generous gift to the north temperate zone. It's what keeps the secret naturalists at their desks and working for the

Man rather than departing for parts west or south. I daydream about the arrival of spring for much of the year. Long in advance, I plan field trips to sample the best of it. Spring arrives and then suddenly it is over . . . done. That explosion of glorious life comes to an end only a few short weeks after the summer solstice in late June.

As a result, the naturalist in me sees the *beginning* of nature's year as the end of June, when the reproductive flourish of spring is done and when the sun starts to parch the lawns of the National Mall. At this time of the year, the world seems to pause and take a summer holiday that lasts a couple of months. Baby birds grow into adulthood. Butterflies lay eggs on their food plants. Oaks begin to grow their acorns for their masting in fall and winter. Humans head to seaside resorts to take an important annual break from the stresses of working life.

These summer doldrums drift well into September. By the autumnal equinox, there are the first stirrings of fall. In September, Broad-winged Hawks soar southwestward along the western ridgelines. Crickets begin to explore basements and make music in the gloaming. Monarch butterflies on the move appear in backyards and along coastlines in numbers. The days alternate between warm and humid versus cool and dry. School buses come to dominate the roadways in mornings and afternoons.

The late autumn comes with the first hard frost and the kick of the northwest wind in November and December blowing the last leaves off the White Oaks. Golden Eagles migrate down along the interior ridges of the high Alleghenies. Large flocks of American Robins show up at fruiting trees here and there. The acorns and hickory nuts fall for the deer, squirrels, and turkeys. A silence passes over the land, as the wildlife begin to bed down for winter. As the trees blaze orange and dark red, an abundance of Palm and Yellow-rumped Warblers and White-throated Sparrows and Dark-eyed Juncos blow in like autumn leaves, either on passage to places farther southwest or looking for a winter home right here.

Full winter usually arrives after Christmas and sets in seriously during January and February. At that time it either snows or it doesn't. In the Mid-Atlantic region, snowstorms are an uncertain commodity. Hard freezes come, though, and usually there are whole weeks or more when the Potomac is iced over, which is the sign of *real* winter in the DC area. At this point one sees down-clad groups braving the cold to skate on the C&O Canal, in timeless fashion. Winter finches in some years rain down on our feeders—mainly Pine Siskins and Purple Finches, but occasionally Common Redpolls and American Tree Sparrows. Backyards become havens for all sorts of wintering birds, dependent on the largesse of feeders to keep tiny avian bodies warm during long winter nights.

In February, invariably, there are thaws—advance notice of the coming spring. By late February the Fish Crows are softly calling their spring songs, a sure sign of better times to come. March brings the Northern Cardinal back to full song, then chickadees and titmice join in to announce that the sun is now peaking higher in the sky. The early spring is an uncertain time for nature and humankind. What weather will next week bring? One never knows. The trees remain naked and stark, yet some days bring a touch of warmth, with a future promise of more. Crocuses and daffodils bloom in neighborhood yards. But then a sudden storm drops a blanket of soggy snow, bound to melt within a day or two.

Midspring begins by April 1 in the DC area no matter the date of the vernal equinox. The earliest wildflowers bloom under still-dormant

Spring Peeper

forest canopies. The resident breeding birds, such as American Robins and Tufted Titmice, are busily singing to stake out their territories. The choruses of Spring Peepers are starting up in the low, damp spots. Flocks of Common Grackles and Red-winged Blackbirds move through the neighborhood, often aggressively commandeering a backyard feeder for a few hours before disappearing to parts unknown. The shad and herring start their run up the Potomac. And the weather zigzags from warm to cold without regard to commuter convenience.

At last comes full spring, the grand finale of nature's year. It starts around the first of May and continues until the solstice in late June. This is the season for which all naturalists anxiously wait. During this period we see the massive influx of migratory songbirds—warblers, vireos, flycatchers, and thrushes. We also see the emergence of butterflies of all kinds—swallowtails, fritillaries, sulphurs, anglewings, skippers, hairstreaks, and others. The trees rush to complete the leafing that started in midspring with their bud-break. Frogs and toads crank up the volume on humid evenings. And the last of the wildflowers bloom in shady gullies facing northeastward. At times, the tree pollen can be overwhelming. But the high sun and warm, bright days make it all worthwhile.

Then, before you know it, it is over, and the doldrums of early summer arrive to bring forth the lazy, glossy days where this annual cycle was initiated. When I was a child, this twelve-month circuit took a painfully long time to repeat itself. Now that I am a naturalist in my sixties, the year in nature remains just as sweet but has been compressed and speeded up. Now it seems that a month zips by in the blink of an eye. The only advantage of this geriatric acceleration of time is that I no longer have to wait so long for spring to come. But instead I must engage each spring with increased attention and care, because it passes so quickly. I must get out every spring morning to take it all in and record its annual surprises. For no matter how many times spring is experienced, there is something new to see as well as a hundred familiar things to savor from years past. That mix of the novel and the deeply familiar is a wonderful combination, and it keeps each naturalist grateful for it all.

In my narrative, the geography of the city of Washington and the Potomac River predominates. Most discussions are based on observations that I made while biking along the towpath of the Chesapeake and Ohio Canal from Bethesda, Maryland, to either downtown Washington, DC, or Arlington, Virginia, to get to my work office at that point in my career. These sylvan bike routes, in which I still regularly engage, give me personal access to the canal, the Potomac, the National Mall, and more—the green spaces that make our nation's capital so nature-friendly.

In the chapters that follow I touch on all sorts of issues—interesting species, urban wilding, the local impacts of climate change, the history of deforestation of the East, and other topics raised by my encounters with nature. I have also included longer entries that recount local field trips to destinations within sixty or ninety minutes' drive to collect fossils, photograph Timber Rattlers, watch birds, or pick a pumpkin in an autumn field. These give readers an idea of the options for nature-based weekend outings within striking range of the city.

Last, I include a number of accounts of longer excursions to very special places for nature that are a one- or two-day drive from Washington. These places should be on every nature-loving person's bucket list. These are nature's East Coast hotspots.

After thirty-six years here, I am fonder than ever of the Washington, DC, area for its ready access to nature. Because the capital city is nestled between the Potomac and Anacostia Rivers on the Potomac's fall line, and because the Blue Ridge foothills lie some twenty miles west and the Chesapeake Bay the same distance east, Washington is a place where nature persists—even abounds—sharing a fertile coastal plain with more than six million people. That is a remarkable thing, and speaks to nature's resilience.

The greater DC environs provide ready access to virtually all of the major environmental and physiographic features that underpin a natural place of interest in the eastern United States—forests, mountains, rivers, freshwater wetlands, major estuaries, coastal beaches, sandy barrier islands, and the deep sea. All of the most interesting natural destinations include one or more of these features. Some combine several—usually, the more the better. For instance, where the granitic outcrops that extend southeastward from the Appalachians meet the Potomac, we find Great Falls, which today features verdant parkland, a rocky gorge, and serious whitewater. Farther west, where the Shenandoah and Potomac Rivers cut through the Appalachians, lies Harper's Ferry, one of the most beautiful piedmont landscapes in the Mid-Atlantic, with plenty of Civil War history thrown in.

Washington would perhaps be rather ho-hum but for its streams and rivers. Rock Creek cuts north-south through the city, and Rock Creek Park is DC's largest greenway—today home to White-tailed Deer, foxes, Coyotes, and other urban wildlife. The Anacostia River courses through DC's eastern sector and provides green space and marshland in an urban setting. The mighty Potomac, of course, defines the city's western border and brings so much to its outdoor environment. Who could imagine Washington without the Potomac? Draining the Allegheny highlands of West Virginia and Maryland, the Potomac is one of the major rivers of the East and constitutes the defining physiographic and environmental feature of Washington, DC, proper.

Forested landscapes also are abundant. Most of the waterways are protected by forested rights-of-way, and many forest tracts have been set aside in parklands scattered across the region. This is all the more remarkable given that by the end of the Civil War, most of the populated land in the Mid-Atlantic was entirely cleared of forest. Since then, forest regeneration has been prodigious, and there is more forest cover in the eastern United States today than could be found in either 1900 or even 1800. Urbanization has led to the abandonment of large expanses of less productive cropland and pastureland over the past century and has inadvertently brought about the recovery of the eastern forests.

Freshwater wetlands abound in the watersheds east of Washington—especially along the Anacostia and the Patuxent catchments and, of course, throughout the western reaches of the Chesapeake Bay. These lead into brackish estuaries in the low country to the east and southeast. The Chesapeake is the largest coastal embayment on the East Coast and, as such, defines the landscape of waterways and marshes interdigitated among the burgeoning suburbs of Anne Arundel and Calvert Counties.

Ancient mountain ridges and valleys dominate the landscape to the west. The first prominent ridge northwest of the city is Sugarloaf, and then there is Catoctin Mountain, followed by South Mountain. Each is aligned southwest to northeast. Between each is a fertile piedmont valley hemmed in by the high ridgelines. These regular and forested ridges pile up, one after the other, in a series that eventually leads up to the Allegheny front, which tops four thousand feet in West Virginia. Where western Maryland meets West Virginia, about three hours' drive from DC, one ascends to a high plateau that forms the continental divide separating the Potomac catchment from that of the Ohio River, which flows southwestward into the Mississippi. The broad and tidal Potomac, at the city's southwestern border, thus rises slowly and inexorably to the high Alleghenies and links the warm and fertile coastal plain to the cold interior and the East Coast's western frontier. This, then, is Washington's physiographic and natural setting—strategically situated between the old but rugged Appalachians and the youthful and gentle Chesapeake.

Closer to home, the city exhibits notable features for the local nature lover. The most important of these is the course of the Potomac. Just northwest of DC, the river passes through a rocky gorge of metamorphosed sandstones and mudstones from Great Falls down to Little Falls and to Fletcher's Cove in the city proper. Below Fletcher's the Potomac broadens and deepens, with a set of rocks known as the Three Sisters, a reminder of this river's rocky passage upstream. The Potomac's west bank features a high palisade that starts at Rosslyn, Virginia, and continues northwestward through Arlington and McLean. This is mirrored on the DC side above Georgetown, forming the gorge of the Potomac.

At Key Bridge and Roosevelt Island, the river becomes tidal and changes in character entirely, as does the landscape, which becomes low and flat—the exception being the height of land on the Virginia side, home to Arlington House (formerly the Lee-Custis Mansion) and Arlington National Cemetery. Historically, the headwaters of the tidal Potomac defined the uppermost access of seagoing ships, and it was here that the port of Georgetown was established in the 1750s. Georgetown, today a popular upscale neighborhood, predates the establishment of the District of Columbia, the site of which was selected by George Washington in 1790 and which was formally established by an act of Congress in 1801.

As with virtually every city along the Eastern Seaboard, Washington was situated because of the critical importance of sailing ships as the most reliable means of moving goods and people at that time. In addition, George Washington envisioned the Potomac as a gateway to the interior. He wanted the new nation's capital to trade and communicate not only with Europe and the Caribbean but with the developing American interior. This was brilliant foresight. Before long, canal-building projects began the struggle to make Washington's dream a reality. Washington himself invested in at least one of these canal-building efforts—to make the Potomac navigable by barge to the western frontier.

President Washington commissioned French engineer and architect Pierre Charles L'Enfant to design the city. L'Enfant's plan had strong

European influences, including squares, circles, broad avenues, and a major greenspace now known as the National Mall. Roger Tory Peterson has written, "The original plan called for fine buildings enhanced by broad vistas, accentuated by avenues of trees." This initial design was completed by Andrew Ellicott, a surveyor of the Mason-Dixon Line and of the original boundaries of the District of Columbia. Both L'Enfant and Ellicott found the design and creation of the capital city a contentious political process, and both departed the effort well before it was finalized. It seems that DC politics then was little different than it is today, human nature being what it is.

An act of Congress in 1899 limited the height of Washington's buildings to 110 feet, which has greatly influenced the nature of the modern city. The restricted building height, in combination with the abundant green space, has helped Washington retain its open and inviting character. The 1,750-acre Rock Creek Park was created by an act of Congress in 1890. It has been joined by an array of parks—Glover-Archbold Park, Battery Kemble Park, Montrose Park, Dumbarton Oaks Park, Palisades Park, Meridian Hill Park, and more.

DC is a naturalist's favored stomping ground. There are places of interest in every direction. It is one of the reasons that Louis Halle, as a State Department bureaucrat and closet naturalist, fell in love with Washington, writing his classic *Spring in Washington*. Published in 1947, the book tells the story of Halle's bicycle-powered wanderings in and around post–World War II DC. It is an evocative compilation of a naturalist's observations and philosophical musings on nature's seasons in an urban setting. In it, Halle sought to demonstrate to his incurious fellow office workers that nature was still all around them—to be appreciated for the inspiration it can impart. Many from my parents' generation read and reread Halle's book. Today *Spring in Washington* is little known, in spite of its wisdom and erudition. Halle's writing has inspired me, and in these pages I revisit many of the themes he raised.

Like Halle, I have spent many days in Washington biking in search of nature. And like him, I have been witness to natural phenomena that have enlivened those days when I saw special features—a beaver, a turtle, a loon, a comet. As Halle knew, a bicycle is far better than a car for searching out nature. Unlike a car, the bike is quiet and slow-moving, and it allows the biker to stop anywhere to take a closer look at something of interest. Moreover, exploring nature by bike allows one to cover a great deal more ground and thus see a lot more of nature than traveling by foot.

So, here, I have taken it as my mandate to reexamine the story Halle told in 1947 and to add some dimensions related to the passing of time, the changing world, and our evolving cityscape. I return to the eternal themes raised by Halle but set them in early twenty-first-century Washington. I have expanded the geographic scope of inquiry by including narratives of a selection of natural history field trips within driving distance of DC. In this way, I can better tell the story of the seasons up and down the East Coast, which is nothing less than the gift of life itself.

Late June and July—Sunny, Lazy Days

> Walking in the silence of the night in the midst of a thousand fireflies is an
> ethereal, almost spiritual experience.
>
> —EDWIN WAY TEALE, *A Walk Through the Year*

It is bittersweet to see the passing of spring. For those of us past middle age there comes the recognition that there are only a finite number of springs in a life. Still, there is solace in knowing that the next season is summer and that the high sun beating down on the tennis court will produce a happy sweat and quickly warm up tight and aging leg muscles of those of us with silvering hair. Some residents like to complain about the heat and humidity of the Washington, DC, summer; yet most secretly love summer's burn, with its long-lit evenings and weekend getaways, capped in August by a week or two at a beach somewhere along the Atlantic Coast. Yes, the heat and humidity are a nuisance during the work week, but we would not trade it for anything on the weekend, when hot summer days make us feel young again. These are lazy times for the naturalist, but there is a sense of satisfaction in having finished with the spring's early morning field trips and that stern alarm clock set for a predawn wake-up.

In fact, the epiphany that brought about my birth as a naturalist and bird lover took place in early summer at a small Baltimore County park in the late 1950s. My mother took my brother, Bill, and me to the park one muggy Saturday evening for a picnic. We roasted hotdogs on a small fire and sat at a picnic table above the lake, surrounded by a smattering of tall trees. I was a timid and frail eight-year-old, literally afraid of rain and a bit uncertain about the wisdom of this expedition on an evening when a rainstorm might have been on the horizon. I can't recall, but I might have even been cowering *under* the picnic table, thinking about rain and my fears (I was frightened of just about everything at that point in my life). Anyway, I heard a strange bird calling out just above us, and looking up, I saw a glorious winged creature, perched improbably on the side of a dead trunk (how do they do that?). It had a bright red crown and nape and a profusely barred black-and-white back. It was the most beautiful bird I had ever seen—an adult male Red-bellied Woodpecker! I was a birder and naturalist from that day on. And I started on the road that eventually led me to spend my career in rainforests. It seems that the bird cured my fear of rain. Here's another reason I start this book at the summer solstice. It's when I started my career as an ornithologist. It's when real life began for me and my fears started to be overcome by my fascinations. Take-home point: careers don't always begin in the classroom.

For the summer, we naturalists tend to take a break and focus on nature in the backyard. That means Red-shouldered Hawks circling and keening overhead, starlings feeding their begging young on the back lawn, the first scold of the Annual Cicada from some tree limb not far off, and the arrival of the fireflies in the velvet darkness of the evenings. That's good enough, because it's summer.

It is now the end of June, and I am biking up the towpath of the C&O Canal, with the sun high even though it is late afternoon. I see other bikers stopped along the path, picking and eating wild blackberries—one of the pastimes of early summer. The blackberry patches thrive in locations where sunlight is abundant at ground level and encourage the more wild-minded bikers to stop and forage. This is one of those direct gifts from nature that everyone can appreciate and many of us cannot resist. Isn't it sinfully fun to consume wild fruit gathered by the Potomac on a warm day in late June?

The summer solstice has come and gone, and we now kiss spring good-bye and welcome the beginning of the Washington summer. Much of spring's productivity provides payoffs in summer. An evening doubles tennis game in Arlington, Virginia, across the Potomac from my Brookmont neighborhood, is yet another opportunity to encounter the fruits of wild nature. First, the tennis foursome is spooked by a Barred Owl winging over the court. The bright court lights illuminate the big ghostly form passing over the court on silent wings. Then, a few minutes later, four Hercules Beetles arrive, one after the other. Two males and two females materialize out of the woodsy darkness and plunk down onto our court—lured in and then bedazzled by the tall court lights. One male is more than two-and-a-half inches long. My frightened tennis mates see these oversized arthropods as dangerous vermin and are amazed when I bend over and pick them up. Holding the imposing but harmless beetles in my hand, feeling their sharp-spined legs strain to escape my gentle grip, I stop the game and explain to my tennis mates that these

Hercules Beetle

beetles are a rare wonder of nature. This is the very first time I have encountered them in life. I knew of this species only through the 1956 Golden Nature Guide to insects, which I had memorized as a child curious about nature. And here I am, communing with these curious creatures a half-century after I first read about them.

The male Hercules Beetle has a pair of glossy, blackish curving horns projecting forward from its face—a larger one above, and smaller one below, forming bowed vertical pincers. The female lacks this prominent and threatening feature, presumably deployed by males to battle each other for the right to mate with a gravid female. The beetle's glossy shell is painted a muted olive-beige with profuse handsome dark markings. This sturdy arthropod is indeed an artful work of nature. The adults consume plant sap and their larvae live buried underground, subsisting on rotting wood. I gather up and place the two males and two females together outside the court so they can get to know one another and, hopefully, produce progeny to boost the local population. My philistine tennis partners shake their heads and tease me about my arcane interests. They are the ones missing out.

It is the very end of June, and two Mallard hens are shepherding batches of tiny ducklings in the shallows of the C&O Canal. These must be second broods because local nesting by Mallards starts in mid-March. Although naturalists tend to ignore the handsome yet hyperabundant Mallards, the fuzzy little peepers are as adorable as any animal babies, with their chocolate-and-gold furlike plumage. I want to pick them up and cup them in my hands, hold my hands up to my ears, and listen to their little sounds. Such are the babies of precocial birds. It is the glory and seduction of fresh young life, radiating across species boundaries. I can see and feel what the mother Mallard must feel.

Here along the canal, the Mallards are outnumbered by families of Canada Geese, each with two large and defensive parents, plus a gaggle of rather ugly young of the spring, no longer little peepers yet still not yet fully transitioned to their proper adult plumage. These family groups, a product of nests placed along the adjacent Potomac, spend time on the towpath because of the abundance of grass to graze along the canal's verges. Feeding voraciously on this grassy resource leads to the production of an abundance of goose poop, which litters the graveled towpath—relatively harmless, but annoying to the many joggers and walkers. Hence the beef against the mess produced by so-called golf course geese, which will come up in various discussions later in the book. These goose families tend to take over the towpath, which is a commuting lane for many bikers. One must slow and edge around the hissing parents, their wings spread and lowered and their demeanor quite fierce.

This time of year, down along the Potomac, few songbirds are singing (most are silently caring for nestlings). But this morning I hear all three of the local nesting warbler species along the canal—Northern Parula, Yellow-throated Warbler, and Prothonotary Warbler. That's a birding hat trick! It is satisfying to hear these three wood warblers singing along the river in late June. These are the reliable three I come to depend on hearing from late April until the end of spring. For most urban dwellers, the many species of wood warblers are primarily a spring and fall experience, as they pass through on their way between their breeding grounds in the boreal forests of Canada and their winter homes in the tropics. My being able to bike to work along the canal towpath and hear the ascending buzz of the tiny Parula or the syrupy sweet, slow musical slurs of a Yellow-throated Warbler or the *swit swit swit swit swit* of the Prothonotary makes my day. The pleasure that these encounters generate is what economists term *existence value*—the measurable enrichment of our lives by the simple existence of something we love. My having resident wood warblers singing for me to hear on the way to work makes my day more pleasant and keeps me happy. I am thus OK with my hefty monthly mortgage payment for a house in a woodsy section of Bethesda by the Potomac, which provides access to daily dividends from nature.

My son, Andrew, receives a smartphone image from his friend Brent Kreutzberg. It shows a small Black Bear mauling a bird feeder on Brent's back deck, about a mile from our house. Later that day, the wandering bear is captured alive in northwestern Washington and then transported, unharmed, for release to a wooded area well beyond DC's western suburbs. The appearance of the yearling Black Bear in Bethesda is a story of urban rewilding. It also exemplifies seasonal wandering by a juvenile mammal leaving its mother's home range and seeking its own place to live. In Louis Halle's day, no Black Bears wandered into the Washington suburbs. The East Coast's great faunal extermination pulse started with the arrival of European settlers in the 1600s and concluded by the end of the Civil War, when most of the accessible forests had been decimated and every edible bird and mammal shot for food or pelt. Hungry settlers and farmers wiped out all but the smallest and most abundant game species. Only now, 150 years after the end of the Civil War, has wild game begun to creep back into the suburban woodlands that have grown up since the mid-twentieth century.

The wooded ridges of the Appalachians, from Georgia to Maine, today host decent populations of Black Bears, and each spring, mother bears throw out their adult young, who then must wander off in search of a place to make an independent life. Finding an unoccupied and productive territory is a pretty messy business, and the young bears wander far and wide looking for a suitable new home. These days it is not uncommon to read reports of a young bear in a suburban backyard in the East. Wandering bears are being joined by other wildlife—the hyperabundant White-tailed Deer as well as Wild Turkey, American Beaver, Coyote, Red and Gray Fox, Striped Skunk, and more. Some urban residents resent this resurgence of wildlife—after all, Coyotes eat miniature poodles and deer eat expensive yard plantings. But many of us salute the return of these creatures. Welcome to the new wild. . . .

By the time July arrives, the best of spring has passed in the low country of DC. For those greedy for more spring, the options are to head uphill or head northward. My solution is to head northwestward and uphill— onto the Allegheny Plateau of western Maryland and West Virginia. My daughter Cary and I go on a photo safari in search of spring, and we find it three hours by car west of DC, via Interstates 70 and 68. First stop, Frostburg, Maryland—a perfect destination to escape the heat of DC in July. Frostburg is a sleepy and rural college town perched two thousand feet above sea level on the eastern edge of the Allegheny Plateau. After settling in to our lodging in Frostburg, we visit nearby Finzel Swamp, a Nature Conservancy reserve that protects a rare tamarack bog typical of northern New England. There is a boardwalk that crosses the bog, which is great for nature photography. Various interesting flowering plants, butterflies, and birds can be found here. Big clumps of Interrupted Fern adorn the wet woodland edge at the head of the boardwalk. A Northern Waterthrush sings its rapid-fire jumble of a song from the middle of the bog, and an Alder Flycatcher buzzes *fee-BEE-o* in a thicket of alders. The blue sky is studded with small white clouds. On a July afternoon, things are typically pretty quiet in a bog, but there are beetles and skippers visiting several wildflowers, and we spend our time happily photographing these accessible subjects.

Nature photography is one of those outdoor pastimes that adds another dimension to recreational travel and helps the observer to get to know some of the more recondite subjects of the natural world. Just as a pair of binoculars helps a birder see more birds, a camera pushes the naturalist to look more closely at the world. In particular, a macro lens draws the naturalist into a world of small creatures typically hidden from general view. One starts examining every flower for a foraging native bee species or a cryptic spider waiting for the arrival of prey. Or there might be a mantis or walking stick, motionless on a green stem, blending in with the vegetation. Seeing is one part eyesight, one part mindfulness, and one part curiosity.

The next morning, we rise an hour before first light in order to shoot the sunrise from Dan's Rock, a few miles south of Frostburg. The receptionist at our motel had told us this was a locally famous place to witness a beautiful sunrise. As we exit the motel, the dark clouds in the eastern sky are lit up in shades of maroon and purple. We have to hurry for the sunrise. I drive to the summit, and we climb up onto the graffiti-spattered granite boulders that provide a marvelous view down into the valley to the east that is backed by rugged ridges obscured by veils of gray mist. Because of the thick cloud cover, sunrise never materializes. So instead we shoot images of row after row of misty ridges tinted green, olive, maroon, and gray. The combination of the brooding clouds and mountaintop vegetation makes for some sublime colors. The ridges have the look of lines of big combers coming in off a late autumn sea on eastern Long Island. Both are mesmerizing, but for different reasons. The combers are truly ephemeral, each lasting less than a minute. The Appalachian ridges have stood the test of deep time. And yet both in their own way create a sense of awe.

The rest of the weekend follows this pattern. We chase down interesting venues for nature photography and keep busy from dawn to dusk. Our next stop is the town of Lonaconing, Maryland, to photograph an iron furnace constructed in 1837 of large sandstone blocks, with a graceful brick-lined arch opening at its bottom. Farther down the road we come upon great heaps of hardwood logs piled adjacent to a paper mill with tall smokestacks billowing white smoke. The mill is nestled in a deep valley surrounded by forest-clad mountains. There will be no shortage any time soon for fodder for this operation. Next, we stop at the sight of a flock of Great Spangled Fritillary butterflies visiting a small puddle at the roadside. Once out of the car, my daughter points out a small green blob beside the pavement, which turns out to be a fledgling Scarlet Tanager, presumably being fed periodically by its parents. I am able to kneel down and photograph this odd little ball of fluff without causing the baby bird any apparent concern. It still has natal down forming comically tall brows above each eye.

We are in Garrett County, Maryland—the land of mountaintop coal mining. Why is the coal perched preferentially on the mountain summits? It isn't. It seems that the fastest and cheapest way to extract the coal is to blast off the mountain summit and then deploy heavy equipment to drag away the overburden to reveal the coal seams. We spend considerable time wandering around the edges of one of these great open pit operations—photographing mountains of rubble, close-ups of the glossy bituminous coal, and taking in the scale of the environmental devastation.

A most remarkable ornithological outcome of this coal mining process is that where the mountaintop strip mines have been closed, then regraded and revegetated in coarse grass, this recovering habitat becomes a mix of grassland and scrub, which is the prime habitat for two of Maryland's rarest breeding bird species: the Golden-winged Warbler and Henslow's Sparrow. Both require early successional grassland–shrubland to prosper, and the postrecovery result of this horrific coal extraction operation ironically offers just what the birds need. Of course, this rather minor species conservation benefit does not offset the massive environmental harm done to regional watershed and groundwater purity.

In the afternoon, we shift base to Oakland, Maryland, an hour's drive southwest of Frostburg. After checking into a motel, we visit Swallow Falls State Park and its featured falls. The falls are worth visiting mainly because of the lovely, dark hemlock glades that one passes through to visit the less-than-overwhelming water feature. Some of these Eastern Hemlocks are among the oldest and tallest trees in Maryland. Ancient hemlock stands can be found tucked away in shady glens here and there in the uplands of the East. They survived the holocaust of deforestation because the species was never a favored timber tree, and often they were hidden and, in essence, forgotten by the timber barons, who greedily focused on the highest-value timber species. These small remnant stands of giant trees are the best examples of virgin forest in the East.

The Eastern Hemlock grove that stands beside the Youghiogheny River near Swallow Falls has never been logged, and its oldest trees are more than three hundred years old. The heavy evergreen canopy creates a dark, damp, and gloom-filled understory environment that causes hikers to pause, take a breath, and look up in silent reverence. There is something about entering a grove of ancient trees that is much like being in a five-hundred-year-old European cathedral. Cary is quiet and impressed, as am I. The silence is broken only by the song of a Black-throated Green Warbler. The primitive and woodsy scent produced by these ancient trees holds us in our tracks for a moment longer; it is the scent of an earlier era.

Now these hemlock groves are under threat, from the Hemlock Woolly Adelgid, a tiny, sap-sucking true bug that has arrived in our country from East Asia. It was introduced to the western United States in the 1920s, but it arrived in the East in the 1950s, discovered near Richmond, Virginia, accidentally brought in from Japan. This diminutive pest kills hemlocks and has decimated hemlock groves through much of the Mid-Atlantic. In the East, it continues to expand its range northward and westward. It will be a sad day for Swallow Falls State Park when this ancient grove of hemlocks succumbs to this novel pest.

On our third day, we head from westernmost Maryland into adjacent West Virginia. Crossing the state line, we reach Silver Lake, headwaters of the Youghiogheny River, and home to Our Lady of the Pines church, the smallest place of Christian worship in the Lower Forty-Eight. Adjacent to the tiny church is a microscopic post office (America's smallest) and a small mountain lake and campground. Daughter Cary is entranced by the two historically diminutive structures. We find no explanation for why these are here in this isolated corner of the world.

Up the road several miles from Silver Lake is the trailhead for the footpath to the summit of Backbone Mountain, Maryland's highest summit. It's peculiar that one has to climb Maryland's highest mountain from a trailhead in West Virginia. We hike this in an hour. The high point of Backbone Mountain, known (mysteriously) as Hoye-Crest, stands at 3,360 feet above sea level. A male Hooded Warbler sings near the summit, apparently defending a mountaintop breeding territory.

Back in the car, following Route 219 (the Seneca Trail) southward to the summit pass on Backbone Mountain, we come to a large wind farm, with dozens of huge white towers topped by giant windmills. We stop and photograph this environmental and visual desecration of the Allegheny front. These tall white monstrosities pollute the view for miles around. In addition, the construction of these ridgetop wind farms in this region resulted in broadscale devastation of sensitive mountaintop habitats that deserved state protection. When rotating, the giant devices make a low haunting sound that further disturbs the peace of this upland wilderness. We are happy to get away from this unfortunate intrusion of technology on once-sacred mountain heights.

We now head down tiny back roads in search of the Fairfax Stone, which marks the headwaters of the Potomac River, in northeastern West Virginia. The original stone was set in place by Colonel Peter Jefferson (Thomas Jefferson's father), in order to settle a land dispute involving the Sixth Lord Fairfax and Great Britain's Privy Council regarding the Northern Neck Land Grant of 1649. The original stone (presumably a natural stone in place on the site) has been lost and today has been replaced by a large flat rock with an inscribed metal historical marker placed upon it. Given how difficult it is to locate this highland spot these days, one can only imagine the travails visited upon the Jefferson party back in the 1700s. Today, much of this mountaintop area is a recovered surface coal mine, a far cry from the grand forest that probably stood here during Jefferson's travels, more than two centuries ago. Nonetheless, it is a special place to visit, and it most definitely is the end of the road— the tiny dirt track leading to the stone ends here. It is cool and sunny and springlike at the stone, and the highlights of our visit to it are a fluttering cluster of Aphrodite Fritillary butterflies and a single Red Eft—the

Day-Glo orange immature form of the widespread Appalachian sala-mander known as the Eastern Newt. This three-inch-long amphibian is moving through a wet spot near the butterflies, perhaps on its migration out of its larval territory. We spend some time happily photographing at close range the brightly colored salamander and the fluttering cluster of butterflies.

Returning to the paved road, we head south to the local winter sports town of Davis for lunch. At this point we turn our focus to Black Bears. Cary wants to photograph a Black Bear, and so do I. I ask the youngsters lounging at the restaurant about bears, and they say they see them regularly. In hopes of seeing a bear, we head to Canaan Valley, perched in a wild expanse of high country in northeastern West Virginia and home to a national wildlife refuge. Much of the valley floor is refuge land—a mix of open marshland and conifer forest. It has a strong New England feel to it. The elevation makes it a snow-accumulator in winter, hence the presence of two ski areas here. During the late spring it is a favored hangout for Black Bears. Today there are an estimated twelve thousand Black Bears in West Virginia (where it is the state mammal) and another two thousand or more in Maryland. I speak to a ranger at the wildlife refuge headquarters and am told we are a few weeks late—the spring dispersal of young bears has already happened.

Undaunted, we exit the valley and then turn onto an unpaved back road that leads up across the high plateau of Dolly Sods, the wildest corner of the West Virginia highlands, set within the Monongahela National Forest. The stony, unpaved road up to the height of land is slow going as we zig and zag through northern hardwood forest. We encoun-ter a Ruffed Grouse at the bend of the road—but no Black Bear. Atop the plateau are lovely vistas across rock-strewn grasslands, mountain laurel thickets, and stands of spruce and pine rising above the dwarfed hardwood stands of cherry and maple. Here we are on top of the world, with no evidence of civilization but for the dirt road. No wind turbines here, thankfully. A stiff breeze is blowing and the temperature here, above four thousand feet, is in the sixties. The season here atop Dolly Sods is at least a month behind that of Washington, DC.

From here we descend slowly eastward, down the switch-backing gravel road, until we connect with a paved country road that leads us back toward civilization—rural Virginia. We stop to get ice cream and to window-shop in the tree-shaded pedestrian mall in downtown Winchester, Virginia. This is where General Stonewall Jackson established his army's headquarters for the winter of 1861–62. After taking in the sights, we push homeward on Sunday afternoon, back into the sweltering heat and humidity of DC. Sweating profusely while unpacking the car, I think wistfully about that cool high plateau in West Virginia, three hours to the west, where spring still holds sway.

Each Fourth of July we like to take in the fireworks display on the National Mall. For years we celebrated with our children, but now they go off with their own tribe to celebrate in their own way, so we are left to our own devices. This year, Carol and I bike down the canal towpath to Water Street in Georgetown, under the Whitehurst Freeway. We have a leisurely dinner at a crowded and festive Georgetown watering hole, and then, as dusk approaches, we walk down Rock Creek Expressway (closed to auto traffic for the evening event) to the Kennedy Center's south patio, where we join a group of families who traditionally assemble here for the fireworks. It is a warm and muggy night, and people are streaming about, looking for the best position to settle and take in the spectacle. In previous years we have watched the fireworks from the Iwo Jima Memorial in Virginia, from near the main State Department building in downtown DC, and from the roof of the American History Museum on the Mall. There are plenty of great vantage points to take in the pyrotechnics.

As we wait for the fireworks to start, we note small groups of Black-crowned Night-Herons passing overhead, heading to nocturnal foraging sites along the Potomac (because of their slow wingbeat, they remind me of the flying monkeys in *The Wizard of Oz*). These birds have a colonial roost in a stand of tall trees at the National Zoological Park, situated up Rock Creek a ways. Seeing groups of these compact and broad-winged herons pass overhead in the evening is always a bit of a surprise. Most would take them for crows, probably, though they are slightly larger. The herons have adapted well to urban life, and they move about unnoticed, mainly. They are part of the DC wildlife underground.

Once the fireworks start, we see flocks of European Starlings heading westward, crossing the Potomac into Virginia. These sociable songbirds are spooked by the noise, smoke, and flashing light. The twenty minutes of fireworks are fantastic—each year is more extreme than the preceding—but, for some reason, the fireworks seem but a minor part of this traditional summer evening, in which the process is so much of the event. Biking in on the towpath, we are always filled with anticipation. Everybody heading into town is in a great mood and is friendly. Dining out makes the night special as well. And traipsing home in the dark by bicycle is always an adventure. It's one of those outdoor events most everybody in town enjoys—an important seasonal marker of the calendar year, announcing the true start of summer.

Speaking of summer, the arrival of the Annual Cicadas is a natural phenomenon that generally peaks in August, but the early birds among them are shrilling by the Fourth of July. The rising buzz of the Annual Cicada has signaled summer to me for six decades. Every July, when I hear the first cicada, I am drawn back to the hot and humid childhood summers in Baltimore—a time without air conditioning, when the world seemed to be a hotter place. The droning cicadas signaled to our brains that it was time to head to the community pool.

More than a hundred species of cicadas (formerly called harvest flies) inhabit the United States. The adult female of the familiar Annual Cicada (or Dog-day Cicada) deposits her fertilized eggs under the bark of small branches of broad-leaved trees. This typically causes the branchlets to dry and fall to the ground. The young larvae hatch out and then burrow into the ground, where they feed for four years on the sap of tree roots before emerging as adults. The larvae of some cicada species remain underground as long as seventeen years. These extraordinarily long development times appear to be an evolutionary mechanism to starve out and then overwhelm their predators. A similar reproductive phenomenon occurs with some oaks, which synchronously produce a large crop of acorns only every few years. Following several years of small acorn crops, populations of squirrels and other seed predators (like Wild Turkeys) will be relatively low. Thus, when the big acorn crop emerges, a larger percentage of the seeds will survive to grow into trees rather than be consumed by the greedy seed predators. A massive emergence of cicadas every seventeen years will have the same predator-swamping effect. In spite of its long underground life, a free-flying adult cicada lives only about a week after emergence: just enough time to mate and produce the next generation of cicadas. This is another extreme by-product of natural selection—producing long-lived larvae and single-use throwaway adults.

Like the shrilling of the Annual Cicada, another iconic sound of summer is the begging call of juvenile European Starlings, pestering their parents in the quest to be fed. This is particularly commonplace on well-trimmed lawns or expansive greens in eastern cities. Here, starling families forage for invertebrates and seeds in the grass, the youngsters trailing behind the adults, begging rather than hunting for themselves. Seeing this, people my age think of their own children, who for years stood by while dinner was being prepared, while the table was being set, while the table was being cleared after dinner, and while the dishes were being washed. Evolution produces the same evolved behaviors. Parents provide and manage. Children consume, then disappear when there is work to be done.

Cutting the back lawn in midsummer, I almost run the mower over a box turtle, hunkered down in a shady patch of grass. I grew up in box turtle habitat and loved playing with them as a youngster. They are handsomely patterned and move slowly, occasionally blundering into the backyard. Young box turtles are small and adorable, and so rural and suburban families often keep young turtles in captivity as a pet of sorts, feeding them lettuce and other greens. We have a single species in the Mid-Atlantic region, the Common or Eastern Box Turtle. This species has declined in abundance, along with all turtles. They suffer substantial mortality as roadkill when on the move in the spring. Their populations have also been reduced by international trade. Fortunately, the international export of box turtles is now controlled by some federal and state regulations. The best thing to do if you encounter a box turtle these days is to admire it, photograph it, and allow it to go about its business.

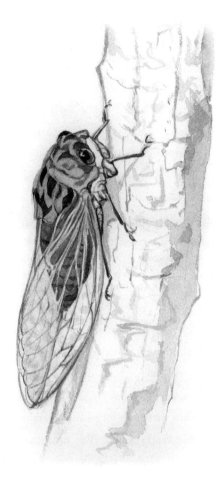

Annual Cicada

Yet another one of those iconic summer sounds is the song of a
Northern Mockingbird at night in the neighborhood. The singing bird
ascends to some high perch and belts out a series of musical phrases in
an ever-changing series of riffs, round and round, somehow soothing

and not annoying, in part because it is a mockingbird. And the effect is different when one hears a mockingbird at night rather than during the day. The night song is so evocative and so subtropical, one naturally thinks of the rural South and the writing of Harper Lee. In former days, before air conditioning, we would sleep with wide-open windows and the song of the mockingbird, along with the sound of katydids and the humid night air, would waft into the bedroom and influence a night's dream-laden sleep. Today we are boxed into our bedrooms, sealed off from the night sounds. That is a shame, though there are obvious advantages to getting a sweat-free night of sleep. These days, I encounter the evening serenade of the mockingbird while walking the dog late in the evening. It is worth quoting Frank Chapman on the subject in 1895: "But listen to him when the world is hushed, when the air is heavy with the rich fragrance of orange blossoms and the dewy leaves glisten in the moonlight, and if his song does not thrill you then confess yourself dead to Nature's voices."

Another evocative nocturnal creature encountered while walking the dog in the early summer evening is the firefly or lightning bug. Neither a bug nor a fly, the common firefly is a soft-bodied beetle with the remarkable ability to signal for mates using "cold light" produced by a chemical reaction in its abdomen. About fifty species of fireflies inhabit the United States. The best way to distinguish the species is by the color of the light produced and the pattern and situation of the nocturnal flashing. In one species, the males fly near the ground, flashing their signal to wingless females hidden in the grass below. In other species, males circle high into the night sky. In New Guinea, I have encountered trees filled with fireflies, some glowing in synchrony and others more like a Christmas tree blinking at all different times.

As a child of a certain age (seven?), I celebrated the arrival of the evening fireflies by joining up with neighborhood kids to scamper about the backyard with an empty glass mayonnaise jar to capture them. Once the jar had a half-dozen of the little blinking beetles, we would add some grass (either for food or habitat or both, I'm not quite sure), and we would take the jar to the back porch and sit and watch the fireflies do their thing. But then, looking out over the backyard, we would see the wonder of the zooming little creatures in the dark, humid night, and we would realize that the fireflies were more entertaining when free to pursue their fate. Quickly, the jar would be emptied of fireflies and grass, and we would happily move on to some other childhood pursuit, leaving the fireflies to their amorous efforts.

These days, children have ready access to the cold light that once remained the sole provenance of the firefly—summer nights at the beach are now illuminated by children throwing plastic glowsticks that produce the same eerie green light as some of the fireflies. My own children, when young, loved glowsticks and invariably begged their parents for them each night at the beach. Believe it or not, these glowsticks are used by commercial longline fishing boats to attract fish to baited hooks set on mile-long lines dragged through the sea. All inspired by the harmless firefly.

During the early summer, tyrant flycatchers are commonplace in woodlands verging the Potomac. On this rather fresh summer afternoon, I hear the voices of five species: Eastern Phoebe, Acadian Flycatcher, Eastern Wood-Pewee, Eastern Kingbird, and Great Crested Flycatcher.

The phoebe, which nests under the pedestrian foot bridges crossing the canal, gives a harsh two-note *fee-bee*!—the source of its generic name. This small tail-wagger has become a human commensal because of its habit of plastering its cup nest under the protection of some permanent cover—the eaves of a porch, ceiling of a tunnel, or underside of a foot bridge. This bird bursts with personality, and I get a happy feeling whenever I see the phoebe in early summer. The Acadian Flycatcher, the smallest of the five, dwells in damp woods. As a result, I rarely see this bird but instead hear its song, an explosive *spit-ta-chee-up*! Hearing this bird reminds me of the bottomland woods in spring. The Eastern Wood-Pewee, like a phoebe but with pale wing bars, inhabits the open canopy of tall forest, singing from a high perch: *pee-a-weeeee . . . wee-yuu.* This is another flycatcher heard more often than seen, but the pewee likes to sally out after insects in clearings, so is less reclusive than the Acadian. The Eastern Kingbird is perhaps the most beloved of the group because of its boisterous and pugnacious territoriality as well as its preference for open sunny habitats. Sooty above and white below, these birds sally for insects across open rural fields and also feistily chase passing crows. Finally, the Great Crested Flycatcher is another vocal canopy dweller, the largest of these five and the most colorful, with splashes of yellow on the belly and rusty brown on the wings and tail. I hear the musical sputters of this local breeder through the warm days of July.

The Tyrannidae, the bird family that encompasses these five, is the most species-rich of any on earth, with more than four hundred species. Most inhabit Central and South America. There are forty-six species of tyrant flycatchers recorded from North America north of the Mexican border. These are suboscine songbirds, which lack some of the vocal specializations exhibited in the higher songbirds. In spite of this, these birds are well known for their voices. Many of the species, especially in the genus *Empidonax* (like the Acadian Flycatcher), are best identified by their voices—because their plumages are drab and so similar.

Each weekday morning when I walk the dog, I make a neighborhood bird count that I upload to eBird—an electronic database of global bird observations. On a typical day, I record probably forty individual birds of about twenty species. On my walk, I often bump into neighbors who, seeing my binoculars, ask me what I have seen. They are invariably surprised by the numbers I record. These neighbors, who are not birders, simply do not notice birds or take note of their voices. The daily avian activity in the neighborhood is mainly invisible to them. They manage to notice the big swirling flock of Fish Crows, but little else.

Not noticing birds in one's daily environment is like being badly nearsighted as well as profoundly hearing challenged. One misses a whole segment of life on earth that can deliver joy each day. Hearing and seeing eagles and hawks and Purple Martins and Red-bellied Woodpeckers is like drinking daily from the fountain of youth—it reminds me of the pleasures of days past, of times gone by, of the summertimes of childhood. People who take up birding as adults visibly grow younger as they engage with the pastime. That is fun to witness.

There are a couple of places along the canal towpath where I have to dodge large green walnut fruits that litter the path in July when I bike to work. The main and proper fall of the walnuts comes in late September and early October. Those falling in July are nuts that have been parasitized by boring beetle larvae or attacked by a pathogen. A tree aborts these doomed offspring prematurely to reduce its investment in them. On the bike path, striking one of these large spheres may cause a biker to fall, so I am always cautious when approaching a mess of walnuts on the ground.

The Black Walnut has a midcontinental distribution that centers on the Mississippi. The species is most famous for its handsome dark and beautifully grained wood, which is favored by furniture makers. Custom gunstocks are typically crafted from a select piece of walnut, not only because of its color but also because the wood is good at absorbing the shock of the gun's recoil. Two loads of freshly cut walnut logs were recently offered for sale on eBay for $25,000. A handsome prepared Black Walnut board was also being offered for $299. It is not uncommon to hear of mature Black Walnut trees being cut and stolen from rural properties in the dark of night. Demand in China is growing for this prized hardwood. The wood is so valuable now that it is mainly applied as a veneer by woodworkers. A veneer allows a valuable wood to be used sparingly by laminating the surface of a less expensive species of wood with a thin layer of a more valuable species.

The Black Walnut may produce fine wood, but it is not a tree most people would want in their backyard. This is not because of the threat of nighttime theft. The mature tree is not particularly handsome, and in autumn the long compound leaves disarticulate and fall along with the large fruit, making quite a mess (especially the long leaf-stems). Moreover, the tree produces an allelochemical called juglone that leaches into the soil under the mature tree, preventing other plant species from growing underneath or nearby. By the way, the walnuts we eat during the Christmas holidays come from commercially grown Persian or English Walnuts or hybrids between these species and other lineages. The edible nutmeat of the local Black Walnut is much favored by Eastern Gray Squirrels and

Fox Squirrels, but less so by humans because of the difficulty of extracting the edible portion from the woody integument.

Walnuts in North America may now be threatened by thousand cankers disease, caused by an interaction between the Walnut Twig Beetle and the canker-producing fungus *Geosmithia morbida*. When tunneling into the tree, the beetle introduces the fungus into the galleries created. The fungus can kill an adult walnut. The disease was discovered in New Mexico in 2001.

Of course, there are other things to see along the towpath besides fallen walnuts. Biking home on the C&O Canal in late July, I come upon a lactating doe White-tailed Deer browsing next to the gravel towpath in Georgetown. I stop and talk to her for several minutes. She looks at me with those big doe eyes while I am parked four feet from her. She continues to forage placidly as I depart for home, energized by the encounter.

In most places, wild creatures are wary and retreat when a human approaches. Not so the deer along the C&O Canal. They have benefited from several generations entirely free of hunting or harassment, and today they are indifferent to humans, even at close range. Just today (I am writing this in October) I stopped to watch a doe and two yearlings browsing right beside the Capital Crescent Trail in DC. They looked at me, then continued to browse, and they did not retreat as I quietly greeted them. This deer population has apparently lost its fear of people. It is not unusual to see one or more deer standing in a small patch of weeds at the head of Canal Road, on the western verge of Georgetown. In the afternoon, they feed peacefully within a few feet of two lanes of outbound traffic that is rushing furiously toward suburbia. Few drivers notice the deer, which are essentially motionless but for the occasional movement of their heads to feed. In the same manner, the speeding bikers on the Capital Crescent Trail often blunder right by one or more deer standing just a few feet from the pavement, heedless of these gentle creatures. Should a deer suddenly move out onto the trail, the speeding biker and the deer could come to grief.

The tame deer phenomenon is not unique to the Mid-Atlantic states. I recently visited a neighborhood in suburban San Antonio, Texas, where the habituated White-tails in this gated community lounged about, resting and foraging, on the front lawns of homes there, entirely oblivious to human activity. In our Bethesda neighborhood, the deer forage for edibles in yards, but they tend to do this only after dark. They can decimate favored plants within unfenced flower gardens. We know the deer have been at work from the clipped plants and the droppings left by the foraging quadrupeds.

Late July. Swallowtails are the largest and most beautiful of North America's butterflies. Twenty-three species of swallowtails breed in North America. Some, like the Spicebush Swallowtail and Eastern Tiger Swallowtail, are commonplace and seen almost daily in early summer. Others, such as the Zebra and Pipevine Swallowtails, are uncommon and seen only under exceptional circumstances or in special places where their food plants grow. And then there are those species seen only in the guidebooks. The Giant Swallowtail, the largest swallowtail in North America, is a will-o'-the-wisp to naturalists living in the DC area. With a wingspan of nearly four-and-a-half inches, it is a huge brute, colored dark brown with a rich yellow racing stripe and parallel yellow spotting on each upper wing and a pale, creamy yellow under wing with scrolling of complex markings. The only Giant Swallowtail I have seen in the area was pointed out to me by my daughter in our backyard. I was inside

Giant Swallowtail

watching some sporting event on TV, and seven-year-old Grace was playing in the backyard. She called out that an unusual butterfly was in the flower garden. I walked onto the back porch and immediately saw this rare creature moving among our flowers. I knew instantly what it was; I had dreamed of seeing this creature for decades. What a treat to be shown the butterfly by my daughter! It moved lazily about in our flowers for several minutes and then lifted itself high into the air and sailed off to who knows where. Grace, my wife, Carol, and I stood transfixed, watching this apparition make its way from our yard and permanently into our memory banks. The only Giant Swallowtails I have seen since have been in southern Texas and the Deep South. I await the day this gorgeous phantom appears once again in my yard.

The Giant Swallowtail has a widespread distribution in the New World, from southern California east to Iowa and Maryland, south to Texas and Florida, and southward into South America. Its favored food plants are in the citrus family—especially the Common Hoptree and Common Pricklyash. The range of this butterfly expands and contracts over time. It sometimes forms isolated colonies north of its main breeding range. As with most species near the edge of its range, it is rare in the DC area.

On an early morning in late July, I approach my office building in downtown DC and am about to enter the underground parking lot when I see a creature in the intersection of Twentieth and M Streets. It is a Gray Fox, paralyzed with fear as cars try to get around this poor beast, frozen in place. As I approach it, I see that it is a fine-pelaged adult, with no signs of physical injury. The creature cowers in the middle of morning rush. It has a gray back from head to tail; its flanks are highlighted with a fine stripe of red-brown from its ears all the way down its neck and flanks to the underside of the tail; its throat and chest are white. The little fox shifts this way and that but cannot make up its mind how to escape. Curious pedestrians on the sidewalk stare in disbelief. After what seems an eternity, it scampers to the sidewalk and scurries down an alleyway to safety.

How does a Gray Fox find itself in traffic in downtown DC? Did it come up from a sewer drain? In the DC area, the Gray Fox is much outnumbered by the Red Fox, which is fairly common in wooded parklands. In more than three decades in the area, I have seen the Gray Fox twice. By comparison, I have seen scores of Red Foxes. My most memorable experience of a Gray Fox took place south of Frostburg bird-watching with my birding buddy Chuck Burg. We were walking

Gray Fox

up to a grassy hilltop in search of Henslow's Sparrows before sunrise on a misty June morning when an adult Gray Fox trotted across the top of the hill in front of us. We watched with binoculars, taking note of the beautiful pattern of silver, gray, black, and rusty-brown fur, the bushy, dark-tipped tail trailing behind. After lowering my binoculars and breathing once more, only one thought came to mind—the perfection of nature.

Encounters like these—brushes with wild nature—enrich a naturalist's life. We tell our friends and loved ones about these encounters, and we even repeat them in our dreams. For a nature lover, these often-brief events recharge the spirit and form the library of experience that builds over a lifetime. Speaking as someone who has been watching nature for more than five decades, the intensity of the experience does not diminish, and the joy derived from a close encounter with a Gray Fox or Giant Swallowtail or Great Crested Flycatcher remains as sweet as ever.

TWO

August—Heat and Poison Ivy

The city of Washington has never had the praise it deserves from those of us
who do not give ourselves over altogether to city life. Unlike New York, it
makes room for nature in its midst.

—LOUIS HALLE, *Spring in Washington*

Late June and July set the stage for summer, but in much of the Mid-
Atlantic, August is the main event—this is when summer reaches its peak
climatologically and sociologically. For north temperate humankind, this
is the summer vacation season, when one or two weeks are spent lolly-
gagging along the Atlantic shore, reading, sunbathing, riding the waves,
and thinking about dinner at a fun restaurant or having a pizza delivered
to the beach house. This is the season with days and days of sun and
heat and enforced lassitude—sleeping late, napping in the afternoon,
and even going to bed early some nights. These are some habits we all
happily adjust to. Nature watching? Not so much . . . except for the
extreme among us. Things may be slow on the nature front, but stuff is
still happening for those who take time to notice. The beach is in my
thoughts on and off for much of the first half of August. It's fun to daydream about a vacation to come.

43

Early August. Work at the office is frantic and hectic today, but like a magic potion, the fifty-minute bicycle ride home dissolves every residual bit of the day's stress. The heat and sweat and the rhythmic movement of my legs create a sense of calm, expelling the toxic residue of some minor office unpleasantness. The familiarity and the repetition and the breeze on the face contribute to the feeling of release. I am heading home, and all of work's cares are left behind.

But there is always some bonus in store. This evening, I discover an adult Yellow-crowned Night-Heron foraging in the water at the edge of the canal, its demure colors combined in a sleek natural pattern—beautiful, not garish. The spirit of the woodlands has sent this phantom my way as a peace offering, to ensure that I arrive home completely relaxed and in tune with the natural world.

I stop my bike and dig out my small traveling binoculars from my pannier. I focus them on the motionless water bird that stands in the shallows. The Yellow-crowned Night-Heron is the most beautiful in a family of beautiful birds. Overall it is soft gray-blue, streaked with white and dark blue on the back, and with deep yellow legs and feet. Its head is black with a white cheek stripe, a creamy yellow crown, and a pair of long, white head plumes that project backward and dangle delicately above its mantle. The eyes are deep red. The bill is thick, black, and pointed. As I note these features, the heron remains poised over the water, waiting patiently for some small aquatic creature to venture within striking distance. After I study the bird for a few quiet minutes, I replace the binoculars, clamber back on my bike, and make my way home, thinking about the beauty of this uncommon water bird and how lucky I have been to spend time with it.

The stately and colorfully plumaged herons and egrets are invariably a pleasure to watch, whether quietly hunting fish, sailing overhead, or perched in a roost tree. The twelve species that inhabit North America are among birders' favorites because of their elaborate plumages, their intricate courtship displays, and their sociable habits. Although the Yellow-crowned Night-Heron is commonly seen in solitude, the other species can be found nesting in noisy mixed-species rookeries and foraging in wetlands in association with one another. A day birding on the Eastern Shore of Maryland or Delaware in August can produce a list of seven or more species. Each has its own habits, and sorting them out can be a fun challenge for a beginning birder.

Although we traditionally think of egrets as different from herons, in fact, the two groups are not distinct evolutionary lineages, according to the most recent molecular phylogenies. For instance, the Great Egret is a close relative of the Great Blue Heron, and the Snowy Egret is a close relative of the Tricolored Heron. The all-white plumage is an ancestral trait that is retained throughout the lineage and is exhibited in selected species of various genera. This is exemplified by the Little Blue Heron. The adult is slate blue with purple highlights and the young bird is all white like an egret.

The heron family has a worldwide distribution, and some species exhibit remarkably extensive ranges. Although the Yellow-crowned Night-Heron is restricted to the New World, its close relative, the Black-crowned Night-Heron, ranges from North America into South America, Europe, Africa, and Asia. The Cattle Egret's range is much like that of the preceding species, extending as far as Australia. These stately birds are indeed cosmopolitan.

Edwin Way Teale, writing in *Circle of the Seasons,* spoke of the many redeeming aspects of nature. Though there are notable exceptions, so much of nature is peaceful. Think of the following things and how they make us feel: the bright green of the growing grass, the murmuring of a stream's waters tumbling over rocks, the blue vault of the sky, the rustling of the leaves, the stars in the dark night, the lapping of small waves upon a bay shore, the bright expanse of beach in the summer sun, the ripples of water on a lake in August. Who is not calmed and relaxed by these simple gifts?

Teale captured the August summer: "No breeze stirs. The cloudless sky seems a vast blue flame pouring its heat on earth. . . . I turn out of the heat onto a path under the trees. The cool woodland air is as welcome to my lungs as the filtered green woodland light is to my eyes."

If you bike through the summer and fall on the towpath of the C&O Canal, there is a good chance you may come into contact with Poison Ivy. It is a native species, ranging widely in the East. It grows lushly and abundantly at the woodland edge as a low ground cover and a climbing vine. The towpath offers ideal habitat for this noxious native plant. Most people are sensitive to the toxin in Poison Ivy, developing itchy blisters on the skin from contacting it. The toxic substance in the sap of Poison Ivy, known as urushiol, causes a chemical burn as well as an allergic reaction on the skin of those sensitive to it. Washington is a hotbed of Poison Ivy, and it can be found in most suburban haunts, such as backyards, playgrounds, parks, and the like. A very aggressive colonist, Poison Ivy is always attempting to invade our yard from the neighborhood park below. We cut it back and pull it up (while wearing gloves and protective clothing). The worst mistake for a homeowner tending the yard is to unwittingly cut up Poison Ivy and then burn it in a leaf pile. The urushiol is then carried into the air and can harm those who pass through the smoke.

Everyone in my family has suffered a Poison Ivy rash. It goes on for days and spreads even after the offending chemical has been washed away. This is very unpleasant, but nothing compared to what happened to a high school acquaintance in rural Baltimore. In late spring, at a nighttime beer bash set in a farm field, this young woman, while chatting with a friend and sitting on an old stone wall, absent-mindedly pulled leaves from a vine and nibbled them without thinking. The leaves were Poison Ivy. She spent some time in the hospital before recovering. Surprisingly, most wildlife species are not sensitive to Poison Ivy. Deer consume its leaves. In autumn these leaves turn yellow and then become a deep burnished red before falling.

Poison Ivy is a perennial. Although it loses its leaves in fall, the woody vine can live for many years. The dark, hairy vines are often seen attached to large trees, allowing the climber to range into the canopy. The fruits of Poison Ivy are important to a variety of birds in winter. I have seen American Robins, Yellow-rumped Warblers, and Pileated Woodpeckers consuming its small whitish-gray fruit.

The other noxious weed that can be found with Poison Ivy down along the Potomac in August is the Stinging Nettle. It is a low forb that grows on damp ground in the shade, typically near a stream. In another Baltimore County memory, my brother and I were on a childhood fishing expedition with our father on a humid Saturday afternoon. Dressed in shorts, I made the mistake of walking through a patch of streamside Stinging Nettles. The pain was immediate, and my tears flowed

Poison Ivy

copiously. From that time on, I knew well the distinct, ominous-looking, jagged-edged leaves of the Stinging Nettle. Nettles are found worldwide. The rainforests in northeastern Australia are home to nettle trees known as Gympie-Gympie whose terrible sting can persist for weeks or even years. In Papua New Guinea, a milder nettle is collected by rural villagers and brushed on the legs to relieve aches and pains—a local remedy for muscle pain that never attracted me because of my childhood memories.

Late August. Our family traditionally takes a late summer vacation at Bethany Beach, Delaware, which lies on the Atlantic Coast south of Rehoboth, Delaware, and north of Ocean City, Maryland. Little about vacationing at Bethany Beach is nature-oriented. Most families, of course, mine included, do not aspire to make the annual summer vacation a nature vacation. It is up to me to squeeze some nature out of what is otherwise a routine, relaxing, family-oriented week at the beach.

When at the beach, surf fishing in the early morning is one way to engage with nature. It is always a pleasure to watch the sun rise east across the Atlantic, and this can be combined with fishing in the surf and watching the birdlife pass by. Typically, I surf fish with my father-in-law, Andy, with assistance from two of my children—Grace and Andrew. We spend an hour or two, before breakfast, with the faint hope of perhaps catching something edible. I say faint hope because mid-August is a bad month for surf fishing in Delaware. So we have to be satisfied with catching anything, because it is so unlikely that we will catch any of the popular sport fish that are good to eat. We do catch things of interest, at least to the children, who are curious about any new sea creature. When we catch a skate or a dogfish, the children dance around the strange-looking and threatening creature, squealing as we struggle to detach it from the hook. We occasionally catch small Kingfish or Bluefish, which Andy keeps, cleans, and has for lunch, pan-seared in butter. As we stand in the swash zone, keeping track of our taut lines, we watch the Royal Terns wing by in pairs, and singletons or small groups of Brown Pelicans, or perhaps an Osprey hunting high above the water searching for the telltale shadow of a fish near the surface. On the beach itself are small clots of Sanderlings, racing with the incoming surf. Up in the dry sand, a few Laughing Gulls wait patiently for bits of stray bait that we discard at the end of our morning of fishing.

Later in the day there is also the afternoon beach watch, in which a group of us sit in the sand reading under an umbrella and periodically looking out beyond the waves. We do this when we are not riding the waves or napping back at the house. The beach watch produces regular observations of pods of Bottlenose Dolphins, which move up and down the coast, usually just beyond the waves. Some pods have young-of-the-year, and to see the little ones breaking the surface brings peals of delight. One summer, there is an infestation of Cownose Rays. In the early morning, these medium-sized rays ply back and forth in the calm sea, exposing their wingtips above the water. This is as close as we ever come to seeing a shark fin protruding out of the sea's surface.

If I need an extra dollop of nature, I sneak off in the early morning with my binoculars and camera to Burton's Island, hidden behind a large marina in the back of Indian River Inlet. This is a little-visited nature reserve in Assawoman Bay, about fifteen minutes' drive from our rental house in Bethany. Crossing the pedestrian bridge that spans a bay channel, I enter a world distinct from the modern comforts of a beach town. The island features a big stand of old Loblolly Pine and is surrounded by salt marsh and small brackish ponds. The understory of the piney woods is American Holly and a species of greenbrier. In August, the area swarms with mosquitoes and horse flies. By 9:00 a.m. it is hot and muggy. But being in nature makes up for the minor unpleasantness. One might find groups of Snowy Egrets foraging with other heron species in a small pond, Great Egrets roosting in tall dead pines, or a Red Fox sleeping in a small declivity in a sandy opening. Brown-headed Nuthatches and Pine Warblers move through the canopy, vocalizing. Ospreys wheel overhead, giving their sad-sounding high-pitched cry. Clapper Rails rattle out in the *Spartina* grass flats. Flocks of Forster's Terns sweep over the bay, diving for tiny fish. A couple of hours spent naturizing on Burton's Island recharges the batteries and provides enough nature to appease me.

Another getaway near the Delaware shore is Assawoman Wildlife Area, a twenty-minute drive from the beach house. One gets there by following a series of winding back roads through corn and sorghum fields and old farm houses with dilapidated outbuildings and operating chicken coops. This old-fashioned inland farming region is slowly being overtaken by so-called resort housing targeting a downscale market of buyers who cannot afford a beachfront house in Delaware. It is sad to see the conversion from rural agriculture to vinyl-sided cookie-cutter housing developments. The lack of land-use zoning leads to this haphazard loss of cherished backcountry I have been visiting for five decades.

We still manage to see interesting things. One time we came upon a male Blue Grosbeak displaying to a female down on the hot black asphalt of the two-lane road. The cobalt-blue male prostrated himself, pressing his breast down on the road and cocking his tail vertically. He held the pose while the agitated female moved about him. They then briefly mated before being flushed by a passing car.

Assawoman itself is a mix of pine forest, salt marsh, and open bay, an expanded version of Burton's Island. It is a popular place for family crabbing, fishing, and birding expeditions. It even features a tall observation tower that overlooks two marshes. During the summer it is infamous for its mosquitoes. In fact, the prime time for Assawoman is spring and fall, when the migration is on. Our summer visits are rarely very birdy, it being August. But Assawoman remains a protected enclave that includes a mix of pretty habitats—a place for the naturalist to escape to for respite from the madding world.

One summer at the beach I go deep sea fishing with my brother-in-law, Adan. Early in the morning, ten of us board a fishing boat, which lumbers eastward thirty miles from Ocean City, Maryland, in search of tuna. I am mainly interested in seeing what seabirds are out in the pelagic zone in August. I am treated to twenty-five Cory's Shearwaters and fifty Wilson's Storm-Petrels—two species that cannot be seen from shore. We also catch five big Yellowfin Tuna. We hook these out in the Gulf Stream, where the water is transparent, bright blue, and eighty degrees. It is striking to see the small hunting parties of tuna rise up out of the deep, following the line of chum we are dropping into the water. They glow silver and green in the bright, sunlit, clear water, moving like torpedoes. That night, we cook fresh tuna steaks on the grill—tasting much finer than anything I have ever had in a restaurant.

At the end of August, having returned home from the beach, my wife and youngest child and I pack the car and head up to northern New England. We are on our way to Waterville, Maine, where we will drop Cary off for her freshman year at college. Our first stop is a rural farm in northern Massachusetts to visit former Brookmont neighbors Josh Spring and Tundi Agardy. Josh works in the film industry, and Tundi is a marine biologist (we did conservation workshops in New Guinea in earlier years). Josh and Tundi have settled outside the hamlet of Colrain to get away from it all and raise their children in the peace and quiet of the countryside.

Josh and Tundi's daughter, Alex, is a former schoolmate of Cary's, and Cary wants to spend an evening with Alex before the two start their freshman year in college. My wife and I are happy to catch up with Tundi and Josh in the country. After an eight-hour drive, we arrive at their house around 3:00 p.m. and are welcomed by the parents, the three kids, plus their two horses, yellow lab, six chickens, three bunnies, and guinea pig.

Colrain, Massachusetts, is a deeply rural natural setting for a family's country life, and we are privileged to experience it firsthand. An adorable Red Squirrel visits the front porch, as does a spunky Eastern Chipmunk—they clearly are treated as family pets. Their small size, dark eyes, and perky demeanor make them irresistible. American Goldfinches give their sweet song overhead, and Downy Woodpeckers come to the feeder on the hour. Ruby-throated Hummingbirds zoom about in the Jewelweed beside the back deck all afternoon long. Here, in late August, this spot seems a bit like the Garden of Eden.

The highlight of the visit is the evening meal, served on a huge rustic table in the dining room, with all-local fare, including many fresh vegetables Josh has grilled out on the back deck. We chatter about mutual friends and our latest travels, the kids speaking to the kids and the adults among themselves, occasionally crossing the divide to confirm a fact or date or name. This is what family visits are all about.

Carol and I spend the night under a big quilt with the windows open, and the frigid mountain air helps us sleep well. Mice race across the uneven pine floors at night. Barred Owls hoot out in the darkened woods.

We rise early, awakened by the bright sun peeking over the hill to the east. I sit quietly on the back wooden deck, listening to songbirds and waiting for the first hummingbird of the morning. Bees of many varieties come to the Jewelweed, making something of a minor racket in the absolute quiet of the morning. At 7:00 a.m. it is about fifty degrees— chilly for August. Low clouds blanket the valley below. The dew on the Jewelweed sparkles in the rays of the morning sun. I savor the domestic side of nature here in northern Massachusetts.

By mid-morning we push on, because we have many miles to go and because our host's eldest daughter has to be driven to college in

Vermont that day. After a breakfast of eggs laid on this property, bacon, and sourdough bread we drive on toward Maine. We race northward up Interstate 91, destination New Hampshire's White Mountains. It is in places such as mountainous and verdant New England that interstate highways are at their prime—few cars, incredible vistas, and a wonderful feeling of absolute freedom. After a quick lunch outdoors in the quiet and rather weather-worn town of White River Junction, we head east via back roads toward our penultimate destination, Jackson, New Hampshire, a hamlet nestled at the base of mighty Mount Washington. This is our final summer stop before the commencement of the harsh reality of college orientation for our daughter.

The White Mountains, in north-central New Hampshire, are the East's most rugged uplands. The Smokys are higher. The Adirondacks are more expansive and wilder. But the Whites are the most imposing. Driving here from Massachusetts, we cross the high passes of Kinsman Notch, the Kancamagus Highway, and Bear Notch and wend our way through deep valleys to a large and porch-girdled country inn offering views of the surrounding alpine scenery. To stretch our legs after the long drive, we wander about, finding a tumbling rocky waterfall right above the inn. Jackson, like so many villages in northern New England, is gorgeously quaint and neatly tended, as if preparing for a postcard photograph. This is a fine place to spend a last family evening together this summer. We are lucky that good weather continues to follow us on our journey northeastward.

The next morning, we stop at the Appalachian Mountain Club's lodge at Pinkham Notch to get a glimpse of Mountain Washington looming in the mists. All around us, conifer-clad ridges rise up toward rocky heights. Even our somewhat skeptical college-bound daughter is impressed by the harsh beauty. And Mount Washington is the most imposing of all—the highest and most extreme summit in New England. The peak is exposed and snowbound for much of each year. The meteorological observatory at the summit recorded the fastest wind speed ever measured on earth—231 miles per hour—back in 1934.

From the Pinkham Notch parking lot, we cross Route 16 and make the half-mile hike up to Square Ledge. This is a short but steep ascent to a rocky overlook that provides a panoramic view up to the heights of ferocious Mount Washington. Climbing that peak is a great experience, but the round trip can take most of a day. Here we spend a brief hour and closely scan the various features of this great mountain—Boot Spur to the left, the Head Wall of Tuckerman's Ravine in the center, and Lion's Head to the right, with the summit peak looming in the background. Much of what we view is above the tree line, rocky and forbidding. Every East Coast mountaineer knows these various features and treasures walking those trails. This is the heart of the Presidential Range—the soul of the White Mountains. I look up with something of a yearning, wanting to be up there yet once again, but I have other mountaineering plans.

As we sit on the flat rocks in the sun, gazing up to the high, rocky summit, Carol and I reminisce about a hike we took here as newlyweds back in the autumn of 1985. We had hiked up into Tuckerman's Ravine, where we observed a crisply plumaged Black-backed Woodpecker we had heard tapping on a dead stub in a thicket of spruces. On today's visit, we had to be satisfied with a glimpse up into the stark mountain wilderness, because we had hours more of back roads driving to get to Cary's college town in Maine.

After getting our daughter settled in at college in Waterville, I drop Carol off at Augusta Regional Airport for her trip home, and I turn the car northward toward Baxter State Park, in Maine's wild northern interior. I am planning to climb Katahdin, Maine's isolated and rugged high summit. Katahdin, like Mount Washington, is a mecca for East Coast climbers, and its summit is the northern terminus of the 2,200-mile-long Appalachian Trail—the famous AT. I have always wanted to climb Katahdin, and here is my chance. Late in the spring I booked a tent site at Katahdin Stream Campground, and without thinking too much I decided to take the Hunt Trail up (which on Katahdin is the Appalachian Trail). I particularly like the idea of doing the last 5.2 miles of the AT—it is the trail's most spectacular ascent.

As I drive into the park, I turn a corner on the narrow gravel entrance road to see the big dark, furred rump of a Black Bear, heading into the bushes. I jump out of the car for a better look, but no luck—the beast is gone. At the top of a rise I get my first stunning vista of the great mountain massif—isolated and imposing. The entire upper reaches of the mountain are gray rock fields. I have a hard time taking my eyes off the summit.

It does not take me long to set up my tent, and by late afternoon I am able to hike two short stretches of the AT—first north of the campground and then south, just as a warm-up for the next day's climb. Both stretches of trail are dominated by conifers—very boreal. The boggy low country south of the campground is almost pure conifer, with a mix of Northern White-cedar, Red Spruce, Balsam Fir, and White Pine. On my afternoon warm-up hike I hear a Hairy Woodpecker, a Black-capped Chickadee, and a White-throated Sparrow. In addition, a few pesky black flies buzz around my head—a hangover from the remnants of summer.

The next morning, I am awoken by the sounds of preparatory movement of other expectant hikers in the campground. By the predawn light in the cloudless sky I quickly breakfast, pack the necessary emergency gear in my daypack, and head off with my Red Spruce walking stick, which I had prepared on the prep walk the previous afternoon.

Baxter State Park is Maine's largest and wildest protected area, but the mountains of the Katahdin range are quite different from the White Mountains that we had recently visited. The White Mountains are more extensive and higher. The Katahdin Massif is a rather compact set of peaks and auxiliary summits, impressive in their own right because they jut up prominently from the low surrounding hills. In addition, because of their northerly location, they boast an extensive mantle of rocky alpine habitat above the tree line. Moreover, wildfire and logging have heavily altered Baxter State Park's low country. The northwestern section of the park is still "scientifically logged" (northern Maine is a logger's paradise). Still, Katahdin and Mount Washington are linked by the Appalachian Trail, and the section of trail between these two high New England peaks is the most interesting stretch of the AT.

From the campground, my ascent trail follows Katahdin Stream gradually upward through young forest. Spruce and fir, and in some spots pure stands of spruce, dominate. I see few large trees, but there is a strong boreal aspect to the forest. The woods are silent except for the wind's rustling of the leaves of the few birches scattered here and there. Looking upward, I see clouds racing by—a hint of things to come. After a while, the trail turns from the stream and climbs steeply up a ridge through Balsam Fir. I am in a tunnel formed by the small trees, and there are no vistas. Birds are few, mainly juncos. Nothing is singing. But when I reach a patch of old aspens, I look up into one of the trees and spot a big North American Porcupine, finely patterned in black and white and curled around a high branch. Up there, motionless, he looks like a big frosty ball of quills.

After a bit more than an hour, I come to two very steep and rocky pitches. These are the meat of the 4,200-foot vertical ascent. The large boulders and cliffs require considerable climbing effort. In some places, permanent metal posts and rungs are embedded in the rock as climbing aids. At the head of the first pitch, I am exposed to a steep ravine that faces northwest. Here, winds of thirty miles per hour nearly blow me off the trail. I stop to put on my heavy fleece pullover and long pants. It is unpleasantly cold. Looking up toward the summit, I see that the peak is now shrouded in fast-moving cloud. The vista northwest toward the rounded and rocky face of the Owl—an ancillary peak—and southeast into the low country are sublime, but the wind and cloud dampen my spirits. The air temperature is probably around fifty, but the wind chill is substantial.

The second pitch is more difficult than the first, and my energy flags. I am now far above the tree line, and exposed. The summit remains enshrouded by the scudding clouds racing out of the northwest. In some places I have to toss my now much-diminished walking stick up above me and use both hands to hitch myself up over a large vertical pitch. Everything is jutting and angular rock. I long for flat ground to stand on without having to use the walking stick as a balance. Then, another gust of wind hits me and I involuntarily step backward to steady myself, but my foot lands on a sharp rock that does not halt my backward momentum. That leads me to lurch back with my other foot, seeking proper purchase on the trail. But no luck. Rump first, I head backward, and for a long second I launch into midair, eventually landing, back first, into a basin of jumbled rocks—the ones I had just clambered over to reach that precarious perch above.

The impact drives the wind from my lungs, and for several moments I lie motionless, stunned. I have fallen perhaps five feet down onto a bed of rough rocks. I feel a sharp, burning pain in my lower back. After a few seconds of trying to get my breath, I curse and mutter, "Let's try to get up and see what I did to myself." I roll to my right side, stagger to my feet, and lurch a few feet forward. I stand there, hunched over in pain, and wonder what the heck I should do. There are no other hikers in sight. I take a drink of water, gather my wits, and start hobbling up the trail. I am already more than two-thirds of the way to the top, so I figure I should try for the summit.

Although I am moving slowly and uncertainly, before long I am up on the picturesque high summit plateau vegetated in the dwarfed, deformed trees known as krummholz, where I can limp along with minimal effort. At this point, I discover that in my fall I have hurt my left wrist as well as my side. The final pitch is gradual but very rocky, and I inch along in the strong wind. I worry about falling again and making a bad situation worse. Now I am moving through a world of cloud and gloom. After three hours and fifty minutes, through the thick, gray mist, I see the large weathered four-legged signboard that marks Katahdin's summit. Several young hikers loiter there. As I slowly approach the summit, two older through-hikers race up from another trail and halloo their joy at completing their 2,200-mile journey. I watch briefly, congratulating them, and then I turn and begin my slow descent. There is no reason to linger: the wind is ripping, I am growing colder by the minute, and the enshrouding cloud wipes out the much-anticipated view. Not having that wonderful wide-open vista is a major downer.

On the way off the summit rise, a confiding Common Raven pays me a visit, flying within a few feet of my head and then settling on a rock, presumably waiting for a handout. I stop and sit gingerly, and then talk quietly to this bird, less than six feet from me. This raven is one of the very few birds I see that day. Resting here, I glimpse a lively Red Squirrel in the subalpine fir scrub—surprisingly high on the mountainside. I take a long break here, and instead of feeling sorry for myself, I come to realize how lucky I am not to have been seriously injured. I am still mobile, and after all, I have achieved my objective of climbing Katahdin, a challenge I had contemplated for decades. I am feeling some serious humility as well as gratitude. The big mountain has dinged me, teaching me that I need to be more cautious when out alone in the woods. This is not the same as watching a TV show about climbing a mountain. I need to show nature (and this mountain) a full modicum of respect.

As my bruised muscles start to stiffen up in the cold, I sit there, contemplating my fate. I am startled from my reverie when another AT aspirant arrives down the trail and, seeing my distress, accompanies me back to the campground. This fellow, my age, completed two-thirds of the AT in 2013 and plans to complete the section from Katahdin to New York State by October. This morning he had ascended Katahdin in two hours and forty minutes—an hour and ten minutes better than my time. For me, getting down is a challenge because of the many places where two free hands are needed to negotiate a vertical drop. I fall three times during this ordeal—each time hitting already badly bruised points on my body. The clouds never abate. Then rain starts to fall. It makes us worry about the several sets of ascending climbers we encounter—naive hikers in shorts and T-shirts who are late, about to enter an alpine environment with strong winds, cold, and blowing rain. We warn them about the risk they are taking and advise that they should consider retreating if conditions worsen.

As I limp into the damp campground, I decide that the best course of action is to pack everything into the car and head to the emergency room of the hospital in Ellsworth, Maine. There I can be examined and have an X-ray taken of my wrist. The campsite ranger comes by my site as I am packing and wraps my wrist with an ace bandage and an ice pack. He reminds me that it is always better to travel with a partner when in the wilderness.

Before dark, I find a campsite just outside of Ellsworth, near the coast. Then I spend a couple of hours in the hospital ER, which on the Friday evening of Labor Day weekend is gloriously quiet. The X-rays are negative. I have a sore wrist and a huge purple bruise on my back and hip that mark where my body hit the rocks. Dosed with painkillers from the hospital, I sleep fitfully in the chilly, windy night. After the near-calamity on Katahdin, my plan is to sleep in at my campsite, then find a seafood shack down the coast where I can get a fresh lobster roll for lunch before motoring on to a birding mecca of my college days— Newburyport, Massachusetts.

In the autumn and winter in New England, one of the most famous birding destinations is Boston's North Shore. And birders' ground zero on the North Shore is the gorgeous, historic fishing village of Newburyport and adjacent Plum Island—now protected as Parker River National Wildlife Refuge. During the 1970s, as a college student in Massachusetts, I periodically visited Plum Island and Newburyport on weekends late in the year. It was there I saw my first Buff-breasted Sandpiper and Snowy Owl, Iceland Gull and Barrow's Goldeneye. I have not visited since the autumn of 1974, so it will be four decades since I last birded this special place.

After a simple but sumptuous lobster roll purchased and consumed at a small shacklike food shanty near Belfast, Maine, I drive south nonstop to northeastern Massachusetts through heavy Labor Day weekend traffic. The northwest wind continues to blow, and puffy cumulus clouds sail across the deep blue sky. It is perfect traveling weather. I exit Interstate 95 just across the New Hampshire–Massachusetts line. Traveling south on Route 1, I look for a campground within striking distance of Plum Island. In Salisbury, six miles north of Newburyport, I snag one of the last tent sites on this busy weekend, nestled under a thick canopy of White Pines. How nice to set my tent on a deep carpet of pine needles—there is no better natural cushion for a sleeping bag.

I am scheduled to bird Cape Cod the following day, so I need to make my visit to Plum Island in the brief time remaining this afternoon. I cross the broad Merrimac River, filled with pleasure boats, and exit onto the main street of gorgeous Newburyport. There is no town in New England quite like it—the stately sea captains' homes, the old harbor section, its many old brick mill buildings repurposed to serve the tourist industry that now drives the local economy. The town is hopping as I creep down Merrimac Street—with lots of street-side dining spots and shoppers moving from store to store. I pass through the urban buzz of this little port town, witnessing the last fling of summer, though today's weather makes everyone feel as if summer could go on forever.

I make a quick visit to Parker River National Wildlife Refuge. Plum Island is a classic barrier island, with a wide, straight beach and low dwarf forest on sandy soil giving way on the back side to tidal marsh and bay. It is much like Island Beach in New Jersey and Assateague in Maryland and Virginia. These barrier islands are wonderful migrant traps—for both land birds and shorebirds—and August and September are when the migrant birds pass through in greatest numbers.

This afternoon, though, the migrants are thin on the ground, one of the perils of the birding pursuit. Sometimes you can be in the right location but not at the correct moment. Yes, there are Gray Catbirds in the thickets and Great Egrets hunkered down here and there in the marshes. A few Least Sandpipers forage in the salt pan famous for its shorebirds. At the wetlands of parking lot number 4 there is a clot of Lesser Yellowlegs and several dowitchers. The evening's only notable sighting is a pair of White-rumped Sandpipers in with some other peeps. It has been decades since I have seen the species, but just like in the old days their slightly larger size distinguishes them, and when they fly there is the telltale all-white rump. I'll have another shot at more shorebirds out on Cape Cod, where I am headed next.

Back at the campground in Salisbury, I cook dinner on my gas grill. I feel as satisfied as those diners in downtown Newburyport. The wind blows and the temperature drops again Sunday evening, but I sleep inside two sleeping bags and remain warm through the coldest part of the night, which dips into the forties. I awaken several times from the pain in my hip and ribs, a reminder of my close call on Katahdin.

Before dawn the next morning I set off for Cape Cod, avoiding the horrors of Boston traffic unscathed because it is Labor Day Monday. I meet local experts Peter Trimble and son Jeremiah at the Hole-in-One restaurant in Orleans. They have agreed to show me some birds this morning—the ones I missed at Newburyport.

The Trimbles are taking me to the flats at Nauset Beach, where we will look for autumn shorebirds (sandpipers, curlews, godwits, plovers, and others). At this season, New England birders make annual pilgrimages to Nauset, Monomoy Island, and Plum Island to witness the spectacle of flocks of the diverse migratory waders as they stop over while traveling from their Arctic breeding habitat to their winter ranges in South America. As I wait in the restaurant for the Trimbles, I think back to a magical day of birding on Monomoy Island in early September 1970. I have never forgotten the intense joy of glimpsing my first American Golden-Plover, Hudsonian Godwit, Baird's and Western Sandpipers, and Wilson's Phalarope, shown to me by the expert guides of the Massachusetts Audubon Society. That was one of the pinnacles of my young birding career.

On this day, Peter and Jeremiah lead me to Nauset Landing, where we drop two canoes into the shallow bay and paddle across to the isolated barrier beach. Here we wander in the sun in search of migrant shorebirds. My companions point out large numbers of Black-bellied and Semipalmated Plovers and Common Terns, but only small numbers of some of the rarer and the more desirable species: four Roseate Terns, one Black Tern, one American Golden-Plover, one Whimbrel, five Piping Plovers, four White-rumped Sandpipers, and three American Oystercatchers. At one point, a big adult female Peregrine Falcon stoops on a cluster of foraging yellowlegs, creating havoc as the skinny shorebirds explode off the flats to escape the speedy predator. Migrant Peregrines heading south to their wintering grounds preferentially move along the coast, probably because of the ready availability of shorebird prey.

The Peregrine perches on a large piece of driftwood by a low dune. This is the falcon prototype—the master hunter of birds in open habitats. This female had presumably bred in the tundra of the High Arctic and is now migrating to a coastal habitat in the Deep South that offers rich bird-hunting opportunities for the long nonbreeding season. We can tell that she is a tundra bird because of her pale underparts with fine, dark barring, as well as the large pale ear spot offset from her black cap and distinctive black teardrop below her dark eye. The prominent dark face markings give her a fierce look. Because she is a relentless hunter, this is the look this bird deserves.

Bald Eagle

By the late 1960s, breeding populations of Peregrines were gone from the East, victims of human pest control practices. The widespread overapplication of a suite of highly toxic pesticides, primarily DDT and Dieldrin, led to the poisoning of Bald Eagles, Ospreys, and Peregrines. Researchers established recovery programs to breed the species in captivity and carefully release individuals in targeted localities, thus engineering their successful return to the landscape: a huge win for conservation. Watching this noble bird, I think about the decades of effort that went into saving this species from the brink of extinction in the United States— wonderful work done by dedicated scientists and conservationists.

Walking the Nauset flats barefoot in the light breeze and under the bright sun is a sublime pleasure. We are alone out here and have nature to ourselves. Birds are moving about and keep us busy identifying them. It is late summer, and the weather is perfect for an outing. As we make our way back to our canoes, a cool fog creeps in and envelops our world. We are now entirely caught in a thick, gray mist, and the sun is a pale yellow disk above, the blue sky obscured. As we paddle back to the mainland through the fog, at one point we can no longer see land in any direction. It is a remarkable sensation, a bit like hovering in a helicopter in dense fog. Only the sound of a nail gun from a house under construction gives us a sense of direction to orient us back to the landing where our cars are parked.

We end our day trip with a quick midday meal of local seafood at the suitably downscale Chatham Squire pub in the prissily upscale center of Chatham town. I then leave my guides and head north up the outer arm of the cape. I arrive in bustling, traffic-choked, artsy, and sand-girt Provincetown at 3:00 p.m. and am able to catch the last whale-watching boat of the day. I have long wanted to do this whale-watch trip off the tip of Cape Cod, and I finally have found my chance.

I board the trim, blue-and-white steel-hulled vessel *Dolphin VIII* with a crowd of eager whale lovers. As the boat passes out of the crowded and sunstruck harbor, we move into the day's fogbank, presumably the same fog I had encountered at Nauset Beach. The enshrouding fog creates a world apart from the sunny, tourist-filled world of Provincetown. Our boat passes in and out of this great, silent fogbank created by the cold water of the Atlantic as we move southeastward in search of whales.

I am here to see whales, but I am just as interested in the birdlife and other sea life. In this season, the seabirds are on the move, and for much of the two-hour cruise I am busy identifying interesting ocean-dwelling birds. First, I see Cory's Shearwaters, familiar from my tuna-fishing trip earlier in the summer. This species—long-winged, brown above and white below, sailing just above the water in long, gliding arcs—is present in small numbers near the northern shore of Cape Cod. Farther east we spy three more shearwater species—Great, Sooty, and Manx. The Great is abundant, and the other two are smaller as well as less common. I find these graceful seabirds either floating in small groups on the calm sea or gliding low over the water with their stiff wings held straight out from their bodies. I am seeing them just off the coast of Massachusetts, and yet all were born on far distant islands. Cory's Shearwater breeds on islands off Spain and North Africa; the Sooty Shearwater breeds on islands off the southern tip of South America; and the Great Shearwater breeds on islands in the far southern Atlantic. These birds are world-class seafarers.

As I am photographing a Great Shearwater sailing low over the glassy water, I am startled to hear a loud "Ahh!" come from the other side of the boat. A whale! The sound of approval rises again and again as apparently more and more whales appear. People rush to that side of the boat, but this is not necessary: we are among an assemblage of perhaps thirty Humpback Whales feeding leisurely in the fog. The boat moves carefully about among the foraging whales for an hour. Tolerating our presence, the whales move back and forth under the boat—great dark forms with white markings passing just below us. Groups of six or eight whales perform bubble-net feeding by rising up from the depths in a tight circle of their own bubbles and then breaking the water's surface with gigantic open mouths, straining the prey-rich water through their baleens. We can anticipate the location of each submarine feeding group by the circle of bubbles that break at the surface. No one on the boat grows tired of seeing the clusters of feeding whales emerge from the depths in a slow-motion demonstration of mass and grace. The fog adds to the experience, making it ethereal and mysterious. Scores of seabirds weave in and out among the surfacing whales. The scene is mesmerizing.

Off the side of the boat a long pectoral fin rises out of the water and then disappears. Then a large adult whale slowly surfaces to grab a breath of air—showing first its head, then its back, and finally its broad tail pointing skyward as the creature then dives back into the depths.

Everyone is captivated by the Humpback Whales in their numbers. I am deeply moved by it all. But we have other sightings of little-known sea life as well. A large pod of Short-beaked Common Dolphins passes the boat at one point. Then a large Basking Shark cruises by our boat at the water's surface, its dorsal fin calling attention to its presence. Finally, the boat passes an Ocean Sunfish that lies on its side on the sea surface. This, the largest of the bony fishes, is one of the most bizarre of sea creatures, shaped like a large silvery dish, all head, no tail, with two stiff, narrow fins protruding dorsally and ventrally. Its small pectoral fin protrudes above the surface, attracting our attention to this strange floating beast. And to top it off, as we motor back to Provincetown, the boat's naturalist, Dennis Minsky, points out a Loggerhead Turtle that has surfaced just off the bow. As the group debarks the boat, we all are spent from the excitement of what we have seen. No one was prepared for this effusion of sea life.

I camp that night just outside of Provincetown. The next morning before dawn I head out to Race Point Beach. I once visited this beach with my father and brother to watch a sailboat regatta in 1962. So much has changed since then. First, I take note of the abundance of Gray Seals, moving in pairs or small parties right along the shore. This is a surprise to me since there were no Gray Seals living on Cape Cod in 1962 (they had been hunted out by sealers and targeted as pests by commercial fishing operations). It took many decades for them to repopulate the cape.

Nor were there Great White Sharks in 1962, which are now commonplace predators lurking off the cape, hunting the now-abundant seals. The Trimbles had told me about the recent arrival of the sharks. I look out over the waves in search of a fin but see only Great Shearwaters foraging low over the water. I bump into a resident naturalist on the beach and ask her if she has ever seen a Great White. Instead of answering, she shows me the shark app on her smartphone showing the location of satellite-tagged Great Whites along the East Coast. On this early morning, the nearest tagged shark is down off Chatham, home to the largest haul-out beach for the seals on the cape. She tells me that the presence of the sharks is why the Gray Seals forage so close to shore. These seals live in holy terror of the lurking Great Whites.

Back home from my trip to New England, I see the first cricket hopping on the rug of my basement office—proof that autumn is on the way in the Mid-Atlantic. Biking to work this week, I start to get back into the groove, and yet I will not soon forget the whales of Cape Cod or that tumble high on Katahdin. Summer travels can create indelible memories.

THREE

September—Crickets and Broad-Wings

And on the mainland, in the waning summer nights, Bobolinks were
taking wing for far-off South America. These were the early ripples of
migration, ripples we would later see mount into the great waves
of the autumn flight.

—EDWIN WAY TEALE, *Autumn Across America*

We tend to absent-mindedly think that autumn begins immediately after
the Labor Day weekend, with the kids heading off to school and summer
vacations wrapped up and the return to the office with a rededication
to the work that had not been completed before the holidays. But this
season is not true autumn—meteorologically, it is still summer, and the
real autumn will not be solidly in place until mid-October or later,
well after the autumnal equinox in late September. Early autumn in
the Mid-Atlantic is the time of Indian Summer days, of vacillation between the warmth of summer and the cool breezes of fall. It's as if the
earth cannot make up its mind about autumn. Frankly, it is a nice confusion, because both alternatives are pleasant ones, as is the variation. And
even though the flood tide of reproduction that peaked in early June is

essentially spent, there are events that make the month worthwhile to a naturalist.

Most people abhor snakes and are terrified of venomous ones, even though these are rarely encountered. Once, many years ago, I stepped on a Timber Rattlesnake on a roadside up in Shenandoah National Park. I jumped a mile. Turned out it was dead—run over by a car. Somebody had cut off its rattle and tossed the dead snake in the grass, where I unwittingly trod upon it.

Biking home one afternoon in early September, I come upon a Copperhead snake on the bike path. The snake—quite alive—is diminutive, presumably born in the spring. Joggers and bikers are passing the little snake by, unseeing. I pass it at speed, jerk to a halt, then walk my bike back to this reclusive little creature that is putting its life at risk on the bike path. Using my bicycle pump, I nudge it gently off the pavement into the leaves and vines pathside. I watch it for a couple of minutes. The little snake twitches the tip of its tail but remains coiled and makes no attempt either to strike at me or to slither off. I am relieved it has not been harmed by some speeding biker.

This is only the second Copperhead I have ever encountered. In both instances I am struck by the sheer beauty of the snake. With its orderly and intricate dorsal pattern of dark brown and beige and its golden-brown triangular head and matching golden eye, this snake is both handsome and cryptic, a marvel of evolution. Its sedate behavior only adds to the animal's grace. When coiled atop some dead autumn oak leaves it simply disappears from view. Its various prey—mice, frogs, skinks, crickets, and the like—don't notice the predator until it is too late. The same goes for humans, but those wearing boots or even stout shoes have nothing to worry about. More likely, the snake will suffer a broken back from the human's misstep. So it goes for most snakes dwelling in the DC area. It's a wonder any survive to reproduce.

The best time to see Copperheads and Timber Rattlesnakes is in April and May, when the Appalachian woods begin to warm and the snakes come up from their rocky hibernacula. So when I encounter this small Copperhead in September, I stop and think of spring and what it would bring. But spring is a long way off. Early September still has the breath of summer, especially on those occasional sweltering days in DC when we all wonder why we are not still at the beach.

The next morning, while biking in to work, I glimpse a Northern Short-tailed Shrew as it quickly crosses the towpath, looking like a tiny gray blur. What's the deal with shrews? I rarely see them except dead on the sidewalk or brought to the doorstep by a cat. Also, it seems that the only shrew ever to show itself is the short-tailed shrew—even though the eastern United States is home to at least eight species of shrews. Shrews are tiny and retiring, yet they have a high metabolism and are very active during the daylight hours. More peculiarly, shrews have very poor eyesight, consume 80–90 percent of their body weight daily, are territorial, and apparently will eat just about anything. Some species, like our commonplace Northern Short-tailed Shrew, are venomous, presumably using the venom to kill the prey animals they attack. Shrews and moles are two common mammals that naturalists typically know little about and see rarely. They both remain mysterious to us.

Northern Short-tailed Shrew

In early September, British birder Andrew Ward visits DC from his home in Abu Dhabi and wants to go out on a Sunday to see some birds. In 2011, Andrew hosted me in Abu Dhabi, showing me two bird families—sand-grouse and Gray Hypocolius—that I had not seen before. Life families! Thus, I owe him, big time. . . .

I had taken Andrew out birding in the spring of 2012, and we did fairly well, but there still is some birding debt owed, it is safe to say. How often have I gotten to see two new bird families in a day? The difficulty, of course, is the season. Finding interesting birds in mid-September in the DC area is tricky. There are birds around, and birds are on the move, but early autumn can be tough birding.

The only sensible option is to get out into some nice habitat and enjoy the day, giving Andrew a fighting chance to see something new. This day is one of those glorious early autumn bluebird days, cool, clear, breezy, and with very low humidity. These are perfect for many outdoor activities (like a walk in the park), but not great for birding. The sunshine and breezes tamp down avian activity. To make matters worse, he is only available in the *afternoon*. Enough said!

These are the days one must loosen the reins and allow the glory of a fine early fall day to take hold. The perfection of a cool day in September can be unparalleled. This sort of day cannot be found in August in the DC area—one needs to be in Maine to experience such glory in that month. And in October, when the northwest wind blows, there is typically a bite in the air—a bit too reminiscent of the approaching month of November. On a perfect September day in DC one can happily wear jeans with a layer or two on top, and yet the sun is warm on the face in a way unlike any other. There is pleasure to be had, in spite of the expectation of rather sluggish birding.

To start our bird walk, we picnic under the trees in a big clearing near the Potomac River at Mason Neck State Park, Virginia. Few birds are calling, but the sounds of children are in the air. And Annual Cicadas continue to sound off despite the cool temperature. This day is perfect for families, and everywhere we go we find small family groups enjoying the day, happy to be outdoors in this weather.

An adult Bald Eagle hangs over the river, making wide circles. This brightens our picnic. Blue Jays and a Red-bellied Woodpecker call out to us. Pleasure boats move about on the broad river. The Black Gum trees scattered along the forest edge sport a few deep red leaves, hinting at the magnificence to come later in the year, when each tree will resonate with deep color.

After lunch, we wend our way along the Bay Front Trail in search of songbird flocks in the woods and water birds over the river. Burly Caspian Terns hunt offshore. A pair of Red-eyed Vireos gorge on the clusters of red berries produced by a small magnolia tree. Carolina Wrens call from thickets here and there. Luckily, Andrew finds butterflies to be of interest! Warm, dry days in September can be wonderful for butterflies. First, we locate an American Lady, with its varied background colors, false eyes, and intricate scroll lines on the hindwing. Then a pair of Great Spangled Fritillaries show up, foraging at the autumn flowers. A Monarch passes by low, with an American Kestrel zipping overhead high up.

Tracking down fall warblers is like pulling teeth. Silent, they keep in small parties in the tall trees, and picking them out from the foliage is nearly impossible. A lone Magnolia Warbler actually shows itself, along with several Tufted Titmice, which are always easier to get in the binoculars than the warblers. A Hairy Woodpecker and then a Pileated call out. The leaves crackle under our shoes. Runners pass us by in the woods, giving us birders a wave of apology for the disturbance.

Huntley Meadows Park, our next stop, lies a few miles to the northwest of Mason Neck in Fairfax County. To get there we had to use a stretch of Route 1—which on this Sunday afternoon is thronged with traffic and slowed by the inevitable accident blocking lanes. Once in the parking lot at Huntley Meadows, we are back in the lovely green world of quiet voices, power-walking seniors, and people exploring nature with their children. What a refuge from the blight and chaos of Route 1 south of downtown Alexandria, Virginia! We make our way out onto

Huntley Meadows's boardwalk. We have hopes of glimpsing a migrating Broad-winged Hawk, which would be a life bird for Andrew. My thinking is that we have a good chance of a Broad-wing if we park ourselves out in the middle of the swamp on the boardwalk, with all that sky above to scan. So we do just that.

While groups of strollers come and go, we take turns searching the skies and the wetlands around us for interesting birds. The blue sky is blotted with white clouds being pushed to the southeast. I find a large kettle of circling vultures, and we search it for Broad-wings, but to no avail. Then Andrew picks up a fast-moving raptor—a male Cooper's Hawk. To the west we catch sight of a Merlin, with its dark and sleek falcon shape. Another Bald Eagle circles. The shallow water below our feet stirs, and there is a large Common Snapping Turtle moving through the muck, its carapace just breaking the surface. Every now and then it drops to the bottom and pokes its head out to take air and look about. In the middle distance, a pair of young Great Blue Herons conduct a stately, slow-motion dance, bills tipped upward and wings slightly opened. Is this dance a first autumnal attempt for these two yearlings at courtship? We watch them circle each other gracefully for more than ten minutes, periodically breaking from them to scan the skies for the elusive Broad-wing.

With the sun low in the sky, we head back down the boardwalk to the visitor center. A passing nature photographer stops us to say that there are Ruby-throated Hummingbirds coming to the feeder there. Andrew has never seen a hummingbird, so that would be a new family for him. Perhaps I can start to repay my birding debt! We find a cluster of feeders behind the visitor center and in the very back is a single hummingbird feeding station. So, we sit at an adjacent picnic table and wait.

Here in the woods it is shady and cool. Andrew sets up his telescope and points it at the nectar feeder. I am hoping that we are not too late in the day for a hummer. The seed feeders are busy with visiting Carolina Chickadees, Tufted Titmice, and White-breasted Nuthatches. We watch the titmice lord it over the other songbirds coming in. The occasional Carolina Wren and Downy Woodpecker add to the traffic. Then a green blur zips from behind the shrubbery to the red nectar station—there is Andrew's desired hummingbird. The dowdy female gorges on sugar water for more than a minute while Andrew feasts on the sight. We watch the little sprite feed twice as the late afternoon shadows gather. A fitting end to a pleasant September day of birding, where birds are just a part of the day's pleasure.

It is now early mid-September, and from my front doorstep this morning I hear a Yellow-throated Vireo singing (it must think it is still early summer). A White-breasted Nuthatch calls as I walk out to pick up the newspaper. Another perfect, cloudless early autumn day, with the temperature expected to reach the seventies. While hitting tennis balls against the backboard in the park behind my house I hear a Red-shouldered Hawk keening high overhead. I also hear a flock of American Goldfinches giving their autumn *wee-hee* call, then the persistent song of the Carolina Wren, the *wheep!* of a Great Crested Flycatcher, and the *churr* of the Red-bellied Woodpecker. This afternoon, the Annual Cicadas are still doing their summer droning. Back from the park, I find a Twelve-spot Skimmer dragonfly alight on the front brick wall of our house before it darts off, and a Common Checkered Skipper feeds on

Carol's flowers in the front yard. Driving down MacArthur Boulevard, I encounter a Red Fox scampering across the road, tail high, from one patch of woods to another, in the Palisades section of Washington.

Sometimes called the catlike canine, the Red Fox is one of those species that has benefited from rewilding of the Eastern Seaboard. As a child growing up in Baltimore, I did not see a Red Fox until I was a teenager, in spite of being out looking. Now, living in Bethesda and without really trying, I encounter this species at least a dozen times a year. This smallish predator has adapted well to suburban woodlots—much better than the similar-sized Bobcat, probably because the fox subsists on smaller prey and has a greater tendency to omnivory, even taking fruit and insects. One spring, I locate an active Red Fox den beside the towpath below Fletcher's Cove in DC proper. I find the fox kits tearing apart a Canada Goose carcass beside the den while the adult, seeing me, retreats into the woods. The feeding kits pay me no mind, and I am able to watch them unimpeded at close range. The four are small and fuzzy and dirty gray-buff, not orange-brown like the parent.

This beautiful predator, because it crosses roads at night when out foraging, puts itself at risk of death-by-car weekly. Was the road-killed fox I see near the DC line a few days later the creature I encountered on this day? My heart goes out to the urban Red Foxes that face peril at every turn. They are no match for the speeding cars shining their bright headlights after dark.

On a warm, sunny day it is great to head out into the field in search of mid-September nature. Things are typically starting to dry out in anticipation of full-on autumn, so it is not wet underfoot, and the last flowers of fall are abundant and covered with foraging bees and butterflies. The cicadas are still noisy, but their sounds are joined by the voices of small groups of Blue Jays and American Goldfinches. Some of the trees and shrubs are starting to show color. This is the time of year to head upstream along the Potomac into western Montgomery County, Maryland, to places such as Swains Lock, Pennyfield Lock, Violette's Lock, or McKee-Beshers Wildlife Management Area. These are all situated along the C&O Canal out beyond Potomac Village, and all are great for a walk at any time. They are super for birds in late spring, when the migrants are flooding through, but they are also pleasant during the early fall, when the world is starting to ready itself for winter and the last breath of summer can be felt.

This turning point, approaching the autumnal equinox, is a time when summer begins to tip into fall. The sun is dropping lower in the sky, and the wood warblers are putting on their washed-out autumn plumages, just to challenge us one last time as they head southward. No bright, complex songs—just chip notes. No bright spring colors—just grays, buffs, olives, and washed-out yellows. This is the real test of a birder's fortitude!

Although birding is my favorite pastime, I also love butterflies. It's always fun to see how many butterflies I can find in a few hours. Jeffrey Glassberg's *Butterflies Through Binoculars* reports that eighty-one species of butterflies have been recorded from McKee-Beshers Wildlife Management Area—an amazing number! Between the birds and the butterflies, a naturalist can really have a field day out along the Potomac (throw in frogs, turtles, snakes, and some wildflowers, and there is a whole year's worth of entertainment—absolutely free of charge).

On this day I focus on photographing butterflies, bees, wasps, and snakes. All of these are most active when the sun is higher in the sky and the air has lost its autumn-morning bite. These cold-blooded creatures need sun to warm their internal engines, unlike the hot-blooded birds. I take my bicycle with me atop the car. On my bike I can cover more territory and stop and drop the bike whenever I encounter something cool. I park my car at the west end of Hunting Quarter Road, where the big wetland impoundment is accessible by a broad path atop a dike. Because it is a weekday, I share the dike with a lone birder of retirement age. The swamp features a Great Egret to the left and a Great Blue Heron to the right. A pair of Mallards swing by overhead. A single Chimney Swift forages high up in the blue. A few plants are in flower— Chicory, Rough-stemmed Goldenrod, Queen Anne's Lace, Thin-leaved Sunflower, and Halberd-leaved Rose Mallow. The butterflies seem to like the goldenrod and sunflowers the best today, but their numbers are thin: a Monarch, a Spicebush Swallowtail, an American Buckeye, several skippers, and four additional lesser species. The bees are more abundant, some of the big black bumblebee types, and quite a few of the smaller types I have never learned to identify. I bike down the main track past crops planted for the deer and turkey (this is a hunting area). At the edge of a sun-dappled patch of grass, a sleek Black Rat Snake is stretched out in that weird fashion where it is all rippled—overall the snake forms a straight line, but it is sinuously laid out like a walking stick made from a curly branch. I drop my bike and get out my camera to photograph the snake, which attempts to move off into the woods. I stand in its way, and the snake gets aggressive—knotting its neck up into a series of stacked bends that will allow it to strike out at me if need be. Undeterred, I take lots of photographs from different angles, and the snake then proceeds to flatten out and starts to make a strange rattling sound—I assume another form of threat. Then in a wink, it bolts for the safety of the woods.

Returning to the paved country road, I come upon a touching scene of sadness. On the drive out here I had passed a road-killed Woodchuck. On my return, from a distance I can see that it is being attended by another Woodchuck—its mate? As I approach in the car, the live Woodchuck—presumably mourning the dead one—withdraws to the side of the road in order to avoid the fate of its dead companion.

Driving the back roads of the suburban and rural DC environs, I pass hundreds of road-killed wild mammals each year—Eastern Gray Squirrels, White-tailed Deer, Raccoons, Virginia Opossums, Eastern Cottontails, Striped Skunks, Red Foxes, and Woodchucks, among others. I see these dead creatures and feel a pang of guilt, even when I know I did not do the killing myself. But seeing a recently dead creature being attended by its living mate is that much worse. We all should make more effort to protect these wild creatures from such a grisly end.

Songbird flocks become commonplace as summer turns to fall. Each passing day I seem to see more of these—flocks of American Robins, various blackbirds, Brown-headed Cowbirds, European Starlings, crows, and more. During the same period, the frequency of avian vocalization continues to decline, to be replaced by the sound of crickets—autumn's leading vocalists. Late one afternoon, coming back into the neighborhood, I encounter a large flock of House Sparrows preparing to bed down in a tall green hedge—more evidence of impending autumn.

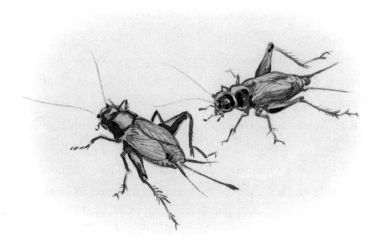

Field Crickets

While playing tennis on Saturday, I casually look up and see a sky full of Broad-winged Hawks in migration. I count fifty-three individuals kettling overhead. One does not need to travel to a hawk watch site to see raptors in the autumn. Given the proper winds, one can see impressive flights passing over the DC area. Moreover, hawk populations in the East have grown substantially over the past half-century, mainly because of effective conservation measures that have reduced the wanton so-called sport-shooting of raptors by hunters and fostered the regeneration of the East's great forests, which offer abundant breeding habitat for many raptor species. I grew up looking for raptors in the Baltimore area in the 1960s, and I can report that today I see many more raptors than I did as a youngster—there are many more to be seen. That is one of the good-news environmental stories we all should take to heart. It is possible to do the right thing and generate measurable results through smart legislation and improved stewardship.

South Mountain, Maryland, is where I first learned about seasonal hawk watches. A hawk watch is a favorable site to watch and count migrating raptors that is usually operated by a group of volunteers who attend the lookout daily during migration (mainly in the fall, in some places in the spring). The hawk watch at South Mountain is one of the oldest and best known in the area. South Mountain is a local high point along the Appalachian Trail, where a stone monument was erected in 1827 by the people of nearby Boonsboro to honor George Washington. The monument looks something like an old stone furnace; inside is a rough stone stairway twisting up to the top of the monument, which features a circular observation platform and a chest-high stone retaining wall. The open-air top deck of the monument is the place where hawk watchers count hawks every autumn. For me, it was a great place to give hawk watching a try. I first visited here with my mother in the 1960s, when we drove up on a windy day in late September and observed a mix of raptors passing by. The most common hawk species then were Sharp-shinneds and Red-tails. Taking a break from hawk watching, it's fun eating a picnic lunch at the base of the monument, where a low stone wall sits atop a talus slope of rough granitic boulders offering a vista out over the broad agricultural valley to the west.

Unaware of the hawk watch, most visitors to the monument are day-trippers visiting the little state park for an outing—young parents with little children who love to be lifted up onto the stone parapet to gaze out at the autumn scenery. In October, this is lit up by the low sun on the yellows, oranges, and reds of the maples, hickories, and oaks that cloak these slopes. The Potomac lurks over to the west, mainly hidden by hills, and Hagerstown sits to the northwest.

I say that South Mountain is a good place to *start* exploring the hawk watching phenomenon for two reasons—it is nearby and it is *not* the most productive in terms of raptor numbers. Best to start low and work one's way up the chart. Next on the list would be Waggoner's Gap, north of Carlisle, Pennsylvania, which is a two-hour drive from DC, and then Hawk Mountain, in Kempton, Pennsylvania, over a three-hour drive. Last, there is Cape May, New Jersey, which offers not only excellent hawk watching but all other forms of birding in the fall—songbirds, shorebirds, and seabirds. Because of these hawk watches, there is now a sizable core of dedicated volunteer raptor watchers scattered through the East. Many of these are not generalized birders but focus exclusively on hawks, eagles, and falcons.

In late September a Northern Mockingbird sings like crazy in a small park in Rosslyn, Virginia, on the north side of Key Bridge. The morning is cool and partly cloudy with south winds. Flocks of American Robins are on the move. There is a touch of chill in the air. Most birds are silent, and most of the common songbirds are not in evidence. Biking home in the early afternoon, I look up in the sky along the C&O Canal to see a swirling mass of Fish Crows high above. They are all giving their high-pitched, soft *kah!* note, and the wind is moving them all about. What exactly are they doing up there? Some sort of social signaling, but precisely what is not at all clear.

At last, autumnal weather is beginning to take hold. As a biker, I welcome the chill mornings of autumn. They make the ride to work invigorating.

FOUR

October—Crisp Days, Northwest Winds

The whitethroats are singing again this morning. As I stand listening to them
repeat their songs, noting how the singing of one male sets off the singing of
another, a memory awakens.

—EDWIN WAY TEALE, *A Walk Through the Year*

Early October. Chill dawns. Clear skies. Northwest winds. Maple leaves
swirling. Autumn is arriving! No one is immune to the transition from
late summer to autumn. It is too bracing to ignore and too pleasant to
dislike. Biking to work in the morning, I notice that the resident birds
are a bit more vocal than they have been. I hear voices of Downy Woodpecker, Blue Jay, American Crow, and White-breasted Nuthatch. It is as
if the birds have been invigorated by the bracing weather.

This evening I witness a curious natural event while biking home
along the Virginia side of the Potomac. Scores of Ring-billed Gulls are in
the air hawking insects along the George Washington Memorial Parkway.
The gulls form a series of linear flocks, all west of the river, mostly thirty to
fifty feet up, actively hawking (swooping upward with mouth opened). What
insects are they hawking? There must be some midautumn emergence of
a social insect worth feeding on. Who ever thought of a gull as a flycatcher?

My bike rides along the Potomac teach me that there is plenty to learn about even the most commonplace species. The lowly Ring-billed Gull is the lay-about gull of Washington. Much of the year—from autumn to early spring—it is the gull we see on the river, on the National Mall, overhead, everywhere. It never seems to be doing too much, so naturalists like me tend to dismiss the species as commonplace, even uninteresting. In fact, over the year, the commonplace Ring-billed Gull does more than lounge about the Mall. In the spring and early summer these birds nest colonially on northern rivers and lakes, well out of sight. During the breeding season they sport a saucy red eye-ring and crisp white plumage with highlights of gray and black. And their fly-catching behavior proves that we naturalists still have things to learn. Good naturalists are always looking and always curious—even about the goings-on of the everyday species.

When cutting the grass one autumn day, I find that the bottom of our back lawn is pocked by the burrowing and mounding activities of an Eastern Mole. There are no visible entrance holes, and the mole remains hidden underground. I have never seen a mole leave its underground lair. Like the shrews, moles are mysterious mammals at our doorstep. Who ever sees a free-ranging mole? But there is a mole ensconced in our backyard now, and it has been creating large mounds of bare earth, with the subsequent loss of grass cover. The mound-building is quite annoying, because the mounds catch on the bottom of the rotary mower. Most homeowners dislike moles, and it's hard for me not to feel the same way. I would be more sympathetic if this wild species made itself more visible. I want to see the wild creatures that live in my backyard! For instance, there is a young Eastern Cottontail that has frequented our yard this autumn. It is probably consuming some of our

Eastern Mole

ornamental plantings, but it is such an adorable little creature that I have
no trouble with it spending time in our yard. When am I going to see
this mole?

Reading up on the subject of moles, this is what I have discovered.
Our common species, the Eastern Mole, is only seven inches long but
may live as long as six years. It inhabits much of the eastern United States,
west to the Great Plains. Besides its tiny eyes (covered by a protective
layer of skin) and nearly naked tail and snout, the most prominent feature
of this species is its broad, paddlelike front feet, set on short and side-
ward-facing limbs, built for plowing earth to each side as the creature
digs its way through the soft earth. The Eastern Mole feeds on earth-
worms, other invertebrates, and plant material. The male maintains a
home range considerably larger than that of the female. The distinctive
molehill is produced when the mole digs a deep burrow, shifting the

earth upward to create the underground cavity. This deep burrow is for nesting, wintering, and escaping periods of drought. The many shallow tunnels just below the roots of the lawn are used for daily foraging.

One of our family's favorite day-trip destinations is Sugarloaf Mountain, about thirty minutes' drive from our home in Bethesda. Sugarloaf is a geologic feature known as a monadnock—an isolated mountain that rises from a plain. This 1,282-foot-high easternmost outlier of the Appalachians rises out of the gently rolling piedmont south of Frederick, Maryland. Sugarloaf is, in fact, the prominent high point in a low ridge that trends southwest-northeast just like all the more prominent Appalachian ridges arrayed farther west. Encircled by a private forest reserve of three thousand acres known as the Stronghold, Sugarloaf was purchased and protected by Donald Strong in the 1940s. For DC residents, it is a splendid nearby hilly patch of forest for hiking, and the rocky promontories at its north and south summits offer panoramic views to the northwest toward Frederick, west toward South Mountain, and southwest toward the Potomac River and Virginia. There are even some rock-climbing pitches that are popular with technical climbers. In the spring, the Stronghold's breeding songbirds are vocal, and salamanders and snakes are much in evidence. There is even a Timber Rattlesnake den hidden on the property. In the autumn, the changing leaves are marvelous, and the leaf-strewn trails and cool temperatures make hiking a weekend pleasure. Vocal Common Ravens loaf around the rocky cliffs the year-round. There are also numbers of resident Turkey Vultures and Black Vultures that catch the updrafts around the summit area.

The Stronghold property supports a good network of color-marked trails that crisscross the forested tract. It also has a winding automobile road that leads to two overlooks, each with short walking trails to the highest summit. Visitors can choose what sort of walk they desire. For a long hike, park at the bottom of the mountain and hike to the summit. For a short hike with a great summit vista, drive to the west view parking lot and go up from there. The mature woodlands support oak-hickory forest with a scattering of pines in the rockier uplands. The owners periodically extract timber from small enclaves in the reserve in order to encourage forest regeneration and the creation of openings for wildlife. In late spring, birders visit Sugarloaf in search of breeding songbirds, especially Black-and-white and Worm-eating Warblers, Louisiana Waterthrushes, Pine Warblers, Wood Thrushes, and Scarlet Tanagers. In autumn, ravens, vultures, and passing raptors attract the most attention, visible from the various overlooks. But really it is the walking through leaf-strewn deciduous woods during the height of the fall colors that brings most nature lovers here.

It is mid-October. As I bike to work on a cool and cloudless morning, the temperature is forty-eight degrees. I find American Robins feeding in a large vine of Wild Grape hanging off a canopy tree beside the C&O Canal. In fact, they are also feeding a group of Common Carp that linger beneath the tree to scoop up any dropped fruit that hits the surface of the water. This is a nice example of incidental species interaction, not quite a symbiosis.

Many nonbirders are convinced that their neighborhood population of American Robins arrives with a flourish in the spring and departs with a *whoosh* in the fall. After all, they were told that by an all-knowing parent, so it must be true. In fact, there are robins in the DC area year-round, though perhaps not the same individuals. In the Mid-Atlantic region, robins are migratory, but this may be manifested mainly in the tendency to join flocks and become nomadic, in search of prime foraging grounds, in the winter. Local birds may move as little as a hundred miles or less during the nonbreeding season. Robins mainly eat invertebrates during the summer and fruit in the winter. This shift to a fruit diet encourages flocking: the spatially concentrated fruit is most efficiently shared by a flock of foragers, and flocks can move around and clean up the fruit resources of late autumn and winter. Flock foraging may also help individual robins avoid predator attacks by bird-eating hawks.

The American Robin continues to prosper in the human-dominated landscape and remains a favorite nesting yard bird. Perhaps most remarkable is that this common backyard nester is one of the most widespread of North American songbirds. American Robins inhabit the boreal conifer forests of Labrador, Hudson Bay, and Alaska, and breeding populations extend, in the mountains, to southern Mexico. I am always surprised when I encounter our familiar backyard bird in the mountain wilds of the Adirondacks of Upstate New York, far from the nearest back lawn.

From mid-September to mid-November, Cape May is an important destination for savvy birders who live within driving distance of southern New Jersey. For me and my friends, the Cape May autumn birding weekend has become a treasured annual pilgrimage, which we started doing regularly in the 1980s. I first visited Cape May in the late 1950s with my family—in the summer as the traditional beach destination at a time when the nearer Delaware beaches had not been fully developed. Then in 1970 I visited Cape May on a birding field trip with a high school classmate to witness the spring migration—excellent but not quite as fantastic as the fall. Since then I have been back scores of times, usually once or twice each autumn.

We begin planning our Cape May autumn weekends in the heat of summer, and we work out the details weeks in advance. Our autumn sojourns at Cape May combine sometimes-great birding with a weekend's camaraderie among close birding friends. But there's more. Cape May in autumn is a most desirable weekend destination. There is always a chance of bumping into old friends and colleagues (visiting for the same reason) whom one hasn't seen for years. And then there are the year-round naturalists living in Cape May who are fun to hang out with and who know all the secrets of the place. Last but not least, there are great restaurants where one can celebrate a great day or, by having a superb meal, wipe away the disappointment of a day just done when the birds or weather did not cooperate.

But first come the birds! In season, the birds at Cape May can be fabulous because of the cape's geography. Cape May is a finger of sand jutting southward into the sea. Murky Delaware Bay lies to the west and the Atlantic to the east and south. Recall that the Atlantic Coast retreats southwestward from New England. The autumn winds favored by migrating birds blow from the northwest. Land birds, migrating southward in the autumn, find that these favored northwest winds steer them to the tip of this peninsula, creating a bonanza for birders situated there. Many,

many birds end up at the cape, surrounded by salt water, wondering how to continue their journey southward but reticent to cross the broad bay waters to Delaware. This geographic conundrum for the birds is a boon for the birders, because the birds swirl around Cape May Point, making themselves easy to be seen and identified. Then the true landlubbers among them (songbirds and many other small land birds) follow the east coast of Delaware Bay northwestward and cross the water at a narrower spot. By contrast, the more adventurous or water-loving species (Ospreys, falcons, herons) rise with the winds and cross the salt water at its widest, arriving at Cape Henlopen, Delaware, via the direct route.

It's not unusual to see a hundred species of birds in an autumn weekend at Cape May: eagles, hawks, falcons, herons, ducks, gulls, terns, sandpipers, warblers, vireos, and sparrows. This is the place to see a hundred falcons in a day in mid-October. Or to see fifteen species of warblers in a morning. But most of all it is a phenomenon of abundance and of concentration—birds in the sky at all times.

Cape May is also wonderful for its range of natural habitats: coastal beaches, salt marshes, ponds, thickets, woods, grasslands, lagoons, canals, bays, tidal rips, open ocean, and more. Each habitat is favored by a particular selection of bird species. So our happy birding group can meander from one habitat to the next, picking up nifty species at each stop.

Then there are the surprises and the rarities. The surprises are birds that are common in some places but rare on the East Coast, such as the Western Kingbird or the Cave Swallow. The true rarities are birds that are nowhere abundant and are always a great treat to encounter, such as Connecticut Warbler or Le Conte's Sparrow. Every good Cape May weekend promises one or two avian surprises or rarities.

The fun of it all, especially in this age of smartphones, is that there are thousands of pairs of birding eyes searching, and news of a rare bird gets broadcast with remarkable speed. This means that more people get to see each special bird. An online posting announces the new finds minute by minute, so the electronically attuned birder can respond quickly. That's a far cry from the technology I grew up with. In the 1970s, the local "Voice of Audubon" recording that listed rare bird sightings was updated once a week—talk about behind the curve!

Cape May is also notable for being one of America's first summer beach towns, and it has a rich history. Because of this, it has many good places to stay and eat, often filled with happy birders. And because it is a seasonal meeting place, one can feel the joy. Everybody is there determined to have fun, and that makes it pleasant for everyone.

The natural phenomena at Cape May are not confined to the birds, though the birds are indeed special. The daytime movement of migrating hawks and eagles is awesome. One can stand on the hawk watch platform at Cape May Point State Park and look up to see scores of raptors of a half-dozen species wheeling about, trying to figure out their next migratory move. Cape May is also a place where Monarchs and other butterflies as well as dragonflies congregate on their autumn journey south, converging on the gardens at the traffic circle near the point. On cool nights the Monarchs assemble in large clusters in the pines along the beachfront. Butterfly lovers visit these clusters as the sun rises to watch the butterflies awaken and disperse for the day. Autumn sunsets and sunrises, too, are stunning, mainly because of the wraparound shoreline. And one can see the weather patterns close-up in a place as exposed as Cape May. There's just a load of nature here. For some of us, this might be the final major nature outing of the calendar year—a last hurrah.

Now to the songbird flight of October 16–18, 2005. Birding friend David Wilcove and I have been traveling to Cape May in autumn for decades, and it was not until the fall of 2005 that we got our first true monster flight, witnessed at Higbee Beach. Because it was late in the songbird season, it was all about the numbers of birds, not the number of species seen—few species in vast quantities. That said, we did record 119 species for the weekend, including 12 species of raptors. But it was the songbird invasion that made the weekend unique. Each morning brought a swirling storm of little songbirds blown in on the northwest winds. These birds had been bottled up by a long period of southerly winds and stormy weather in New England. Once that weather dissipated and the northwest wind began to blow, it unleashed a hurricane of songbirds desperate to get to the southlands before winter was upon them. Most remarkable about this four-day phenomenon was that each successive day was bigger than the preceding one. Each morning, the sky was littered with Yellow-rumped and Palm Warblers, Northern Flickers, American Robins, and Sharp-shinned Hawks. There were birds in the sky, on the ground, atop parked cars, and whipping past stunned birders. Once we realized the magnitude of the flight, we played hooky from work and stayed over on Monday to get another morning of the mass migration. Although we were not present for the last day of the flight, we were told that Tuesday was even more amazing than Monday.

On a typical fall day at Higbee Beach, one might look up into the sky to see two or three birds on the wing at any point. By contrast, on these monster days, one would look up and see scores or hundreds of birds in the air, being buffeted by the strong northwest blow. Binoculars were of no use because of the strength of the winds and the numbers of birds. It was best just to stand and watch them all swirl about. This was not so much a fallout as a big blow—one we will probably never witness again. Here are some of the counts from that weekend that boggle the mind:

October 15: 1,418 American Kestrels, 342 Merlins, 41 Peregrines

October 16: 2,000 Northern Flickers, 25,000 Tree Swallows, 1,500 Palm Warblers, 40,000 Yellow-rumped Warblers

October 17: 2,000 Palm Warblers, 30,000 Yellow-rumped Warblers

October 18: 955 Northern Flickers, 200,000+ Yellow-rumped Warblers

In late October I like to go camping at Greenbrier State Park, in Frederick County, Maryland. Car camping with the kids in October in the mountains west of DC is a treat if the weather cooperates. So long as the sky is blue and air is cool, camping will be a winner. The cool weather makes sleeping in a tent a pleasure and also makes the ritual of a campfire at dinner and breakfast both practical and fun. Greenbrier is about an hour's drive northwest of Bethesda. The park is situated on a high basin on the western side of South Mountain ridge, not far from Washington Monument State Park. In late October the leaves are starting to fall and the weather tends to be dry and clear—great camping weather. The kids love having a big campfire and having fire sticks, which are nothing more than dry switches that can be stuck in the fire to create a bright burning ember on the tip. The stick can then be waved about to make glowing designs in the dark or to threaten another fire stick–wielding child. Naturally, for the supervising parent, this is marginal behavior—potentially dangerous—so limits have to be maintained. Hotdogs are cooked in the evening and marshmallows roasted, but the true highlight of the campout is breakfast, during which a whole pound of bacon is roasted to a crisp on a skillet over the fire (for some reason it tastes better cooked this way). Doughnuts, crispy bacon, and hot chocolate make an irresistible feast for the kids on a cool October morning.

Naturewise, it is mainly a blizzard of autumn leaves—which range from not quite prime in the lower zones to almost finished atop the ridge. A side trip to the monument atop South Mountain is a featured exercise, which takes us along a winding and very hilly road where we try to make the car "fly" over the highest humps in the road—bringing out shrill shrieks from the kids. This time of year, the forests are pretty quiet. Barred Owls often hoot at night, but not much else is in evidence. Here one gets a preview of the months to come when winter descends over the countryside.

As the end of October approaches, the morning chill intensifies, the days shorten, and the end of Daylight Savings Time creeps ever closer. For the year-round biker, the seasonal shift in the declination of the earth has a substantial impact, especially if one departs for work by 7:00 a.m. and gets home at 7:00 p.m. The biker must start preparing a bicycle lighting plan that will render the biker visible to others and illuminate the bicycle path when it is dark. I prefer a couple of headlights and at least two flashing red rear beacons—one for the back of the helmet, the other for the rear of the seat-post. One cannot have too many bike lights. For a bit more than four months a year I travel in the dark for at least part of the day's ride. It is a major annual adjustment.

Riding home at night along the gravel towpath of the C&O Canal involves getting used to biking blind. Yes, the front lights provide some illumination, but not nearly enough to allow the rider to truly see the way. One must take a leap of faith that the path is clear on the evening ride home just as it was clear on the morning ride in. If a limb has fallen across the towpath in the afternoon, the nighttime biker will encounter this barrier with little time to see it, for the brain to interpret what is being seen, and for the biker to apply the brakes or to dodge the obstruction. Surprisingly, though I have fallen quite a few times when biking to or from work, I have never fallen after dark.

A few times I have found myself engaged with an evening social event downtown that forced me to bike home after midnight. This is a distinct experience altogether, because the biker is in unfamiliar territory, timewise. Biking the several miles down along the wooded Potomac is a bit eerie but also invigorating. In the deep of night, the senses are alert. One rarely encounters another biker after midnight, but there are other encounters to be had, such as with homeless men who camp in the woods along the river. More common, and perhaps a greater threat for mishap, are the abundant deer foraging along the towpath. They generally do not move or retreat as the biker passes. My concern is that my bicycle spooks a big buck and it crosses my path, taking me and the bicycle down. Luckily, this has not yet happened. Some late nights I have counted a half-dozen or more deer on the path, so the worry about human-deer contact is not unrealistic.

Perhaps the greatest threat to night biking is a large American Beaver, perched silently on the towpath, like a big black boulder. The deer have eyeshine, so it is pretty easy to see the deer in advance. Not so with the beaver, whose small beady eyes are less reflective. I missed a huge beaver one night by a hair and was past him before I even knew what I had avoided. If I had struck the beaver head-on, it would not have been pretty for either of us.

By the end of October, the sapsuckers arrive in the Mid-Atlantic from their nesting grounds in the mixed deciduous woods of New England and Canada. They filter in like snowflakes, settling one by one in woodlots and backyards. Their arrival is marked by the distinctive high and nasal squealing note *Kiiyyyanh!* that the solitary wintering birds give every now and then. Hearing this note strikes a chord in longtime birders, announcing that full-on autumn has arrived. It has a touch of the bittersweet. Yes, it is a treat adding a new bird to the autumn list, but with it comes the acknowledgment of the impending arrival of winter and the passing of another calendar year of birding.

There is nothing quite like a sapsucker. First, the name—it's a bit out there. . . . Our eastern species is infelicitously named Yellow-bellied Sapsucker, a bit like what a school bully might call a boy he's about to beat to a pulp in the playground. Names like sapsucker make birdwatching a pastime many people in America still mock. What right-minded teenager would voluntarily want to spend time outside, in the woods, with other like-minded souls, in search of something named Yellow-bellied Sapsucker?

In reality, among the insiders who know about birds and birding, Yellow-bellied Sapsucker is, indeed, a silly name, but the bird itself is more than worthy of the strange moniker. It *is* yellow bellied. And it does drill sap wells in certain species of trees for the express purpose of both drinking the exuding sap and consuming the insects attracted to the sap wells. These sap wells are drilled in series of rows, each horizontal row neatly arrayed down the trunk of a tree. No other woodpecker perma-

Yellow-bellied Sapsucker

nently tattoos tree bark like the sapsucker, although apparently the
Downy Woodpecker is also known occasionally to construct sap wells
for the same purpose.

For me, the Yellow-bellied Sapsucker is special for three reasons.
First, it is a summer denizen of the forests of the North Woods and thus
very much associated with the summers I spent as a boy in the Adirondacks. Second, the herky-jerky staccato drumming produced by the
territorial male is both memorable and amusing—it sounds as if the bird
is sending a signal in some kind of drunken Morse Code (by comparison,
the drumming of other woodpeckers is smooth and continuous and
easily distinguished). Third, as I mentioned, in our area the sapsucker

is a harbinger of year's end. Hearing the sapsucker's squeal, along with the sad song of the White-throated Sparrow and the sight of a Palm Warbler in a countryside hedge, always reminds me that it is time to buy a pumpkin for Halloween.

On Thursday, my wife and I sneak off with the kids to a local pumpkin patch in northern Montgomery County. In the Mid-Atlantic this is a seasonal rite of passage (in what Carol calls agrotainment). Local farms expand their customer base by offering festive seasonal events that typically revolve around wandering outside in the country and selecting and buying some agricultural product, such as a pumpkin or Indian corn or apple butter—things you probably would never think to buy if you were in the supermarket on a Saturday morning. When I was a child, a single pumpkin was plenty. Today, each family member, it seems, gets to choose one. I enjoy these rural excursions in late October because I typically encounter White-crowned Sparrows and Palm Warblers in the overgrown hedgerows of the pumpkin patches. And usually there is a Red-tailed Hawk or two blowing around overhead in the autumn wind. And, of course, the autumn colors are at their peak, and, for once, the children are behaving instead of fighting. . . .

In late October 2012, the hurricane known as Superstorm Sandy struck New York City and the New Jersey coast with a ferocious punch—more than three million people were left without electricity. Our beloved Cape May was lashed but survived with only minor damage. In the DC area, the storm was mainly rain and wind, but we still got two days off from work because of downed trees and powerlines.

Late spring to late autumn is the hurricane season. Sandy struck in late autumn, but then again, Sandy was a cross between a hurricane and a nor'easter, something of a perfect storm. The damage wrought by Sandy was horrific. By zeroing in on New York City, Sandy wreaked havoc on the most densely populated urban area of the East Coast. The flooding of lower Manhattan and Brooklyn was catastrophic. And the northern Jersey Shore took the biggest hit of all, with entire beachfront communities being demolished, along with boardwalks, shorefronts, and the livelihoods of hundreds of thousands.

The severe impact of major storms on barrier islands and beaches is nothing new to the East Coast. I remember well the great Ash Wednesday storm of March 1962, which made a direct hit on the Delaware shore. My mother drove my older brother, Bill, and me down to Bethany Beach to inspect the damage firsthand. Many of the great creosote-shingled shorefront summer residences were cast about like little toy houses on a tipped Monopoly board. Much of the beach was thrown across the ocean highway into the bay. The highway itself was closed between Bethany Beach and Rehoboth by storm-tossed dunes of sand astride the road. We thought it was all fantastic and surreal, but of course, we were not homeowners who had lost everything.

Storms like that of 1962 and Sandy move a lot of water and sand. The funny thing is that the Mid-Atlantic coast and its barrier beaches and islands are the natural end product of this storm-wracked history. The beaches, barrier islands, inlets, and bays are all created by a mix of calm and catastrophe. And nothing stays in the same place for long. Everything moves, even the dune grass. It was only after the mad beachfront summer-home-building orgy of the 1960s and 1970s that governments began to invest in the impossible dream of coastal "permanence."

That delusional effort, costing tens of millions of dollars annually, continues to be the folly of beach town mayors and foolish statehouse governments. Remember the greedy mayor of Amity Beach in the movie *Jaws*? Think every East Coast beach town mayor and their planning sessions with the US Army Corps of Engineers. The corps has been tasked with the demented mission of stilling the seas—King Canute redux.

The big-time losers here are the American taxpayers, whose money is swept away like sand, *and* the coastal birdlife, the coastal fishery, and the magnificent and purposely ephemeral natural coastal environments that evolved in concert with the stormy sea. This interplay of sea and shore produces a complex mix of dune, beach, flat, and barrier island that creates foraging, roosting, and critical nesting habitat for Wilson's and Piping Plovers, Least and Sandwich Terns, and migrating American Golden-Plovers and Hudsonian Godwits, as well as a host of nearshore migratory fish species. Because of the widespread depredations of the Army Corps of Engineers, many habitats have been wiped from existence or much degraded, replaced by the barren dune habitat and the kind of impoverished littoral zone that can be re-created by bulldozers and sand-dredges. Luckily, a few natural places remain in the National Seashores—the likes of Assateague Island, a few hours' drive from DC. But the rest is not what it once was because of the dark partnership of the corps and greedy seaside developers.

Few people get as excited about the passage of a hurricane as meteorologists, the staff of weather.com, and the Army Corps of Engineers. Add birders to that short list. Certainly, birders do not celebrate the arrival of a hurricane, but they do attempt to take advantage of a ghastly meteorological phenomenon that they cannot influence in any way. The swirling mass of wind and airborne water carries with it clots of pelagic seabirds that normally never make landfall on the East Coast. These are the jaegers, phalaropes, shearwaters, storm-petrels, frigatebirds, boobies, and tropicbirds—feathered gold to land-based Mid-Atlantic birders.

These mysterious and striking birds of the far ocean are literally carried aloft for days, often borne along with the storm scores of miles into the interior. Once the storm subsides (which happens rapidly after landfall), the birds do the only logical thing. They scramble about in search of a stream, then follow that stream until it joins a river, then follow the river until it joins a bay, and then follow the bay out to the open ocean. The smart birders line up on the windward shore of the nearest coastal river or bay and watch with binoculars and telescopes as the oceanic waifs trickle down toward the sea. There is no better way for land-based birders to see these elusive birds other than on their distant island nesting grounds. After the passage of Sandy, the storm-blown seabirds coming down the Delaware Bay were amazing: 125+ Pomarine Jaegers, Band-rumped Storm-Petrels, and much more. Stationed south of Philadelphia on the Delaware River, my birding buddy David Wilcove and his graduate students watched dozens of jaegers and a phalarope pass downriver on the way back to the sea. We have done this at East Potomac Park in DC after Hurricanes Irene and Isabel passed by. It works! Try it the next time you want to see a Sooty Tern or a Parasitic Jaeger.

It is Halloween day in Brookmont—very cool and cloudless. Walking the dog, I admire a spectacular sunrise across the Potomac. The

White-throated Sparrows are noisy in the thickets this morning. Stubby-tailed and chocolate brown, a Winter Wren hunts for arthropods in a small bush by my home office window. I watch it as it preens and fusses only eight feet away from my computer as I write.

The arrival of the Winter Wren in our neighborhood signals the approach of frosty mornings of early winter. These little wrens like to hunker down in a jumble of fallen branches in a ravine for the winter. During this time, they do not give their marvelous reeling song, but they do make their presence known by quiet *jib* notes when they are disturbed. This is a bird we search for during our Christmas Bird Counts, come December.

FIVE

November—Tumbling Leaves

November is berry-bright and firelight-gay, a glittering night, a crisp blue day,
a whispering wind and a handful of determined fence row asters.

—HAL BORLAND, *Sundial of the Seasons*

In the DC area, true autumn, with the blaze of bright leaves, does not generally arrive until the end of October or early November. That's why I divide autumn in two. One is the autumn of Indian Summer. The other is the autumn of brilliant leaves and frosty dawns. This is another bonus of living in the Mid-Atlantic. We can revel in an extra fall season. The late autumn sees morning temperatures in the thirties and forties, deep blue cloudless skies, and flurries of falling golden or deep red leaves. A taste of this in early autumn has prepared us for the real thing. We break out our autumn clothing and have it ready for the first really cold mornings, when two layers of fleece are required on the bike ride to work. By the time late autumn arrives, we are ready and even happy to see its arrival, much like the long-anticipated football game between two ancient rival schools.

Earliest November. Today I take my office staff (of two) on an outdoor work retreat to Sugarloaf (heralded with soaring ravens). After our three-mile-long hike along the ridgetop forest, I show Sarah Banks and Lela Stanley the small saplings of American Chestnut still subsisting in the forest understory, scattered among the oaks, hickories, and beeches. Millions of small saplings arise from living tissue found in rootstock and old stumps where a mature chestnut tree once stood many decades ago. These clonal saplings remain susceptible to the blight and thus die back when they reach sapling size—rarely exceeding twenty feet.

In the 1960s, the woods where I played as a boy in Baltimore were littered with fallen chestnut logs. These survived for decades because they were resistant to rot, reminder of a forest catastrophe that forever changed the forests of the East Coast. The Asian chestnut blight arrived in the United States in the early twentieth century. Over several decades the blight decimated chestnuts throughout the upland forests of the East. The chestnut was perhaps the most common tree species in forests from Mississippi to Maine. Nearly a third of the mature trees in the northeastern forests in 1900 were American Chestnut. Those mature canopy-dominating chestnuts are now gone, all gone. It is difficult to imagine the full extent of the impact of the disappearance of some three billion American Chestnuts from the eastern United States. Because of its annual production of a large crop of chestnuts, this loss must have severely affected the mammals and birds that subsisted on this reliable staple—species such as Wild Turkey, White-tailed Deer, and Black Bear. The chestnuts have since been replaced by oaks, many species of which produce crops of varying size from year to year and are thus a less reliable food source for these woodland creatures.

Our house in Brookmont was constructed in 1938. It features a fireplace and window trim of chestnut, which was used extensively in construction even after the arrival of the chestnut blight. Chestnut wood

American Chestnut

makes wonderful building material. It is straight of grain, strong, easy to saw, and readily split, and it is highly resistant to decay. Chestnut wood was traditionally used for furniture, shingles, home construction, flooring, piers, plywood, and paper pulp. These days, woodworkers who want to use chestnut need to harvest it from old barns and ancient abandoned homes.

The American Chestnut exists today only as a few blight-resistant mature trees scattered in various corners of the United States. It appears that many of the once-giant trees killed by the blight will continue to rejuvenate themselves in the woods as sapling clones of the parent, their cells never dying out—much like the immortal HeLa cells of Henrietta Lacks made famous by cancer researchers. Will these chestnut cells live forever? It would be nice if they outlived the pathogen of the chestnut blight, growing to restock the forests of the East at some point in the future.

At evening dusk, above Fletcher's Cove, I watch a pair of Barred Owls sail across the towpath of the C&O Canal in the gloaming—like two beige ghosts—to perch in the floodplain forest of Boxelder and sycamore. I see a single Spicebush in flower—it must be confused! And I find a Woolly Bear caterpillar on my back patio as I come into the house this evening—an enduring symbol of autumn.

Whenever I spot a Woolly Bear I always think of the old wives' tale that the thickness of its red-brown middle band predicts the severity of the coming winter. I never took much stock in this belief. Anyway, the Woolly Bears themselves are harmless and amiable creatures that come along at just the right time of year to cheer us up on a cold and gray November day. The natural history of the Woolly Bear is curious in its own right. These caterpillars hatch from an egg in the fall and then forage into winter, eventually hibernating under a log when it gets too cold to forage. In the spring, the caterpillars thaw out, come back to life (like the chestnut saplings), make a cocoon, pupate, and then emerge as an Isabella Tiger Moth—handsomely patterned yellow and orange with dark speckling. Unlike the caterpillar, the moth has a very brief period of life before reproducing and dying. In the far north, Woolly Bears require several growing seasons to forage enough to be ready for a spring pupation. These individual caterpillars may survive several winters to entertain us in autumn.

Late in the fall, my father-in-law, Andy, loves to go surf fishing. For several successive autumns, when my son, Andrew (Andy's namesake), was old enough to appreciate it, the three of us would pack Andy's car and drive down to Lewes, Delaware, to fish for two days at Henlopen State Park, on the wide, sandy beach facing the Atlantic. The last year we did this was our most productive ever for fishing. We arrived later in the season than normal (we typically went in late October). It seems that early November is a better time to catch fish in the surf.

Lewes itself is an interesting spot, where the Atlantic shore meets the mouth of the Delaware Bay. Taking advantage of the protected harbor behind the curving sand peninsula of Cape Henlopen, the Dutch established a whaling and trading post there in 1631, thus making it the first European settlement in what would become Delaware. Named Swan Valley (Zwaanendael), presumably because of the vast flocks of Tundra Swans that wintered there, the settlement was decimated in an attack by the Lenape Indians a year later. A second Dutch settlement was wiped out by the British in 1664. The British bounced the Dutch. Subsequently, the Delaware colonies were handed over to William Penn by English sovereign Charles II in payment of a family debt. Penn changed the settlement's name to Lewes. The town was bombarded by a British fleet in 1813 during the War of 1812. A cannonball from that bombardment remains embedded in a town building—young Andrew always enjoys touching this relic when we visit the charming old downtown. Today, Lewes is a popular upscale summer destination as well as a desirable year-round community in which to retire.

This year, as always, Andy spends several days preparing the three surf rods and all the attendant tackle for fishing. We pack clothing for the cool and windy weather on the exposed beach. The drive takes about two and a half hours. As always, we stay in the same decrepit but clean motel in Lewes—the only one open in November. We dine out both nights at a local watering hole that features deep-fried food delivered weekly by the SYSCO truck—food ideal for a young and growing boy, though not so great for the two older boys in the party. The restaurant also features several video game consoles in the outer foyer, which Andrew feeds multiple quarters in order to eke out a few short minutes of entertainment.

Of course, we are there for the fishing, which we get to the next morning after a fortifying fisherman's breakfast at the small old-fashioned diner adjacent to the motel. In my case, this always features a big portion of well-browned scrapple—a local dish that can only be prepared properly at a greasy spoon. By nine we are on the beach baiting our hooks (recall that at this time of year the sun rises late).

Surf fishing is an art that requires superior amounts of patience, something my father-in-law has in spades. One does not go out and find the fish. One must wait for the fish to find you. Some days they never find you and you catch nothing. In the autumn, when the fish are on the move (they migrate up and down the coast much like the birds do), conditions become ideal for surf fishing.

Spending hours on the beach next to the breaking surf in early November requires some stamina and a number of layers of clothing to keep warm. One baits the several hooks with squid or minnows and casts the set out beyond the breakers. A heavy lead weight keeps the set from being pushed around too much by the roiling water. Then, if you are lucky, bottom-foraging fish that hunt in the surf zone take the hook. If you get a strike, it is one of the finest outdoor sport feelings there is. It is like a jolt from a live wire as the line grows taut and the tip of the fiberglass rod bows. At that point you are in direct contact with a wild fish in the sea. There's nothing more primordial than that.

It is then a matter of setting the hook in the fish's jaw by giving a sharp, quick tug on the rod, and then coaxing the fish in, which can take a while if the fish has some fight in it. It is satisfying to haul a big fish onto the shore; maybe all of us guys have a fishing gene in us, perhaps stuck somewhere on that tiny and shriveled Y-chromosome.

If the weather is fine, being on the coast in November can be sublime. The breeze is at your back, the surf is roaring, the sun is warm on your face, all sorts of birds are on the move, and there is always hope of a fighting fish on the line.

This weekend starts out perfectly. Lewes is quiet because it is late in the season. This is a summer town, and by November much of it is shut down for the winter. But there are thousands of Tree Swallows staging in the marsh grass in preparation for their departure south. In the foggy early morning they get active, swirling about in large tight flocks, making the air alive with green-and-white darting birds, each making its soft *jiit* call. Down on the shore, things are even more active. Dozens of Northern Gannets, like black-and-white jet fighters with their six-foot wingspans, sharply bank to and fro out beyond the breakers. Strings of blackish scoter ducks skim just above the waterline, headed down the coastline. Gulls of several species hang around our encampment on the beach, hoping to steal some of our bait; their compatriots circle high overhead. Double-crested Cormorants in small parties wing past, headed to a favored foraging ground. And southward-migrating

Sharp-shinned and Cooper's Hawks race with the wind, their short wings beating hard. We could not be bored or lonely under these circumstances.

And we catch some fish. First, Andy brings in a foot-long Bluefish. We have broken through! About ten minutes later, little Andrew tugs in another Blue about the same size. Its flanks gleam silver and green-blue as he raises it up off the wet sand and brings the bowed rod back to our little encampment above the wave line. Bluefish are gorgeous, and their dark meat is oily but good eating when consumed within hours of catching them. Suddenly, I find I have on my line an eighteen-inch Red Drum (known as a Redfish in the Deep South), which takes me several minutes to haul in through the surf. Another good eating fish. Finally, Andy snags a big one—a five-pound Black Drum that takes more than five minutes to land—what a brute. We donate our cache of fish to a resident surf fisherman, who happily drops these trophies into his ice-filled cooler. His family will be feasting on these after dark this evening.

Sunday morning arrives with winds and tides that are not benign. The high point of the day is breakfast and the crispy scrapple. A heavy fog sits on the beach the whole morning, and the wind is from the due east. Casting into the wind, with the surf coming on hard, is no treat. With the heavy mist, we see few birds, and the east wind is not ideal for them anyway. With surf fishing, one must take the bad with the good. By noon we are ready to cut bait, literally. We catch not a single fish and see little of interest. The other fishermen on the beach are having little luck either.

On days like this, it is best to retreat to the motel, change clothes, and head out for a good and hearty lunch, which we find in downtown Lewes. Andy and I savor a thick crab bisque that restores our spirits while little Andrew tucks into an oversized cheeseburger. That gives us the strength to pack up and hit the highway back to DC. On the way home, driving in the warm car, listening to a Redskins game on the radio, we think about the Atlantic beach in late autumn—a far cry from the crowded summer shores where nature is in retreat. It is the beaches of autumn and winter that offer the most to the naturalist—a variety of sea ducks and other water birds, broad, empty expanses, blowing sand, surf fishers, and hardy folk walking their dogs at the ocean's edge.

This afternoon, in Georgetown, as I pass through the Potomac waterfront park below Whitehurst Freeway, I encounter a Cooper's Hawk with a small bird in its talons. It sails low into a sapling Willow Oak by the water and begins plucking the bird's torso, the small contour feathers floating downwind like Dandelion fluff. The loafing Ring-billed Gulls on the water by the park take no notice of this bloody act of predation.

Washington, DC, has come to be viewed as a dog-eat-dog world of cut-throat competition, populated by unsympathetic government bureaucrats, greedy K Street lobbyists, and malevolent elected politicians. Like the DC bottom-feeders, the killer instinct of bird-hunting raptors comes straight from nature, and predation of the small and weak by the large and swift is the law of the land in parks, woodlots, and nature reserves. And among the very best predators are the accipitrine hawks, typified by the handsome and fierce-eyed Cooper's Hawk. It has one main job in life, and that is to hunt down, kill, and consume birds.

The latte-sipping urban elite decry violent death of any kind—a reason for PETA's ascendancy in recent decades. But nature, be it urban, suburban, or rural, is based on the Darwinian rule of eat or be eaten. Whereas the East Coast urban elite works to foster cooperation and altruism, no predator in nature will survive by letting one get away. To a naturalist, predation is vital and urgent and exciting. To watch a stooping Peregrine Falcon hit a Mallard and drive its limp body *THUMP* down onto a riverside field is a mesmerizing sight, and it is 100 percent organic. Moreover, it is a driving force of natural selection.

The tense interaction between predator and prey is conceived by evolutionary biologists as an evolutionary arms race in which the predator brings about the evolution of faster and more elusive prey and in which these faster and more agile prey in turn bring about the evolution of faster and sharper-eyed predators. That is why naturalists tend to cheer when they see an act of successful predation in the wild. For it is evolution in action, nothing less, and naturalists love the mechanism of evolution, especially when it is on display, firsthand, and not in an exhibit case in a museum or a proffered example of so-called intelligent design.

It's for that reason that I long for the successful invasion of the DC environs by the wily Coyote. Reviled by farmers and ranchers across the West, the Coyote is the poster child of the Anthropocene's most successful predator. Why should we hate a Coyote if we love its nearest relative, in the form of the harmless and affectionate Golden Retriever? They both evolved from the same lineage—one an example of directed unnatural selection (the retriever) and the other of undirected natural selection (the Coyote). Which do you think has a better chance of survival in the wild?

We should appreciate the arrival of the Coyote in town for at least one reason: the White-tailed Deer. The influx of a healthy population of urban Coyotes may diminish the problem of White-tailed Deer in DC. The overpopulation of deer is problematic for two big reasons. Cars hit them with frequency (insurance companies paid out four billion dollars in 2012 because of car-deer impacts, and during the twelve months ending in July 2015, there were 1.3 million claims made for deer-automobile collisions). And our peri-urban deer have not only nibbled to nothing the expensive plantings of myriad yards but have done the same with a vengeance in DC's forests. Deer have decimated native wildflowers from the region and also seriously harmed the recruitment of tree seedlings needed to ensure natural forest succession throughout the Mid-Atlantic. Coyotes may help rebalance a system badly out of whack. Here's to a wild predator that can reform our artificial suburban Bambi-nature run amok.

On this morning, a heavy frost encrusts the front lawn. Coming out of the house, I hear Fish Crows giving their flight call in the neighborhood. Individuals are doing what appear to be display flights. A first hint of the spring to come?

Crows tend to get no respect, and most urbanites don't like crows. These big black birds seem to be cocky and irreverent. They hang around garbage cans and aggregate at recent roadkill. In spring they pluck songbird babies from nests and smugly consume their prey while the hapless songbird parents noisily and ineffectually gabble about them. On the other hand, crows are clever and wary and mysterious in their social life, which appears to be inordinately complicated. In the years just after West Nile Virus arrived in the United States in 1999, crow populations in the East were decimated. Now the crows seem to have bounced back.

The reader may think a crow is a crow, but that's not so, at least in the DC area. Two species of crows are common here: the American Crow and the Fish Crow. Both are all-black and large and are difficult to distinguish unless one hears them vocalize. The American Crow, the better known of the two, gives a harsh and guttural cawing. By contrast, the marginally smaller Fish Crow gives a soft and high-pitched, throaty note or notes, *kah-hah* or a quiet *kdra-kdra-kra,* similar to, but less harsh than, that of its better-known cousin.

Both American Crows and Fish Crows can be found in my neighborhood year-round. Given how similar the two are, the question is how they manage to coexist. Their diets do not seem to differ. They sometimes join up in mixed flocks. Ecological theory posits that very similar species must evolve ecological differences in order to coexist. It is not clear what those differences are in the case of these two familiar crows. Here's a ready-made field project for an ambitious doctoral student.

In our neighborhood in Bethesda the Fish Crow is the more common crow. It is probably predominant here because of our proximity to the Potomac. Here in Brookmont, the Fish Crow is an important harbinger of spring. To see these birds overhead, sailing gracefully in the winds, chanting softly, is to think of spring. And they apparently begin signaling in November the anticipated arrival of spring, which seems hard to believe. It may be that they are establishing nesting territories long in advance of egg-laying and that they do this by their song flights, if song is the right word for a bird with such a minor-league vocalization. Nonetheless, these crows carry out an important seasonal function as sentinels of spring. And why should not birds start anticipating spring in November?

There's more. Near the boathouse at the Watergate Hotel, a big bushy *Ilex* hedge has an abundance of small white flowers that are giving off a lovely fragrance. It reminds me that I saw the yellow twirly flowers of a witch hazel in the woods the other day. That's the weird thing about fall! Sometimes one gets a foreshadowing of spring in November. And one also realizes, in spite of the white *Ilex* and the yellow witch hazel blooms, or even the romantic crow vocalizations, that there is no shortcut, and that although spring is coming, it is by way of winter, just around the corner.

On a Sunday in November in the year 2000, with some birding colleagues I visited the reservoir at the intersection of R Street and MacArthur Boulevard in Northwest Washington. Our purpose was to check out the gull flock there for rarities. Among the mix of Ring-billed and Herring Gulls was a Lesser Black-backed Gull, an immigrant from Europe and a life bird for me. I had been hearing about Lesser Black-backs, and I decided that I needed to get out and see one for myself.

The changing status of the Lesser Black-backed Gull in the United States tells the story of a world in flux. If you look in the 1947 edition of Roger Tory Peterson's *Field Guide to the Birds*, you will find that its main account of the gulls does not mention this species. In a small section in the back labeled "Accidentals," there is brief mention of the species, which states: "Although there are a handful of sight records of this European Gull, there is no specimen for North America." Chan Robbins's *Birds of North America*, published in 1966, noted that the Lesser Black-backed Gull was "casual on the East Coast"—a small step up in abundance. By 2003, as reported by David Sibley in his *Sibley Field Guide to Birds of Eastern North America*, the Lesser Black-backed Gull was an "uncommon to rare visitor from Europe; small numbers found with other large gulls." Sibley's revised guide, published in 2014, states: "Locally fairly common at a few locations in the Atlantic states." So, over my lifetime, this species, on its own, without any direct intervention from humankind, has expanded its range from Europe into the Western Hemisphere and is now recorded year-round, most commonly in fall and winter, along the East Coast. We now expect to see it every autumn on our visits to Cape May. Why did this gull invade the eastern United States? So many things in the environment change over time that it would be difficult to pinpoint why the Lesser Black-backed Gull has chosen to settle more permanently here, but one possibility is the proliferation of solid-waste disposal facilities—once known as dumps. Gulls are able to forage happily year-round in these dumps. Gulls of all kinds have prospered in the eastern United States of late, the Lesser Black-backed along with the rest.

The colonization of the United States by the Lesser Black-backed Gull is a particularly noticeable change, but there are hundreds of others just like it. More common are the species declines documented over my lifetime. For example, the lovely Regal Fritillary butterfly was once a regular resident in old fields across the eastern United States. I remember hunting for it in fields north of Baltimore with my brother in the 1960s. It has now all but disappeared. It is difficult to tease the natural changes from those caused mainly by human impacts on the environment. A take-home point is that *change* is perhaps just as common as *stasis* in nature, and we should be taking note of both. Part of being a naturalist is looking out for the eternal and documenting the ephemeral—denoting the unchanging patterns as well as the short- and long-term shifts and the rare or one-time events.

Speaking of the eternal, in mid-November my son, Andrew, and I visit Randle Cliff Beach, in Calvert County, Maryland, to search for marine fossils. The high clay and sand cliffs on the western shore of the Chesapeake Bay are the famous Calvert Cliffs, which erode during winter storms, shedding blocks of marl that are rich in Miocene marine fossils. Finds can include shark's teeth, ray dental plates, bones of porpoise and whale, and loads of fossil shells of many types. The cliffs, in some places reaching one hundred feet, extend for about thirty miles from Chesapeake Beach in the north down to Calvert Cliffs State Park.

Fossil hunters walk the beach and search the rubble at the cliff base for fossils. Most are found in the swash zone, where the small bay waves strike the beach. Here the moving water sorts articles of different sizes and specific gravities, and the hunters bend over looking for shapes that distinguish the fossils from pebbles and other detritus. This can be done year-round. The summertime is the most fun for families because the hunting can be combined with playing in the bay shallows. The wintertime is better for finding prize fossils because there are fewer people out in the cold and this is when winter storms peel fresh, fossil-bearing material off the cliff face.

In the early 1960s my family occasionally took weekend trips to Calvert County to search the beaches at Plum Point and Scientists Cliffs for natural treasures, mainly in the form of the glossy blue and gray teeth of a wide array of now-extinct species of sharks. We also picked up giant scallop shells (*Chesapecten*) often five or six inches across, many of the weird, black grinding dental plates of several genera of extinct rays (their excuse for teeth), and the occasional crocodile or porpoise tooth.

For a ten-year-old boy interested in all things nature, this was a marvelous pastime. The dream of every collector at Calvert Cliffs is to find a pristine, fresh-from-the-cliff tooth of the extinct giant shark *Carcharocles megalodon*—the bigger the better. Known informally as the Meg or Megalodon, this great shark produced teeth that today are the gold standard of Calvert Cliff fossil desiderata. Meg teeth come in all sizes, from less than half an inch to more than six inches long. The smaller ones are uncommon. The biggest ones are vanishingly rare. The finest examples of the largest teeth sell on eBay for thousands of dollars. These great teeth are perhaps one of the most beautiful and admired of nature's creations. Moreover, the largest Megalodon tooth is considerably larger and heavier than the largest *T. rex* tooth. Megalodon, a sixty-foot-long saltwater predator, employed these giant teeth to grasp and tear apart whales, porpoises, giant turtles, and seals.

Fossil teeth of most vertebrates are rare. Not so shark teeth, because of a developmental peculiarity of sharks. They produce several rows of teeth that periodically push forward in their mouth when mature, forcing out the older row of teeth, which are shed to the bottom of the sea. Each row comprises 60 teeth or so. And a mature shark might possess four or five rows of teeth in its mouth at any time—more than 250 teeth. Each shark, then, would produce hundreds or thousands of teeth in a lifetime, all of which are being collected today in places like Calvert Cliffs. That lucky fact has made the finding of a fossil Meg tooth a possibility even for a small boy walking on a Calvert County beach.

Here's the remarkable thing. Many of the teeth were shed from the shark's mouth after barely being used. These fresh, undamaged teeth fell to the sea floor and became safely entombed in rapidly deposited sediment. Millions of years later, when they are eroded from the cliff, they can look as fresh as if they had been extracted from a live shark today. But it gets better. The fossil teeth, trapped in the sediments over time, become opalized and gather mineral coloration from the matrix that surrounds them. The fossil teeth are thus not the pallid white of a modern shark tooth. Instead they come in many hues—dark blue-gray, rich brown, reddish-orange, and sometimes multicolored. They have become gemlike.

Holding a large Meg tooth in one's hand is a bit like holding a well-crafted obsidian spearpoint. The sharp, serrated cutting edge is intact, narrowing down to a sharp distal point. The triangular shape of the tooth is iconic, and the combination of the rough root, the shiny, blackish chevron that separates the root from the tooth, and the glossy enameled foretooth is mesmerizingly seductive. A big tooth makes a savage paperweight that looks good on any desk. Every visitor to my office cannot resist picking up the big tooth at mine and hefting it (some teeth weigh more than a pound), running a finger along the sharp, serrated cutting edge. Even nonpaleontologists understand that this is a tooth that came from a top predator that devoured large prey in the manner of *T. rex*. It sends chills down the spine.

I have collected at Calvert Cliffs on and off for fifty years, and I never tire of the hunt. The anticipation is great. On many occasions I have had waking dreams of finding "the big one." In fact, I have found only two perfect specimens larger than three inches in my amateur paleontological career. They have pride of place in our fossil exhibit under glass in the living room.

The amazing thing is that an object ten million years old can be so pristine. The tooth remains sturdy and fine. Few other fossils can compete. The shells we collect are dull gray or pallid white and usually quite fragile. The bones are gray or blackish and invariably incomplete, with the processes broken off. The only thing that perhaps can compete with a shark tooth is a crocodile tooth—but they are so much rarer to find. I have found only a single intact croc tooth in all my years of collecting at Calvert Cliffs.

OK, so the large Megalodon teeth are hard to find. Thank goodness perhaps thirty other species of sharks also deposited teeth in these Miocene sediments. A trip to Brownie's Beach in northern Calvert County can turn up more than two hundred teeth in a day. This trove would include the teeth of five or ten species—tiger sharks, mako sharks, hammerhead sharks, lemon sharks, sand-tiger sharks, snaggletooth sharks, and more. The only thing is that the teeth are mainly tiny, less than half an inch long, with the vast bulk a quarter inch or smaller. Still, many are in perfect condition, showing gloss and beautiful color. These are perfection in miniature. And children love to collect them. The kids walk the swash line looking for small teeth being tossed up and sucked back by the wave action. Their distinctive triangular shape gives the searcher a general form to look for. After collecting a few of these teeth, one never loses the search image. Our family has collected thousands of fossil shark teeth over the years.

The highlight of our day's outing is that Andrew finds a 2.75-inch-long Meg tooth—his largest ever. Also, we locate a number of fossil porpoise vertebrae in the cliff. We also combine our shark-tooth collecting with seeing lots of nature at the water's edge, including swans, ducks, eagles, and cormorants. It is a purely natural experience one can do year-round.

In mid-November, I bike down Constitution Avenue, headed to my research office at the Natural History Museum. I stop at the Constitution Gardens reflecting pool on the National Mall, where I find a flock of Ring-necked Ducks sharing the pool with various Mallards. The woodland-dwelling Ring-necks will spend much of the winter here, as long as the pool does not freeze over completely.

What lovely birds Ring-necked Ducks are! The hens are demurely drab, but the drakes, with their black, white, and gray, are as neat and handsome as DC lawyers in their dark suits in November. But they may be newcomers to downtown. The ducks of autumn and winter in Louis Halle's day were indeed populations from a different century. In his book he talks of dozens of species of ducks in big numbers on the Potomac in the DC environs, but he never mentions the handsome Ring-neck. Washington was a different world back in the mid-twentieth century. And I have some data of my own from back then. In the winter of 1961, my father drove my brother and me to National Airport in Alexandria for a Saturday excursion. We stood on the roof of the terminal and watched the planes take off and land (people did that sort of thing for fun in those days). Even back then, my brother, Bill, and I were bird crazy. Our dad was sympathetic because he had been a youthful naturalist growing up north of Baltimore. So we could not visit National Airport without also stopping off at the little wetland across the highway called Roaches Run. There we saw flocks of Redheads, Canvasbacks, and Pintails, among others. I remember clearly seeing these birds after a half-century. The open water was filled with ducks, and we were excited as two young kids could be to see them up close.

Now fast-forward a few decades. For five years (2007–12), I biked by Roaches Run each workday morning and evening to and from work. Over that period the little wetland reserve boasted cormorants, gulls, Mallards, and Canada Geese, but I recorded few other species of waterfowl during those years, and not one Canvasback, Redhead, or Pintail. The world has changed and the waterfowl with it. Whereas Canada Geese have ballooned in numbers, mainly because of the rise of golf course geese that now live and breed in the DC area, most of the wild duck species that we all appreciate are not nearly as much in evidence in the area as in Halle's day.

Continentwide, waterfowl populations are in pretty good shape (so the US Fish and Wildlife Service tells us). But in the DC area, the habitat and food resources for waterfowl just are not what they were in the 1940s. Ironically, the Ring-necked Duck is one species that is probably doing better today than in Halle's day, as is the Wood Duck. These are two woodland-loving ducks, and forests are much more widespread today than they were in the early postwar era of Halle. But the bay ducks—scaup, Redhead, Canvasback, Pintail, and the like—have much declined. I have a report of a March 1925 count of forty thousand Canvasbacks on the Potomac below Washington, DC. By contrast, the midwinter summary count for the species for the whole of Maryland in 2012 was only fourteen thousand. And the compiled count for the entire Eastern Flyway was twenty-seven thousand birds. The submerged aquatic vegetation that formerly supported vast rafts of Canvasback no longer exists in the Potomac or the Chesapeake. Will it ever return? Only after the nutrient load in these waters is reduced to proper levels. And that will not happen until the farmers in the Potomac and Susquehanna watersheds reduce their use of fertilizers and take steps to keep these nutrients from entering their streams—the ones that flow into the Potomac and Susquehanna and ultimately the Chesapeake.

One Saturday morning in November, taking the dog for a walk, I have a close encounter with a foraging pair of Pileated Woodpeckers. One dangles under a Poison Ivy vine, plucking and swallowing its pale gray fruit; the bird is just ten feet from me. Its mate drills into deadwood on a large tree limb above.

The Pileated Woodpecker is the DC area's best backyard bird. Nobody can believe that this big black woodpecker with the red crest would deign to settle in our neighborhoods, but it does. My wife and I see it warily visit our suet feeder from time to time each winter, but we never tire of watching it, no matter how often it swoops gracefully into the yard. The species is naturally shy, but somehow it manages to insinuate itself in our more sylvan suburban neighborhoods. Not long ago, while biking across Key Bridge (linking Georgetown and Rosslyn, Virginia), I saw a Pileated high overhead, winging from DC across the Potomac, in the middle of one of the most urban spots in the region. I stopped to admire this winged creature, with the elegant black-white-and-red patterning and wonderful undulating flight. It took me back fifty years to a moment when I was on a high bridge over the Shenandoah River at Harper's Ferry, West Virginia. I was nine years old, on a Saturday outdoor adventure with my father and brother. Looking down into the wild, rocky gorge, we saw a Pileated flying across the river below us. It was the first time my brother and I had seen the species, and we were transfixed. Birders tend not to forget their first Pileated.

On an unusually warm day in late fall, it is fun to think of spring. It is easy to do this, because with the warmth the birds come to life and our local world is changed for a day. On this day, I encountered several bird species of a Carolinian bent that have moved substantially northward since Louis Halle's day. Even in the 1960s, before the term *global warming* came into vogue, naturalists talked about southern birds moving northward into the Northeast. We did not know why they were moving northward, but we were nonetheless intrigued. The most prominent of these subtropical travelers were the Black Vulture, Red-bellied Woodpecker, Northern Mockingbird, Tufted Titmouse, and Carolina Wren.

The Black Vulture—the smaller and more aggressive cousin of the better-known Turkey Vulture—is today common in the DC area. Biking to work, I have regularly seen both species circling in the sky over the C&O Canal. In former decades, this vulture was a bird of the South. Here is what Frank Chapman had to say in his handbook published in 1895: "Breeds from North Carolina southward." In 1958, Stewart and Robbins, writing of the birdlife of Maryland, noted that the species was a common year-round resident only south of the DC area. In the latest edition of David Sibley's field guide, the range map for the species shows its breeding range extending north to Massachusetts.

Regarding the Red-bellied Woodpecker, Chapman's 1895 work noted that on the East Coast the species ranged north to Maryland and that in Massachusetts it was an accidental vagrant. Stewart and Robbins in 1958 noted the bird to be fairly common north to the upper Chesapeake. Sibley's current range map shows the species breeds now in Vermont and New Hampshire.

How do we explain these changes in the distribution of so-called southern birds? The answer is probably nothing more than change itself. Bird breeding ranges have probably always been in flux and will be changing for centuries to come. Yes, a myriad of factors is driving that change—rarely is it one thing. Along the East Coast, several known factors have influenced the movement of bird populations over the past half-century. Widespread winter feeding of songbirds allows southern species to survive northern winters. And the construction of the national interstate highway system has created linear strips of edge and shrub habitat leading northward to New England: human-made range expansion corridors. These highways, moreover, have created a largesse of roadkill from south to north—encouraging the expansion of the vulture. The human-led alteration in food availability and the structure of natural habitats have profoundly affected where birds live today. And, yes, global warming has clearly nudged birds northward.

To return to our group of Carolinian birds, as a naturalist who grew up in the 1950s and 1960s, I still think of this group as southerners, and when I see them today I think of the South. I recall a spring vacation in 1962 with my grandmother, mother, and brother to Williamsburg, Virginia, to see the reconstructed colonial buildings, the giant azaleas, and an array of southern birds like Red-bellied Woodpeckers and the others mentioned. My historical knowledge baseline ties me to that earlier century. I suspect that my grandchildren's view of the world will be substantially different, based on growing up in a substantially different world, with different memories. Scientists call this *shifting baselines*.

You know how some sunsets end with a green flash, a last hurrah that signals the very end of the day? Well, autumn has an analogous signal, with the bright transition of poplar, oak, and maple leaf coloration just before the trees drop the last of their leaves. It seems to be a signal, like a wink of the eye, letting us know that the death of our green world is only temporary and that good things are to come, even if not in the immediate future.

The turning of the leaves in the Mid-Atlantic is a thing of glory on those days when the sky is a cerulean dome and the sharp breeze slaps the exposed cheek. The botanical phenomenon is well explained, but the mystical nature of it all is not. Why this last burst of glory? Is some spirit of the forest sending us all a message that all will be reborn come spring? The glory of the leaves does revive hope in the life force, but of course, it is a temporary burst, followed by the blizzard of falling leaves, the endless raking of yards, and finally the ranks of bare gray trunks of trees with awkward naked branches reaching up to the cold blue heavens.

At about this time, we get another jolt, this time from high above. That is the migration of the snow-white Tundra Swans, headed to the Chesapeake Bay for the winter. One first hears the birds in the distance at the very end of the day or early evening. It is a high yodel, given by all the birds of the V, and together it has something of the quality of sleigh bells, but not quite. More like nature's sleigh bells calling out for winter. To look up and see that formation of great white birds winging southeastward is to know the approach of winter. The birds are telling you so—they could be the precursor of the snowflakes to come.

In early November, birders' thoughts also turn to Golden Eagles and Northern Goshawks. To see these two uncommon and majestic raptors, it is best to head north and west up onto the long Appalachian ridges. One good option is to drive to the Waggoner's Gap hawk watch, situated a few miles north of the bucolic college town of Carlisle, Pennsylvania. Carlisle is home to Dickinson College, founded by a signer of the Declaration of Independence, the Philadelphia physician Benjamin

Rush. The Waggoner's Gap hawk watch is perched on a sharp, rocky crest with vistas south and north. Southerly winds send the birds south of the ridge, and northerly winds send the birds north of the ridge (because of the updraft produced). The lookout and surrounding forest are owned by the Pennsylvania Audubon Society. Volunteer hawk watchers are in attendance from 9:30 a.m. to 4:30 p.m. each day during the fall migration, from September through November. Northwesterly and southerly winds produce the most raptors. The hawk watch at Waggoner's Gap tallies some twenty thousand migrating raptors each autumn. Most notably, it annually records more than twice as many Golden Eagles as the more famous Hawk Mountain, which lies about forty miles to the east. The young Goldens come through first, in late October, and the adults follow in early November. The goshawks pass through at just about the same time as the Goldens.

Waggoner's Gap lies on a prominent ridge of the Appalachians—the very same Kittatinny Ridge that leads eastward all the way to Hawk Mountain and thence to the Delaware Water Gap. These ancient, worn-down mountain cores composed of uplifted and metamorphosed marine sediments form a series of long, almost continuous ridge lines from the Hudson River southwest to Georgia, but nowhere are they so even and regular and sinuous as in central Pennsylvania. These geomorphological relics of an ancient Himalayan-scale mountain range now rise steeply above the intervening valleys. The ridges are wooded, and the valleys are mainly tidy farm fields. The long, continuous ridges generate strong and reliable updrafts that aid the flight of the migrating raptors heading south for the winter, forming a raptor highway.

Most of the southward-migrating raptors follow the ridges of the Appalachians for three reasons. First, the ridges trend southwestward, which parallels the coastline. They are thus a well-marked pathway that keeps the raptors from ending up over the Atlantic when the northwest wind blows. Second, they provide the lift that allows the birds to sail for miles and miles with minimum effort. Third, since many of the ridges are protected watershed forests, they offer the raptors a green space where they can roost at night in safety and hunt for prey during the dawn and dusk when they are not migrating.

Hawk migration in the Appalachians is very much about the autumn and the year's end. One heads to the watch sites when the autumn leaves are in their glory and when a decent wind is carrying big clots of raptors down the ridges. Serious East Coast birders try to visit both Cape May and the Appalachians for hawk watching every autumn. It can be one of the birding high points of the year. Participating in a day of hawk watching on a windy ridgetop engages one in the changing of the seasons because it takes place on a high ridge where one comes face to face with the prospect of advancing winter.

The glory of an autumn day with the trees turning and the northwest wind blowing is self-evident. The sun is shining, the sky is cobalt blue, and the great hunting birds are tearing by at ridge level or perhaps circling high if the wind is not so strong. There is no scent of summer. Everything is clearly heading toward December and a first snow. The blood is pumping from the hike up from the parking lot, and the breeze on the face banishes any feeling of summer lethargy. This is full-bore autumn, vigorously engaging all the senses. Perhaps the only thing that can compete with this type of experience is a small-town college football game on a blustery day with clouds and sun and wind and several hundred alcohol-fueled, screaming students—something one might experience right in Carlisle on a Saturday in November.

This particular November day at Waggoner's Gap has all the proper meteorological necessities and produces a decent count that includes the raptors we are hoping for. I see lots of Red-tailed Hawks and Turkey Vultures, some Sharp-shinned and Red-shouldered Hawks, a few Bald Eagles, and small numbers of the two target species for November: Golden Eagle and Northern Goshawk. A single juvenile Gos powers right by the watch at eye level. I am struck by its bulk and profuse dark streaking. It has the menacing look of a hunter. The watch crew tallies seven Golden Eagles on this day. My best bird is a big dark adult Golden that teases us with a promise of a close approach. The hawk watch has four minutes with the eagle. First it is far to the northeast—just a black speck, identifiable only to the most seasoned hawk watchers; then it seems to be headed directly at us; but at the last moment it turns and sails north of us, gaining speed as it passes to the west and southwest. I see the golden neck ruff and the all-dark tail, with just a smidgen of white at the base. I try to get a sharp image of this regal bird with my long lens, but it never circles or shows itself except in profile. But that's hawk watching! No guarantees, even when the proper wind is blowing.

Driving home, with my cheeks red and burning from the affront of a day's worth of cold breeze, there is no confusion that I have participated in nature firsthand that day. And I got my Golden Eagle for the year. The drive home takes me by Gettysburg, where a large crowd, including President Barack Obama, is celebrating the 150th anniversary of Lincoln's Gettysburg Address. Such is the enduring impact of 274 well-chosen words, soaked in the blood of Union and Confederate soldiers. The Gettysburg Address will remain in our collective memory for a long time to come, mainly because of our long and repeated engagement in killing wars, generation after generation. Perhaps war and violent death are as much a part of our human DNA as the instinct to kill is embedded in the DNA of the raptors I watched this day. What else can explain our participation in more than fifteen violent conflicts, in which American blood was spilled, in the fifteen decades since Lincoln made his address?

One year when our three children are young, Carol and I hatch the harebrained idea to spend Thanksgiving on Chincoteague Island, Virginia. The idea is to get away and enjoy the natural pleasures of Chincoteague and Assateague Islands with the kids. This is a complete change from the standard afternoon family-focused big-meal event, which is stuffy and exhausting, what with the excessive eating and travel to and from Baltimore, where the traditional Thanksgiving Dinner would be held. So we drive down to Chincoteague and stay in a ramshackle motel for three nights. The idea is to bird-watch and naturize during the daylight hours and then celebrate the season by dining out in the evenings. The kids are young enough to be up for anything, and they love to climb into the car and go.

Chincoteague Island is a bit over four hours' drive from Bethesda if you stop for lunch. That's about as far as a family with small kids would wish to drive in a day. By 3:00 p.m. we arrive at our motel, which turns out to be a dump, and since there is little to do at the motel besides sit on the beds and watch TV (no indoor pool!), we opt to spend as much time as possible outside exploring.

The general Chincoteague setup is as follows. Chincoteague is a small island in Chincoteague Bay, sandwiched between the mainland of the Virginia Delmarva and the southern end of Assateague Island—the long, sandy barrier island that stretches southward from Ocean City inlet, Maryland, ending at Tom's Cove, Virginia (famous historically for its oysters). Chincoteague is private and developed and a working island of watermen. Assateague is mainly a National Seashore, but with a National Wildlife Refuge situated at its southern extremity. One sleeps and eats on Chincoteague and spends the day birding, biking, fishing, or walking on Assateague in the refuge. There is a wildlife drive and various walking trails. In the late autumn, the waterfowl descend on the refuge in big numbers, providing a noisy and colorful show.

The natural highlights of our sojourn are various. We watch a Merlin stoop several times on a flock of Dunlin sandpipers. It moves with incredible speed and drives the small shorebirds wild. The Merlin veers and banks in various attempts to knock a Dunlin down, but without success. The Dunlin are literally running for their lives. We also encounter a friendly family of River Otters. They emerge from the brackish water and move along the bank in a playful fashion, entertaining quite a few spectators in cars. The watered impoundments are filled with ducks and geese, and groups of these come and go through the day, as they move about to forage in different habitats. The sound produced by the large aggregations of waterfowl is quite a sensation and never seems to end. And if a big raptor, like a Bald Eagle, appears overhead, the large flocks explode into flight while calling out, raising the sound level to a roar. These waterfowl are the main wildlife attraction this time of year on Assateague.

The downside of Assateague in late November is that it can be cold and raw and cloudy and windy, and that is tough on kids as well as adults. One needs to prepare for the weather because the barrier islands are so exposed to the elements that it will always be colder and windier than back at home. Another option is to visit in late May or early September, when the migratory shorebirds and songbirds are streaming through and when the weather requires fewer layers. No matter what, a visit to Chincoteague and Assateague is worth doing for those interested in nature. Of course, Thanksgiving is very much about the big meal. We can safely report that Thanksgiving dinner at a restaurant on Chincoteague is truly horrible and to be avoided at all costs. From our experience, we recommend pretending there's no such thing as Thanksgiving and ordering the chicken fingers or a cheeseburger.

In the very last days of November, the Cedar Waxwings and American Robins are foraging on the overripe fruit in the small ornamental crab-apple tree right outside my office building in Crystal City, Virginia. As I bicycle into the parking lot these mornings, I am happy to see the groups of fruit-eating birds in this little tree. It's wonderful that a tree is so generous at a time of scarcity and cold. Biking home that evening I come upon a big buck White-tailed Deer, standing on the verge of the path. It looks at me impassively and returns to its browsing. It is a thing of beauty, especially this time of year, in its gray winter coat and with its impressive rack. The big dark eyes, the muscular shoulders and hips—this is indeed a big and sexy creature during the time of the annual rut.

In an earlier section, I spoke disparagingly of White-tailed Deer in the DC area, complaining of the overpopulation of this, our biggest local game animal. Perhaps I should not complain. In Louis Halle's day I am guessing that there was not a single free-ranging wild White-tailed Deer nearby. Halle does not mention White-tailed Deer once in his book. In 1947, essentially all the big game animals had been extirpated or much reduced in the environs: deer, American Beaver, Black Bear, Wild Turkey, Red Fox, Gray Fox, American Otter. A century or more before then, the even larger game had been culled to local extinction: Elk, Bison, Grizzly Bear, and Gray Wolf. The eastern United States first saw the killing off of the largest predators and game species, then the razing of its great forests, followed by the defaunation of the remaining remnants of forested lands. The final blow was certainly the five years of Civil War, in which virtually every DC area woodlot was felled for cooking fuel, winter warmth, and the construction of battlements. The Mid-Atlantic region, where many of the Civil War battles were fought and where large armies had to survive long winters out in the open, must have been a barren sight in 1865—probably the nadir for wild nature in the Mid-Atlantic, given the appetites of the various armies of young men on the move.

Comparing the DC environs in 1865 versus today strains the imagination. Today there are trees and parks everywhere. Large wooded tracks are commonplace. Virtually none of those woodlands were extant in 1865. They probably did not start to regenerate until around 1930, when domestic small-scale agriculture began to wane. Today we are seeing a rewilding that no naturalist predicted in 1947 or 1960. In spite of a burgeoning human population, the area has more forest cover and more wildlife than at any time in the past century.

Because of the absence of game hunting and the absence of top predators near DC, the wildlife has returned to levels probably higher than ever known for the region since the establishment of human populations in North America. That is why deer are present in plague numbers now. We like to complain about the deer, but it is remarkable that we share the land with this handsome game animal today. Growing up in Baltimore in the 1950s, we neither saw nor spoke of deer. I finally saw my first deer in 1964 up in Shenandoah National Park on an October family field trip. I was stunned and thrilled. This was a rare creature then. Today, deer forage on the planted flowers in my front yard. My wife recently saw a big buck sauntering down the street in front of our house in broad daylight. Barred Owls hoot from the backwoods, and their nestlings sometimes end up in our yard. We often hear a Red Fox giving his blood-curdling cry late at night. And even Black Bears, as noted earlier, are showing up in the area. Wild nature is back, and we should be grateful. We now live in a richer, more diverse natural environment, a far cry from the empty and toxic suburban landscape described by Rachel Carson in 1962.

One final point. The return of deer and forests has been a long-term phenomenon of many decades. Nature's evolutions are slow and steady. Human-caused devastation can come rapidly (witness the impacts of DDT on eagles and Osprey in the 1960s), but restoration is much slower (reestablishing those raptors took half a century, with some serious human assistance). The take-home message is that our conservation actions need to have a time-horizon of fifty or even a hundred years. We need to invest in actions today that will benefit our grandchildren and great-grandchildren. That is the challenge of our time.

Today's big surprise, on the last day of November, is a fallen Weeping Willow—eleven inches in diameter and thirty-five feet tall—in the grass beside the Mount Vernon Trail across from Roosevelt Island. It was felled over the weekend by a beaver.

The American Beaver is yet another species that suffered a catastrophic decimation followed by a slow recovery across the United States. The decline of the beaver in North America was driven by European and American demand for pelts to manufacture beaver hats, which were popular among stylish men for nearly three centuries, starting in the late 1500s. First, the populations of the European Beaver were wiped out, and then American populations were harvested to economic extinction, from East to West. Much of the early exploration of the West and of Canada was driven by the global demand for beaver pelts. The beaver hats, which were produced in a range of styles, were made of felt constructed from the underhairs of the beaver, which were shaved from the skin and then soaked, heated, and compacted into a flexible felt fabric that was stretched over a frame. The demand for beaver pelts began to decline before the Civil War, when the most popular hats were made of silk.

Wild beaver populations did not return to the DC area until the 1970s. One belief is that the massive flood in the Potomac watershed caused by Hurricane Agnes in June 1972 carried with it a small founder population of beavers from West Virginia. Today, beavers are common and widespread throughout the area. Their toppling of trees and damming of waterways cause problems for land managers on both private and public lands.

Most land managers abhor the beavers' large-scale environmental engineering. Beavers dam streams to create ponds in which they place their stick-mound houses. Having the beaver house situated in the middle of a pond creates a safe haven from predators. The flooding of

American Beaver

bottomlands drives land managers to distraction but is an ecological boon to the wild landscape. These new wetlands open up the forest, create water features, and expand habitat for all sorts of wild species—ducks, mammals, frogs, fish, and invertebrates of many kinds. For a local DC naturalist, there are few wild places as rich as a beaver swamp. This is a great alternative to the beaver hat.

As we shift into a new month, we start the run-up to the winter solstice and the last weeks of autumn.

SIX

December—Approach of Winter

> Every man looks at his wood-pile with a kind of affection. I love to have mine
> before my window, and the more chips the better to remind me of my
> pleasing work.

—HENRY DAVID THOREAU, Walden

Many DC area bikers are seasonal. Come December, they pack away
their bicycles and bike gear and start commuting to work by other means.
Not me. I see no reason to stop biking unless the weather forces me off
the road. There are too many things to see and too many experiences to
undergo to give up the daily habit. A true naturalist wants to experience
all of nature, not just the pleasant bits. I get a kick out of biking home in
the dark during a snow squall or feeling the sting of hard rain on my face
from a wind-driven storm. It is instructive to suffer the power of nature
firsthand. That said, I have never intentionally put my life at risk in
pursuit of nature in the raw.

On a day in early December, I bike to work under a light drizzle, with
the air temperature in the fifties. Above Key Bridge I look out over the
river to see an adult Bald Eagle winging majestically down the Potomac.
About fifteen minutes later, I again find this big bird perched atop a giant

Red Oak at the Humpback Bridge on the Virginia side of the river, where the eagle has water views in two directions. As I will discover, this Red Oak is a favorite perch for this eagle and other large raptors.

In Louis Halle's day, the Bald Eagle still frequented the Potomac below Washington. That said, its population then in the Lower Forty-Eight was probably much lower than it was at the time of the Civil War. The population would drop further to fewer than a thousand birds in 1963. Through much of the twentieth century, raptors were shot adventitiously across the country. Legislation protecting eagles, along with cessation of the widespread use of DDT and other organochloride pesticides, brought about the slow recovery of the species in the United States after 1972. By 1989, there were at least five thousand eagles in the United States. Today, there are four times this number. This is one of the great wildlife recovery stories in the United States, along with that of the Peregrine Falcon and Osprey. Today, eagles regularly pair up and build big stick nests in prominent sites along the Potomac both above and below DC. A pair recently nested in National Arboretum in northeast DC. Seeing an eagle remains an exciting encounter, but no longer because of the great rarity of the species.

As I walk the dog in early December, I see a pair of adult eagles (white head, white tail) circling high over our neighborhood. I watch them through my binoculars for a few minutes, entranced. Seeing the first bird out of the corner of my eye, I know right away it is an eagle because of its very long wings. Eagles are not like other raptors—they stand out. As I glass the first bird, another moves in and greets the first bird. They play about, high in the sky. One bird, presumably female, looks larger than the other. Perhaps this is a mated pair, or perhaps the smaller male is courting this female. Eagles start nest building early in

February. It is not too early for this pair to be dallying in anticipation of a pair-up to produce spring nestlings.

Why do we go gaga over eagles? Size matters. Also majesty. And the symbolism. With the silver eye, the yellow bill and feet, and the chocolate body offsetting the stark white head and tail, there is a lot to appreciate in this bird with a wingspan of eighty inches. Ask a cross-section of American citizens what bird they most would like to see at that moment, and most will quickly answer "eagle." These folks should be spending more time looking up in the sky. The eagles are there, moving about in the breezes, even over the nation's capital.

As pointed out by Louis Halle in his book, there are three dominant winds proffered by nature in the Mid-Atlantic—northwest, southwest, and east. The northwest is the wind that brings in the cold fronts and clear skies and starry nights. It is the wind of autumn. By contrast, spring is defined by the southwest wind, which brings us warm temperatures and migrating songbirds. The east wind brings stormy weather. We never forget this, because "east wind, rain," was the Japanese government code to announce the impending break of diplomatic relations with the United States leading up to the attack on Pearl Harbor in early December 1941.

It is December 8, and the high is expected to reach thirty-four degrees. An American Robin on the front lawn this morning is fluffed up to fight the chill. Walking the dog, I hear a sapsucker's squeal in the neighborhood. Biking to work, I sight an adult Bald Eagle on the Virginia side of the river. Lots of Canada Geese have moved in to their regular Potomac loafing spot at the south end of Roosevelt Island. Finally, in the late afternoon as I bike home for the day, I note that the Barred Owl is roosting in its regular perch hidden in the greenery of the leafy vine on the big Eastern Cottonwood above Fletcher's Cove along the canal.

The Barred Owl is the common nocturnal predator of bottomland hardwood forests in the East. Because of our proximity to the Potomac bottoms, this owl is a year-round visitor to our neighborhood. All our neighbors are familiar with this species and love hearing its distinctive strident hooting at night. Who can resist the charms of a wild owl? This species subsists on small mammals mainly, but also takes some birds. In our neighborhood, the owl probably takes mainly mice, voles, and squirrels (and perhaps the occasional small pussycat). Its presence in the neighborhood seems to fluctuate seasonally and year-to-year for reasons unknown. At times, especially when the young owls are fledging from the nest, Barred Owls can appear to be commonplace. Then months go by when the owls are neither heard nor seen.

Presumably, the productive core population of the species lives down along the river where the bottomland forest is extensive. The birds in our neighborhood are probably subordinate individuals pushed out of prime habitat, squeaking by with little resource margin to spare. The scientific term for the marginal breeding habitat is *sink*. It is where breeding pairs typically fail to raise their offspring to adulthood. So long as the Potomac bottomland forest remains productive, then our neighborhood will continue to receive migrants from that richer, more extensive, and more productive source population. It is a bit sad to think of pairs of owls (or other noble vertebrates) striving to reproduce year after year in marginal habitat and coming away with nothing. Nature can be cruel.

This time of year, I get a naturalist's version of cabin fever. The customary field trips of spring and fall are done, and I have few plans for getting out into nature. I stare out the window of my basement office and daydream about field outings of the future. On days like this, it is best to retreat to a fat book, which inevitably leads to a nice afternoon nap, followed by time spent cooking dinner while a basketball game provides background sound in the room and the winter birds make one last visit to the feeders out back as dusk sets in early.

Ah, that first snow of the season and looking out the window to see a world transformed! In our region, there are three steps to full-on winter. First comes the hard frost (usually in late November). Then comes the first light covering of snow (usually in December). Finally, when the Potomac freezes over, one has reached stage three, where there is no mistaking the season—deep winter. So here we have reached stage two, with our first all-white morning. Something about the sun on the thin layer of white snow has an emotional impact. It speaks to the child in us, taking us back to early memories of winter snows and all that this meant to a child's sensibilities. Even as a senior, I react with a primal excitement. When I see snow in the backyard I think of Evening Grosbeaks arriving in tight flocks at Baltimore feeders in the early 1960s. My mind drifts to pond skating followed by hot chocolate at the Valley Inn in rural Baltimore County. And of course, I think of evening sledding as a child on the great hill on the golf course of the Baltimore Country Club. First snows evoke rich reveries of childhood in so many ways.

The annual Christmas Bird Count (CBC) is a national phenomenon that sees the participation of tens of thousands of birders across the country. During the December–January count period, parties of birders do

Fletcher's Cove, C&O Canal in snow

a daylong survey of birds within a designated circle with a diameter of fifteen miles. Usually, the territory within the circle is subdivided into sectors, with each sector being assigned to a particular team of birders. The mandate is to count every individual of every bird species within the circle. At the end of the day, these are tallied and an overall master list is produced for that named CBC circle. When this annual count effort is applied across the country, a snapshot is obtained of the US winter bird fauna for that year. Most count days end with a festive dinner followed by a light-hearted count tally during which the sightings of the rarest and most amazing birds are saved for announcement at the very end of the event. So the CBC is something of a cross between a national survey and a daylong winter-season festival celebrating birds.

Although the end-of-year bird fauna around the DC area is a bit thin, it is nonetheless fun to head out to a patch of habitat to try one's luck at putting together as big a list as possible to win the approval of the other members of the CBC team. It is also a great excuse to get outside at a season when most activities are indoors. This year, John Lamoreux and I participate in a count in Brooke, Virginia, an hour south of DC, and our count sector includes some frontage on the Potomac, where it is tidal and baylike. The daylong effort is much like a scavenger hunt for birds, totaling up the common birds and searching for the species that are present in the area in tiny numbers, hidden in brush piles or stream tangles, or bobbing far out in the middle of the great river. We have a sector that includes large tracts of oaks, extensive marshlands, and expanses of river. The diversity of habitats means we will find birds with three distinct ecological requirements. We are lucky with the weather, which can determine whether the day will be a success.

I have participated in a quite a few CBCs over the years, scattered far and wide across Maryland and Virginia. It is often the only birding one does during the winter period. It also is a social event, permitting old friends to see each other and catch up during the evening CBC tally and dinner. It can be one of the nicest events of the holiday season for a birder.

Everyone who has birded for a long time has an interesting CBC story to tell. Mine comes from Baltimore in the early 1970s. I was doing a sector in the city quite near my childhood home. It was a party of two—my mother and me. We were counting birds on the woodsy campus of a small Roman Catholic college. It was cold and clear and windless. As we stood listening for woodpeckers in an open grove of ancient White Oaks, we heard a loud report, sounding like a gunshot (it was early Sunday morning so we doubted that it was the product of gunplay, even though it *was* Baltimore). Instantly on the alert, we looked around to see the canopy of one of the massive White Oaks begin to shift. This great tree slowly began to tilt and, gathering speed, crashed to the ground a mere hundred feet from us. The sound of destruction that it produced seemed to go on for seconds as we stood frozen in our tracks. After the sound finally ceased, we whooped our relief, for we had, a few minutes before, been standing just where the tree had crashed down. We had dodged a bullet, figuratively. I remember nothing about the birds seen that day—only the treefall that almost killed the two of us. I have had similar close calls with treefalls while camping in New Guinea's old-growth forests. Ask a greenhorn what poses the greatest danger to a person camped in the woods, and the response would probably be: venomous snake or Black Bear. Not correct. A falling tree or tree limb is probably the greatest threat. There are precautions that one can take regarding the snake or bear. Not much can be done about the falling tree or limb aside from being very careful about placement of the sleeping tent.

On this weekday morning, I bike to my office in Crystal City, through the bright, windless, cloudless, and cold day. Many flocks of geese laze about the Potomac. A flock of House Sparrows has started to inhabit the basement parking lot of my office building. There is also a large flock of this species wintering in a tall evergreen hedge in our Bethesda neighborhood.

In the United States, the House Sparrow is nobody's favorite bird. As I write this, I can see a half-dozen sparrows stripping one of my backyard feeders of seed as the less aggressive native species perch in the verges. Initially translocated from England to New York City in 1851 and 1852, the House Sparrow, long known as the English Sparrow, expanded its United States range rapidly, much in the manner of the European Starling. Both have been very successful invaders of the New World. The House Sparrow today ranges from the Canadian Maritimes west to northern British Columbia and from south Florida west to Baja California and thence southward into Central America.

The House Sparrow is mainly associated with urban areas and is often seen begging at the patio tables of outdoor restaurants in the spring and summer. Although the male in his breeding plumage can be considered handsome, the females and young birds are very plain. That said, this resourceful species has amusing and attractive traits as well. As I mentioned, during the winter a flock of House Sparrows retreats to the underground parking lot where I park my bicycle in Arlington. This is the only species I have seen do this to get out of the cold. The House Sparrow flock escapes the severe cold for weeks on end by overnighting in the underground lot—not a stupid thing to do. The naturalist John K. Terres described reports of the species entertaining itself by repeatedly dropping small pebbles onto a tin roof and listening as they rattled down the sloping metal sheet. Sounds like something a group of bored children might do on a lazy summer day back in the 1950s.

A birding colleague, Bob Hahn, had for many years conducted the annual Christmas Bird Count on the White House grounds. I wanted to do that, so I emailed the White House with a proposal about serving as the volunteer ornithologist for the White House grounds. The proposal came to naught, but it was amusing to think about. That brings to mind a 1910 article from *Bird-Lore* magazine that published Theodore Roosevelt's bird list from the White House grounds. Roosevelt was probably the best birder of all the presidents, although apparently his cousin Franklin also liked to bird-watch, and Jimmy Carter remains an active birder. The list of ninety-three species provided by President Roosevelt to writer Lucy Maynard included both birds recorded on the White House grounds as well as species the president observed in his travels around the city. Focusing strictly on the species Roosevelt listed for the White House grounds highlights three things: first, many species that were common in 1910 are still common today—most of them, in fact. These include the Carolina Chickadee, Downy Woodpecker, Chimney Swift, Fish Crow, Baltimore Oriole, and Song Sparrow. Second, some species common in 1910 are rare or absent today from downtown DC and the White House. These would include the American Kestrel, Red-headed Woodpecker, Saw-whet Owl, and Wood Thrush. Last, some species absent from the list of 1910 are common today in urban DC. These include Canada Goose, Pileated Woodpecker, Rough-winged Swallow, European Starling, House Sparrow, and House Finch. The take-home point, once again, is that stasis and change are two sides of nature that are always there for those who are watching. Both are of interest, and why some things stay the same while other things change is of interest to most of us. We appreciate both, but often struggle to explain the driving forces underlying either.

Of course, with regard to the annual seasons of nature, most of us like our seasons to remain the same, with the same annual display of natural phenomena. We like to hear the voices of migrating flocks of Tundra Swans in late November. We like to see snow on December 24 or 25. Our memories appreciate the annual appearance of seasonal signposts, things that recur, year after year in season, from childhood to our senior years. These give a rhythm to our lives and offer environmental reassurance in a world filled with unpredictable political events and unpleasant surprises. The permanence and resilience of nature is comforting.

On Christmas Eve, my birding buddy David Wilcove and I make a morning dash out to Riverbend Park, Virginia, along the southern bank of the Potomac. It is sunny and cold, with two inches of snow on the ground. In the wintery oak woods, we discover a rufous morph Eastern Screech Owl hiding in a small tree hollow. We are alerted to the owl by the mobbing behavior of Blue Jays and Tufted Titmice. We see the little predator in its narrowed "freeze position" in the dark hollow of the tree. Spending about ninety minutes walking the trails, we also see a Winter Wren, Brown Creeper, White-breasted Nuthatch, fifty Ring-necked Ducks, a Gadwall, and a Red-tailed Hawk.

On Christmas evening, my wife and I hear two Great Horned Owls calling behind our house. This is a new species for our yard list. Yard listing is a common practice among birders—think of Teddy Roosevelt, building his own yard list at the White House. He did the same at his summer place near Oyster Bay on the north shore of Long Island. It combines two popular pastimes, birding and record-keeping. A yard list is nothing more than a cumulative list of the birds recorded from one's yard over the years. It is fun mainly because of the challenges and opportunities it offers the homeowner who happens to be a birder. The yard list can be worked on while raking leaves or gardening or simply sitting in a lawn chair, looking up into the sky or listening carefully to the ambient sound. Countable birds can be flying high overhead (think Common Loons migrating north on a mid-May morning) or calling from a patch of woods down in the hollow (think Great Horned Owl). It is an open-ended pursuit and can be worked on for decades. People love to brag about their yard list (mine is a paltry ninety-three species). It's one more way to bring nature home to yard and family.

Washington is south of the Mason-Dixon Line. But it is neither south nor north. It's just sort of amorphously subtropical. And thus, the arrival of winter is always here and there interrupted by dissonant signs of spring, as if the earth cannot make up its mind about winter—at least in this corner of the earth. For the naturalist residents of DC, this is definitely a good thing. We get strong doses of winter interspersed with brief doses of pseudo-spring. That makes the winter more bearable, because nature is hinting to us that something better is coming.

By contrast, think of Duluth or Traverse City or Bismarck or Bemidji. In such places the winter locks down and there is no escape for a good three (or more) months. No respite. Grim deep-freeze winter. Yes, the major snowfalls are fun for a while (just like they are in DC), but the relentless winter tedium wears you down. Especially for a naturalist, the long winters of the north country are particularly tough, and it seems that spring can never arrive soon enough. Think of this: on April 24, 2014, 60 percent of Lake Superior was covered by ice. Winter still rules there in late April. Winter in northern Michigan: December, January, February, March, April—too much for many of us.

In subtropical DC, we almost root for winter's arrival. A good snowy winter means perhaps twenty to thirty days with snow cover, and perhaps five or six days with a measurable fall of snow. Any tenderfoot can survive that. Spring is always just a string of warm days away.

Biking home at the very end of the calendar year combines satisfying physical exertion with an unambiguous benchmark—another year logged. The achievement is mixed with anticipation and anxiety concerning what the new year might bring and the challenges to come. And then there is nature . . . some things are seasonal but timeless: a Winter Wren making one of its winter vocalizations, trilled *j-d-d-d-d-d-d-d* notes from a brush pile; White-throated Sparrows foraging on the verge of the bike path in the gloaming; a stunning technicolor postsunset light show in the sky. At those moments, nature trumps work.

SEVEN

January—River Ice

> The beginning of another day; the beginning of another year. The wind no
> longer rages but the silent cold continues on.

—EDWIN WAY TEALE, *A Walk Through the Year*

Sure, there are cold winter days in the DC area from time to time, but to experience a real winter day it is worthwhile driving up to snow country in northern West Virginia during the Christmas–New Year's holiday season when a snowstorm is predicted. This entails an automobile-powered environmental transect from the subtropical lowlands of the Chesapeake basin into the nation's interior heartland, crossing the continental divide into a highland zone of winter extremes. The trip up to Canaan Valley, West Virginia, in January, is a jolting climatological relocation. There is no other like it in our region.

It's just a matter of loading the SUV with winter gear, bundling the family into the car, and driving westward for about four hours. One departs a DC environment typically with dreary and cloudy skies, temperatures in the forties or fifties, and drizzle expected. Snow is an unknown commodity during most DC Christmas seasons. One drives west for at least a couple of hours, gradually rising higher and higher up toward the Allegheny Plateau before seeing the first patches of snow on north-east-facing slopes. Our experience has been that as you approach the higher passes on West Virginia Highway 48, the flurries start. As you cross the continental divide into the Ohio–Mississippi drainage, suddenly the wind picks up, the flurries transition to blizzard, and the car enters a shroud of blowing snow. The ground and road surface become snow covered, and the snow-filled sky is a uniform gray. Welcome to continental winter! Drifts of varying size form where the blowing snow hits a roadside landform. Traffic slows to a crawl as traction and visibility degrade. Before long, we are on a winding two-lane road in the mountains, and the spruces and pines on the hillsides are encrusted in snow. We now have departed the DC zone and arrived in our local version of montane Colorado. This is what winter is truly meant to look like, and suddenly we are all excited as can be to be headed into the snow zone to do some skiing and getting our teeth sunk into full-on winter of the continental interior (even if it is only West Virginia).

One should make the pilgrimage to real winter once every year, because it is unlikely that DC's weather is going to offer up the real thing, with all the trimmings. The thing about Canaan Valley and the West Virginia high country is that it does offer everything to transport you to a world so different from DC that a three-night sojourn there seems like a whole month, and you go home feeling somehow changed. The pinnacle of distinction comes when you are standing atop the highest summit of the ski area, and the dwarf firs and spruces are all buried under a deep covering of powdery snow or rime ice, and then you gaze out in all directions to a world of frosted mountains and white-blanketed valleys. This is what the marketing folks mean when they promise a *Wild and Wonderful* West Virginia.

Canaan Valley in January is a far cry from what my daughter and I experienced in late June when we searched for Black Bears. A silence has come over the land along with the thick blanket of snow. Not much need for the binoculars. The only birds are the Black-capped Chickadees that frequent the slope-side chalet feeders in the ski area and the occasional Rough-legged Hawk out over the open ground at the bottom of the valley. Then there are the track marks made by Snowshoe Hares and Red Squirrels atop the snow. Here a snowfall of ten or fifteen inches is commonplace, and huge mounds of snow are created by the busy snowplows. The sky can be slate gray with steady snow falling for days at a time. Now that is what I think of as *real* winter.

Having returned from snow country, one is now prepared for some winter weather, which in the DC area normally does not settle in until sometime in January. One can gauge the arrival of true winter by the river. When a thick and picturesque layering of ice covers the Potomac from bank to bank, then winter is here in earnest, and one's blood begins to thicken from the mornings and evenings of biking in a cutting headwind with afternoon temperatures in the twenties. Throw in a few inches of snow, and the whole of Washington is in winter mode, reveling in the brutal truth of the remorseless weather. For this is the signal that the scales have tipped and that autumn is forgotten; the next hope is for spring to be making its first, tentative signals.

It is early January, clear and twenty degrees at 7:00 a.m., and as I bike down the towpath to work, I encounter a Red Fox silently padding over the ice of the canal. When it sees me, it quickly changes course and crosses into the woods bordering the river. A bit later, on the Virginia side of the river, I see a Bald Eagle perched at the south end of Roosevelt Island. Here, many geese aggregate daily along the Potomac, clustered near the west bank, upstream from Gravelly Point. They are the reason for the Bald Eagle's presence. The big predator is scanning the goose flock for a sick or dying bird—the wintering goose flock is the eagle's cafeteria.

The Canada Goose is one of the commonplace birds in the DC area year-round. This, however, is a relatively recent phenomenon. In my boyhood, Canada Geese bred in the wilds of Canada and migrated in November in great skeins to the bays and coastlines of the Mid-Atlantic region, to be hunted by my grandfather and others like him. I remember hearing the haunting musical sound of geese flying overhead when I lay in bed at night as a boy. At that time, no geese loitered on the Washington Mall. No geese swam in the Potomac in May and June with goslings. No herds of adult and adolescent geese clogged the towpath in July. If you wanted to see geese, you needed to drive down to the Chesapeake in mid-December, and there they were in skittish rafts out of shooting range from the hunting blinds along the shore. Geese were wild. Seeing geese was special.

What happened? States started breeding and releasing the captive-bred nonmigratory Giant Canada Geese (a large southern subspecies). These prospered, began breeding locally without help, and mixed with the thousands of wild geese marooned in these parts after being lightly wounded by hunters deploying the less-lethal steel shot to shoot these big birds (lead is heavier and deadlier but also becomes a toxic addition to wetlands). All of a sudden, there were geese pairing up and not migrating. They came to infest urban parks, greenways, and golf courses. And here we are today. The Canada Goose is no longer Canadian, and very much an urban and suburban American. When, in late autumn, one hears the high strains of a skein of geese at night, one can't be sure whether it is some truly wild Canada Goose or just some golf course geese making a local move. Somehow, this is disappointing to the purists among us. I suppose it is because now this species is taking on some of the characteristics of the House Finch, House Sparrow, and European Starling—omnipresence, overabundance, and excessive urban familiarity. In most instances, we don't like our nature to be overly abundant and familiar.

Biking to work in January produces treats and challenges, day by day and night by night. Before sunrise, the pinky clouds are superb in the early gloaming. A Belted Kingfisher perches on a twig beside the river right across from the Washington Monument. An all-dark juvenile Bald Eagle sits atop the big Red Oak that normally is home to a majestic white-headed adult. There are skeins of geese on an ice-free section of river. Scaup are bobbing on the river near the Virginia shore. As I bike along, I hear the occasional songs of Carolina Wren and Carolina Chickadee. Moonrise in early evening is spectacular, just over the Capitol building.

Another morning is cold and windy—a tough bike ride. At Key Bridge, the Potomac is covered in large rosettes of ice. The rosettes have accreted to form a geometric pattern across the river. I find a juvenile Cooper's Hawk near National Airport; I approach to within twenty feet before it flies. A flock of two hundred American Robins passes through Crystal City. There are still patches of snow around, and everything is frozen. The bike path remains treacherous in places.

On another morning, superb sunrise colors fill the sky before dawn—mackerel clouds suffused with purples and pinks. I hear a flock of American Crows, see a small flock of Brown-headed Cowbirds, and hear a Red-bellied Woodpecker churring.

View of Lincoln Memorial and full moon from across the Potomac

Then the cold retreats, and it is springlike and balmy. Northern Cardinals and Carolina Chickadees are vocal and active. A single Fish Crow perches high atop a sycamore giving its *ha-heh* spring song. Then I see a pair of crows futzing around an old nest in a tree behind the tennis court. More Fish Crows are active at the nearby shopping center, noisy and sociable—up on the eaves, down in the parking lot—real mall rats! They are behaving as if spring has arrived.

On January 11, a fantastic flaming sunrise glows pink-salmon at 7:10 a.m. I see an adult Bald Eagle atop a high canopy branch above Roosevelt Island. The surprise of the day is a party of six Black-crowned Night-Herons roosting in a thicket by the river near the Gravelly Point playing fields. House Sparrows are still hanging out in the underground parking lot. Remnant seed husks on the concrete are evidence that some soft-hearted soul has been feeding them down here.

A couple of days later, the cold returns. Snow flurries are expected this afternoon. Three hundred Canada Geese loaf on the ice of the river. White-throated Sparrows and Dark-eyed Juncos forage beside the bike path. They are like little dark mice on the verge of the right-of-way. I hear the call of an American Crow. But in spite of the outdoor activity, my mind wanders to other things. . . . I am about to retreat southward with my wife and leave the cold behind.

Captiva Island, the northern sister island to the more famous and more crowded Sanibel, lies off the west coast of southern Florida, near Fort Myers. To get there we take a flight from DC and drive our rental car across a long causeway from Fort Myers to Sanibel. Then we slowly proceed northward along a narrow, traffic-filled two-lane road up the middle of Sanibel to a small bridge crossing a narrow water passage to Captiva. About four miles long and a half-mile across at its widest, Captiva is home to an old-fashioned and comfortable resort with ready access to a lot of nature and lots of salty water. The gulf and a long, white beach lie immediately to the west of the inn property, and Pine Island Sound lies immediately to the east. To walk from one shore to the other in bare feet takes about three minutes. My wife and I have visited Captiva several times over the years. We love to stay in one of the small and quaint old cabins that are named for some tropical flowering plant (such as Hibiscus or Frangipani). The whole experience is informal and low-key. It is the perfect winter vacation couched in nature.

For the naturalist, the three most compelling features of basing at Captiva are the access to the long stretch of Gulf of Mexico beachfront (especially Bowman's Beach on north Sanibel) for shell collecting; canoe access to the mangrove forests of Buck Key within Pine Island Sound; and the presence of the J. N. "Ding" Darling National Wildlife Refuge on northern Sanibel, just a fifteen-minute drive by car. Between the big shell-strewn beach on the gulf, the waters of the sound, and the trails and nature loop of Ding Darling, there is plenty to keep a naturalist active in mid-January.

Walking the gulf beach in the early morning is very productive for wintering birds. Brown Pelicans loaf in the water offshore and cruise the wave line in search of fish schools near the surface. Ospreys are always in the air, often uttering their high, plaintive notes (a voice not expected from such an imposing predator). These fish hawks hunt just offshore, but usually at greater heights than the pelicans. The occasional Magnificent Frigatebird circles highest of all, its long, pointed wings and forked tail creating a distinctive dark, angular silhouette. Seeing this strange wayfarer always makes me think of some distant tropical island. Snowy Egrets forage daintily right in the swash zone, ignoring passing pedestrians like me. The shorebirds, however, are the main feature of the morning beach avifauna—Willets, Black-bellied Plovers, Sanderlings, Red Knots, Dunlin, and Ruddy Turnstones. Added to these are the occasional Short-billed Dowitcher, Killdeer, and Wilson's Plover. Of course, there are terns here—mainly Royal and Sandwich Terns, but also the smaller Forster's Terns. Small silvery fish are abundant in the shallows of the gulf. These are prime tern food. On one occasion, we spy a remarkable Calico Crab that is handsomely variegated with assorted dark colors. When threatened, it compacts itself into an armored spheroid with its little pincers tucked perfectly into the front of its carapace, its seamless design allowing no point of vulnerability. It is a treat to pick up and examine this pretty subtropical creature before putting it carefully back into the sea.

We visit Bowman's Beach, a popular public beach on the gulf side of northern Sanibel Island. This is a wonderful place to walk the shore, hunting for shells. It is a regional park and is isolated from the mainland by a mangrove-fringed channel. One can walk north a couple of miles to the passage that separates Sanibel from Captiva. At this time of year the beach is littered with windrows of shells of many kinds. We collect cockles, scallops, small whelks, murexes, boat shells, olive shells, and cones, always looking out for the famously rare Junonia—the island's Holy Grail. There is something particularly relaxing and satisfying to shell collecting on the beach in south Florida. It is at once productive and acquisitive while being little more than a form of dawdling in the sun. Few can resist the charms of collecting shells on Bowman's Beach.

J. N. "Ding" Darling National Wildlife Refuge lies on the sound side of north Sanibel, with bike paths, kayaking, and a drivable wildlife loop. It is 6,400 undeveloped acres featuring mangrove forests, submerged seagrass beds, marshes, and West Indian hardwood hammocks. It is famous for its long-legged wading birds—Wood Stork, several egrets and herons, two ibis species, and Roseate Spoonbill. It also hosts American Alligators in good numbers, lots of turtles, and more. My find of the field trip is a Gopher Tortoise, a large terrestrial reptile of the Deep South that inhabits piney woods with sandy soil. The tortoise I encounter moves slowly across a grassy clearing beside the main road—surprisingly large to one used to seeing Eastern Box Turtles. Gopher Tortoises are most famous for the burrows they construct, which they use for roosting and breeding, but which also are taken over and used by a wide array of other species—making this tortoise an important habitat creator in the Southeast. I have been hunting for this species for years and am pleased finally to have a chance to see this prehistoric-looking creature. Carol and I have one additional nature encounter back along one of the waterways of the refuge. We come upon a small Bonnethead Shark in shallow water, consuming a crab. The shark is no longer than three feet, and it spends quite a bit of time with this crab. This is our only shark of the trip.

Early one morning, Carol and I rent a twin kayak and paddle across Pine Island Sound to Buck Key Preserve, following the marked canoe trail. We are in search of West Indian Manatees, which winter in and around this area. I have never seen a manatee, so I am anxious to see what we can find. The wind is light, the sky is cloudless, and we glide easily across the sound to Buck Key and its mangroves. Double-crested Cormorants are out and about, and a single Anhinga soars high above us, almost raptorlike. A bird of the Deep South, the Anhinga is a relative of the cormorants and is always fun to encounter for northerners. It typically nests in colonies of egrets in swampy thickets.

A Tricolored Heron perches at the edge of the mangroves, near the entrance to the canoe trail. A Belted Kingfisher rattles and flies low over the water as we paddle up to the entrance of the trail that leads into an open lagoon. Here we look up to see nine White Pelicans soaring in a circle high over us. These are huge—Florida's biggest bird. In flight they are remarkably long-winged, graceful, and handsome. A Little Blue Heron flies up out of the mangroves that we are passing by. An Osprey sits on a dead snag above the mangrove forest. He is eaglelike, perched there, with plumage patterned dark brown and white. A small remnant of what appears to be a fish is held under his left foot. We are disturbing this bird's breakfast, it seems. Ospreys are here in southwest Florida in winter in big numbers—presumably a mix of wintering birds from the Mid-Atlantic plus local breeders. It is such a pleasant surprise to see this big raptor up in the sky virtually every time you look up. When we return our kayak to the marina staffer, we complain about our failure to locate any manatees. She pauses, and then says off-handedly, "Manatees regularly loaf about right here next to our landing. Try tomorrow, early in the day before the sun is high!"

The next morning at 7:00 a.m. we stand at the water's edge, with the boat dock to our left and a small patch of mangroves to our right. There is no sun hitting this part of the island yet. Within a minute of our arrival, we see the surface of the water break about twenty yards out. It is just a slight movement of water, but we are instantly on needles and pins—maybe a manatee. As we sharpen our senses, we begin to see disturbances of the water in several directions; three or four of the beasts are here with us. For a brief moment we see the slightly curved back of a manatee break the surface and then submerge. Then we see a broad and rounded tail flipper poke up. Then a head, which is shaped a bit like that of a bulldog, but dull gray and with two prominent nostrils opening straight up to draw in air.

Then Carol looks down into the shallow water just in front of us, and there is the shadowy silhouette of an adult manatee, more than five feet long, no more than fifteen feet from us, in water that is less than four feet deep. We can practically reach out and touch it!

These gentle herbivores grow to a length of thirteen feet and a weight of three thousand pounds. They forage mainly on seagrasses in shallows of the Gulf of Mexico, the Caribbean, and the northern South American coastline. At times, individuals wander northward as far as Rhode Island. Carol and I are mesmerized by the presence of these mysterious will-o'-the-wisps in our midst. To think that they were right under our noses all along and that we had not been sharp enough to detect them.

We stand on the beach for more than an hour watching this small group of manatees lounging and feeding. Only a few times do they bring attention to themselves by raising a flipper or tail fin high out of the water. The rest of the time they could easily have been overlooked. I'm sure that's the way these retiring beasts would have it. Our manatee close encounters are the high point of our Captiva sojourn.

On January 21, 1996, the Potomac River rose eighty-five feet in forty-eight hours at Great Falls, in the fifth largest flood of the Potomac in a century. The flood was produced by a combination of events—the rapid melting of a local snowstorm, heavy local rain, melting of the deep snowpack in the Potomac's headwaters, and a heavy ice pack in the river blocking water flow. The Potomac at Little Falls, just above downtown Washington, crested at nine feet above flood stage. The canal towpath just below our neighborhood was inundated. I was forced to bike to work on the sidewalk of MacArthur Boulevard for several months because of the damage to the towpath, the canal, and lower parts of the Capital Crescent Trail. We have witnessed several Potomac floods over the years, and I am always stunned by the volume and power of the rushing water and the amount of damage that it can do. At these times the Potomac becomes a truly wild and rampaging river as it attempts to pass through the gorge of the Potomac between Great Falls and Little Falls.

In late January, Carol and I go to Gravelly Point to scope out a Snowy Owl that has taken up residence at National Airport. At least a hundred people are there to see it. We find the owl perched atop a small mainte-nance building beside the airfield. Toward the end of the day, a lovely sunset adds to our pleasure.

During the winter of 2013–14, hundreds of Snowy Owls emigrated from their Arctic territories to coastal areas of the East. An invasion like this happens only every six or seven years, and this particular invasion was especially large and widespread—a hundred-year event (like the flood). Although Snowy Owls do occasionally show up in downtown DC or at the nearby airport, most of these Arctic wanderers, when irrupting south, are drawn to habitats that approximate the Arctic tundra where they grew up. Aside from airports, coastal marshes seem to be the most popular habitat analog in the Mid-Atlantic. Most wandering Snowy Owls end up near the coast.

This airport Snowy Owl is what we call a stake-out bird—a rare or desirable species that arrives at a public place, stays around for at least a few days, and gets observed by many birders. Stake-out birds tend to be easy-to-locate species in open habitats that for some reason establish a temporary territory for a while. The Snowy Owl is a classic stake-out bird because it is easy to see (a giant all-white bird) from a distance and typically perches in the open.

Because of their rarity and showiness, Snowy Owls that arrive in the DC area always draw a crowd. They are even more popular since the Harry Potter movies featured owls in a big way. Stake-out birds often make it into local newspapers and TV newscasts. This positive publicity is great for bird-watching and can lead to recruitment of new cohorts of birders joining the pastime. Who can resist a big white owl?

A few days after our Snowy Owl adventure, it is sunny but bone-cracking cold—twelve degrees at 7:00 a.m. I hear the voices of a Carolina Wren and an American Crow. On the river, I see geese and Mallards and not much else. Ice covers the canal and some verges of the Potomac. The goose poop has frozen into rocklike pellets on the bike path in

Virginia. There is very little bird activity. A flock of Bufflehead ducks bobs about in the open Potomac off Gravelly Point. There is an inch of snow on the ground, and more snow is expected.

Biking home in the dusk, I see clots of geese on the edges of the Potomac and a flock of Ring-billed Gulls in the parking lot of Gravelly Point. While biking, I have a close call on a patch of slick black ice on the pedestrian bridge by the airport. As it grows darker, I pass through a band of heavy snow, and the flakes hitting my cheeks feel like the cold breath of winter.

End of January. The morning temperature is eighteen degrees, and snow cloaks the bike path, but I somehow avoid skids or tumbles. A Tufted Titmouse and a Carolina Chickadee are singing in the woods in DC. The Potomac boasts three Hooded Mergansers, two scaup, some Mallards, and five hundred Canada Geese. The morning headwind at Gravelly Point is brutal, but I get to pass through three big flocks of birds at ground level—Ring-billed Gulls, Canada Geese, and European Starlings—swirling wings and sound. That is the treat of the day.

In the latter half of January there are occasional hints of spring, but mainly we are centered deep in winter. Now we will move into February and see what that month brings.

EIGHT

February—Last of Winter

> The snow lying deep on the earth dotted with young pines, and the very
> slope of the hill on which my house is placed, seemed to say, Forward?
> Nature puts no question and answers none which we mortals ask.

—HENRY DAVID THOREAU, *Walden*

Early February is a time of short days, gloom, and the hint of death. At
the same time, there are preliminary indications of new life to come.
This is nature at its least sympathetic. The sky is steel gray; a snowstorm
is headed up from the south; a strong south wind is blowing at Gravelly Point in the afternoon. The storm has brought in birds—four Redhead ducks, two Pied-billed Grebes, three Hooded Mergansers, and I
finally get a positive ID on a Lesser Scaup (shape of the crest and the
purple sheen to the head). On the towpath I hear a Red-shouldered
Hawk calling and a Red-bellied Woodpecker in a locust tree is giving
its spring call—*prrrd!*

The next morning I bike in to the Natural History Museum along
the towpath. Two inches of fresh snow make my ride in a challenge:
patches of ice hide underneath the snowy blanket. My attention to my
balance is suddenly drawn to something else, a terrible sight—a

floater in the canal in Georgetown, a dark reminder of life's brutality in winter.

I stop in my tracks to gaze at a clothed corpse submerged in the C&O Canal. The corpse, with its layers of raggedy clothes, looks to be that of a street person, and I see no evidence of foul play. It is a grisly sight, throwing a dark blanket over the new day—one that is already gloomy and dank. A few DC police are beginning to filter in and are taping off the scene. That said, my clear view of the body suspended motionless in the dark water is a shock and something not quickly forgotten. It is a sharply drawn image that my conscious mind involuntarily returns to a number of times over the next few weeks.

Thankfully, it is not often I come upon corpses when biking to work. Over three decades I have witnessed three floating bodies in the canal—all in the urban confines of Georgetown. I suppose this should not be surprising, because the towpath and canal area in Georgetown is a retreat favored by homeless folk. Many are aging and not in good physical condition. Some suffer mental illness. Death hovers over them. Presumably bad winter weather takes these victims at a weak moment. Now, at this low point of winter, it is not that surprising to be reminded of our mortality. The approaching celebration of spring is really something of an attempt to battle back against life's darker half. Spring is, in some ways, a joyful announcement of having survived grim winter. And this body floating in the canal reminds us that life is perilous and that those of us smiled upon by life's fortune should, in fact, celebrate life every day.

In early February, needing to escape the Mid-Atlantic gloom of Washington, I decide to head north into the more cheerful white snowy landscape of a Canadian winter. I drive twelve hours to Algonquin Provincial Park, in eastern Ontario, and camp for four nights at Mew Lake Campground, which is open year-round and provides the luxury of hot showers and campsite electricity, making tent camping a possibility in the Canadian snows of February. After spending the day out in the cold, it is good to be able to recalibrate in the evening with a hot shower. And having campsite electricity allows me to run a power cord into my small tent to run a space heater. With the space heater turned on at night in the tent, I can sleep in real warmth. The only additional winter necessity I require for comfort is a four-inch-thick foam mattress that keeps me off the icy tent floor. Although some might consider winter camping in Canada a challenge, it is voluntary, *and* it is no hardship when compared with what homeless folk face every night on the mean streets of Washington in February.

I set up a large tarp over my picnic table, which I clear of snow. I also put up a feeder of sunflower seeds. Within twenty minutes Black-capped Chickadees are coming to feed, and this is followed by a rambunctious group of Blue Jays, presumably able to spend the winter here because of the largesse of winter campers. I cook and eat at the picnic table, under the tarp. Needless to say, I have to dress for the conditions, and mealtimes outdoors are necessarily brief. From time to time I duck into the car, which remains warm after being used, in order to write up field notes and to read.

Tent camping in Ontario in February requires picking dates that promise decent winter weather. Using weather.com, I select a set of days when the daytime temperature hovers around freezing, at a time when the park is snowy. Winter camping would be a waste without the presence of snow, but not *too* much snow. During my four days in the park it snows about four inches, on top of about a foot of snow already present. This provides beautiful winter conditions but also allows me to move around the park at will—something I could not do if the snow were deep. And had it been much colder, I would not be able to camp in a tent and eat my meals outside on a picnic table.

I am here in Algonquin Park for five things: the winter weather, winter solitude, winter finches, winter mammals, and winter wilderness. The weather is pretty easy to plan, as I've noted. Winter solitude and wilderness are guaranteed. I checked for the presence of winter finches on eBird (it said "yes"). And the presence of winter mammals is much improved by a rare winter event announced on the Algonquin Park website—the presence of a Moose carcass in the valley below the visitor center. This is a road-killed individual that had been towed into the open boggy valley, providing a distant but unimpeded view from the large wooden observation deck of the center, high above the valley floor. The park staff do this to give visitors an opportunity to see local predators that are normally vanishingly difficult to observe.

The weather is perfect for a winter lover like me. The temperature never drops below twenty-five degrees. It never rises above thirty-two. There are periods of light but steady snow every day. For most of my stay, the sky is a leaden gray. The ground and the conifers are blanketed in white. And the snow on the walking trails and side roads is not too deep for a pedestrian naturalist. I spend each day walking trails and back roads of the park in search of winter nature. With the snow on the ground I can see the tracks of Moose, Eastern Wolf, Red Fox, and American Marten. Seeing the tracks assures me that these creatures are up and about and gives me hope of chance encounters.

Winter walking in Algonquin sometimes can be done by boot and at other times requires snowshoes. I do a little of both, depending on the conditions. The more popular trails are so well packed by visiting nature lovers that they can be walked in boots. Going off trail requires snowshoes. Just being out walking in the snow in the deep woods is a near-religious experience. The beauty of the scenery, especially the stands of snow-laden White Spruce and Balsam Fir, as well as the Tamaracks and Black Spruces out in the boglands, is so absolutely tranquil that it is like being in an empty cathedral. No music, no chatter, no plane sounds, no smartphones, just solitude. A winter walk in Algonquin is mainly a silent experience. The birds are few, and their voices are typically muted this time of year. That's OK. I am here for winter. If I wanted cacophony, I could come back in early June.

At one point, walking the old railroad grade heading east to the Mizzy Lake Trail, I come upon the busy prints in the snow of a wolf pack. Just like me, wolves enjoy being able to walk the old rail grade, which is flat and reliable. Following wolf tracks for half a mile is an experience I do not get in suburban Washington. Later, I find the tracks of a cow Moose and her youngster. I follow these for a while. Near Wolf Howl Lake I hear the wolf pack sound off for a couple of seconds. It is over before my brain recognizes what it was. Afterward, I stand there, straining my ears, hoping to hear more, but that is all there is.

My main activities each day are nature walks and nature photography. A large flock of Evening Grosbeaks regularly visits the feeders at the visitor center, so I return there at least once a day to check in at the feeders and take yet more images of those boreal-dwelling yellow, black, and white seedeaters. I also walk the Spruce Bog Trail once a day in search of other boreal birds. Finally, I venture out along the Opeongo

Lake Road or Mizzy Lake Trail to get away from it all. Most of what I encounter is the stillness and silence of winter. Wildlife is very scarce, except at the feeders.

But every now and then I come upon something of interest. Flocks of White-winged Crossbills pass overhead, chipping excitedly as they hunt for conifer cones bearing ripe seeds. They perch atop the spires of the tallest conifers and vocalize. I find their cousins, Red Crossbills, on the surface of the park's main east-west road one morning, harvesting rock salt scattered by the snowplow. On one occasion, I locate a small flock of Pine Grosbeaks feeding on the seeds of American Ash trees. I round out my list of winter finches through encounters with small numbers of Purple Finches, Pine Siskins, Common Redpolls, and Snow Buntings. My search in the snow for Spruce Grouse and Black-backed Woodpecker does not bear fruit, but I do locate Boreal Chickadees and Canada Jays.

Along the Opeongo Road and on the Spruce Bog Trail, three species of birds are habituated in winter to humans—Red-breasted Nuthatches, Black-capped Chickadees, and Canada Jays. Presumably, these birds have been spoiled by generous nature lovers who, winter after winter, bring pockets full of birdseed for these adorable scamps. Thus each time I walk the Spruce Bog Trail, I am followed closely by endearing but demanding Black-capped Chickadees. The second I bring seed out of my pocket, they descend to my hand and even sit atop my woolen watch cap. It is difficult to resist the close encounters with these little songbirds, which have a lot of personality.

Coming back to my camp one afternoon, I see an American Marten in the Red Pine where I had placed a suet feeder. The lithe predator watches me cautiously from the pine and does not retreat for several minutes. This is an oversized weasel, about three feet long from head to tail and with thick, lustrous red-brown fur, an ocher throat, dark brown feet, and pale frosting on its face and ears. It is the most beautiful and graceful of the American mustelids—fast on the ground and agile high in trees. I encounter martens a number of times on this trip, and each encounter is entrancing.

It turns out there are several martens living in the campground this winter. They have found the campground to be easy pickings because of the year-round occupation by campers, who apparently do not refrain from (illegally) feeding the wildlife. Moreover, there are many Red Squirrels in the planted pines, the primary natural prey of the marten.

I spend several mornings and afternoons on the big outside deck of the visitor center, keeping a lookout on the distant Moose carcass. The most common visitors are American Ravens and Red Foxes. Every now and then a large form lopes across the open snow—an Eastern Wolf. On four occasions I watch pairs of wolves harvesting meat from the carcass. On another occasion, one of the wolves carries off a large limb bone into the distant woods. It is sublime to watch wolves moving across the snowy winter habitat of the open valley floor. Seeing these big predators moving about, undisturbed, in the open winter habitat is a rare treat. Most wolf encounters tend to be brief and unsatisfying roadside glimpses. These encounters are minutes long and give me a real sense of the wolves' daily foraging behavior.

Even more special for me is the arrival of a Fisher, the largest of the American weasels. As a youngster in the 1960s, I had studied the Houghton Mifflin mammal field guide and had latched on the Fisher as my favorite wild mammal. For decades I had longed to see this big dark brown and bushy-tailed hunter. And finally, here it is, humping across the snow with its distinct mustelid gait, heading to the Moose carcass. I set up a telescope on the Fisher and watch it work over the carcass. Looking like an oversized Mink, the Fisher has thick dark brown fur and typically a face frosted with pale fur. After feeding for fifteen minutes, it retreats across the valley to the safety of the woods. That day I observe Red Fox, American Marten, Fisher, and Eastern Wolf—one of my very best mammal-watching days as a naturalist. Because of some dumb luck, my winter visit to Algonquin Provincial Park provides a rare combination of winter solitude, a rich assemblage of winter birdlife, and maximum predator encounters.

Today, February 8, it is twenty-nine degrees at 7:00 a.m. in Brookmont. A Mourning Dove vocalizes at dawn. At the backyard feeder, the juncos are foraging on the ground while cardinals and titmice are taking sun-flower seeds above. I am surprised to see a tiny mite of a bird—a Ruby-crowned Kinglet—come in to forage at the hanging suet feeder. This is a first for my yard.

Biking to work, I find a female Bufflehead duck, then a pair of Hooded Mergansers, in small water openings on the icy C&O Canal in DC. Finally, I count sixteen Lesser Scaup drakes in the Potomac River off Gravelly Point, waiting out the bad weather. I hear a male Northern Cardinal singing his full spring song in the patch of woods by the point.

There is nothing quite as cheering as the male Northern Cardinal's spring song early in the year. Cardinals are permanent residents, so one does not have to wait for their return to hear them in song. It's just a matter of the sun rising sufficiently high in the late winter sky to nudge the cardinals to start preparing for spring. The male's variable song is always bright and musical and uplifting. And, of course, year-round the male is a brilliant red and has his black face-mask and perky red crest. The sights and sounds of this bird produce a one-two punch in anticipation of spring.

The following day starts at fifteen degrees, with clear skies. Ice stretches all the way across the Potomac at the Lincoln Memorial. This morning, I see two adult Bald Eagles circle low over the DC side of Key Bridge, then wing slowly over me to perch on the concrete tower of the Georgetown University Library.

I depart a bit early from work, and biking home, I encounter a mixed foraging flock of land birds along the towpath. Bird flocks are usually where the action is on a February afternoon in the low country beside the Potomac. At these times the various hungry land birds gang up when they are out foraging. In the leaves by the bike path are a bunch of White-throated Sparrows, shuffling their feet in search of seeds and other edibles. A Carolina Wren rasps a scold in a tangle of honeysuckle. A female Downy Woodpecker taps on a hollow stem to drive out hibernating ants. Higher up, a male Red-bellied Woodpecker searches the bark of a locust tree. Several Carolina Chickadees and Tufted Titmice move about, actively examining twigs in the middle stories of the woodland. Given the open nature of a winter woodland, lacking the protective cover offered by summer's greenery, one assumes that these birds flock together as a response to the ever-present threat of predation from Sharp-shinned or Cooper's Hawks. By clustering together, the birds can share the job of vigilance—the many eyes can more readily pick out a lurking raptor. The flocking may also benefit the members of the group through the effect of beating the bush and driving insect prey from cover, permitting one of the flock members to recover a prey item frightened up by another forager. In the Potomac bottomland woods, birds flock together throughout the nonbreeding months. It is clear that they must be deriving some benefit from this cooperative activity.

Mid-February. Because the bike path is iced up, I am forced to bus in to work. It takes me seventy-five minutes. Moreover, I am unable to make any natural history sightings from the bus. Ugh! It's not that I am against public transportation. I like it as an alternative to driving to work in a car. I just like biking better for a number of reasons. There is no daily fee to bike or to park my bike. I am outside in the fresh air. I get to see nature. I can come and go at the time most convenient to my schedule. I get exercise. I am not adding to a traffic jam or harming the urban environment. And I arrive at work in a good mood and with my body revved up for a productive day. That said, most people do not have the luxury of being able to bike to work year-round. I am one of the few who can put the necessary pieces in place—a home near a bike path, proximity to the office, and an employer who tolerates biking. I am very fortunate.

Although I consider it a privilege to bike to work year-round, there are times when biking to work is a physical challenge. Of course, with snow and ice it is hard to get to work without periodic falls. It is hard to control going down on such falls. During a fall, only time will tell whether you are going to go down easily or badly. Given that the tumble comes unexpectedly, it is impossible to plan a good fall. So it is best simply not to ride if there is glare ice on the path or fresh snow sitting atop an underlayment of ice. If there is no ice, and only an inch of fresh snow, biking to work presents no problem.

More commonplace than snow or ice is the strong and persistent headwind on the ride home. For me, the toughest section to ride in wind is the open landscape of Gravelly Point, on the west side of the river and just upstream from National Airport. There, the northwest wind blows with a vengeance. Such winds are not uncommonly accompanied by snow showers. The combination is ferocious. One needs to keep the body low and head down, but this is hard to do on a winter's night when the snow is obscuring the bike's puny headlight. One labors on, eager to escape the open riverside landscape for the protection of the wooded trail on the DC side of the river.

One morning, in late February, I simply cannot bike to work. After reaching shady areas on the bike trail, I am defeated by a combination of crusty snow, ice, and slush that is impossible to negotiate. Then it is back to home, changing clothes, and out to the bus stop.

Late February is a time to look at the dark side. It is a time of pessimism. The glass is mostly empty. The warmth and music of spring are still distant, and memories of that floating corpse continue to rise up from the depths of my dreams. Late this month I read a seminal environmental book published in 1948 and entitled *Road to Survival*, by William Vogt. It is most interesting to gain a grasp of the outlook of an American environmentalist just after World War II and well before the advent of the Earth Day revolution. The oft-repeated themes of this important but now-forgotten book are twofold: (1) the earth is overpopulated, and (2) humans need to reduce their overuse of natural resources (especially croplands) to ensure sufficient food and fiber. These two admonitions sound eminently reasonable today, because the earth now holds more than three times as many humans as in Vogt's day, and much more land is being cropped now than in 1948.

What is remarkable is that Vogt's alarming suppositions about the future of the earth sixty-five years after writing the book have, in general, *not* been borne out. He spoke of regular cycles of famine in India—and predicted much worse to come. Yet the opposite has occurred—more population and yet less famine. He predicted a maximum limit to the earth's capacity to produce food and that this limit would soon be reached, with dire results. This has not occurred. He made no prediction about climate change, something that most definitely has come to the fore in 2019.

Vogt must have written the last page of his book in a dark and dreary late February. This is what he says: "Unless . . . man readjusts his way of living . . . to the imperatives imposed by the *limited* resources of his environment—we may as well give up all hope of continuing civilized life. Like Gadarene swine, we shall rush down a war-torn slope to a barbarian existence in the blackened rubble." Thank heavens, his vision has not been borne out in the second decade of the twenty-first century!

For some strange reason, it is difficult for brilliant environmentalists to envision the future clearly. Both Vogt and Paul Ehrlich (in his 1968 book, *The Population Bomb*) got it very wrong, happily for us today. To both Vogt and Ehrlich, the future decades appeared dire because of the raw numbers being analyzed. And yet, civilization managed to dodge the bullet and continue forward on its merry way.

What are the take-home points of this story? First, the raw numbers can alarm; second, the future is a little-known world behind multiple veils; and third, regarding the earth and its ability to support humankind, things seem to work out better than our best minds can predict. This is reason for optimism, even in February. That said, we should not continue to expect nature to bail us out. We need to act in the best interests of the planet. Being optimistic is no reason for inaction or procrastination on pressing environmental issues.

In search of pelagic seabirds, I take a boat trip out of Lewes, Delaware, in the latter half of February. Perhaps the most extreme birding activity is the wintertime oceanic boat trip in search of pelagic seabirds, mainly gulls and auk relatives—black-and-white sea-dwelling birds that nest on rocky islands in Maritime Canada. Here is another chance to experience the rigors of winter out in nature!

I join three birding buddies (Stacey Maggard, Chuck Burg, and Olivier Langrand) aboard the *Thelma Dale IV,* sailing out of the small harbor in Lewes, Delaware. Led by Paul Guris, the boat, loaded with forty intrepid birders, heads due east in relatively calm seas, cold temperatures, and deeply overcast skies. We depart the harbor before dawn and start birding not far offshore as the dim light announces the uncertain start of a dreary February day. Near shore we see mainly scoters flying in lines as well as a few Northern Gannets.

The main challenge of the pelagic boat trip is seasickness. There are plenty of landlubbers aboard who do not find the movement of the boat pleasurable, and for them, the day probably seems interminable. For the seasick, low-grade nausea makes doing anything difficult, and it is only made worse by the periodic need to throw up. The afflicted are instructed to blow their lunch on the lee side of the boat, not in the tiny and claustrophobic toilet. Those susceptible to this malady who have taken seasick medication in advance do better. Luckily, none of our little party of four suffers too much from seasickness, so we are able to spend the bulk of our long day on the ever-moving upper deck in search of interesting sea life.

The boat rocks continually, and the top deck sees the most movement, so one must be careful when moving about and must steady oneself with the aid of guard rails and other handholds at all times. Of course, this makes it difficult to pinpoint the birds moving over the surface of the choppy sea. Luckily, Paul, our leader, employs a number of able young spotters to point out the best birds. Other members of the team toss out chum behind the boat. Chum is a combination of fish parts and fish oil, which draws in many of the seabirds, who find this revolting mix delectable. As a result, swarms of gulls follow the boat. Apparently, the sight of this aggregation of white seabirds attracts other species from afar. Thus we employ the presence of common birds around the boat to draw in the rarer and more desirable species.

The most common species are Herring and Great Black-backed Gulls and Northern Gannets. Joining them are individual Thayer's and Lesser Black-backed Gulls, both rather rare (Thayer's is now considered to be a well-marked subspecies of Iceland Gull). Also rare and new for me is the Northern Fulmar, a shearwater relative that has the look of a gull but soars about on long and stiffly extended wings. Small parties of fulmars sweep in, pass the boat, and then quickly disappear in the gray distance. They never hang around for the scraps. We see both pale and dark morphs of the fulmars but never get any photographs of them. We also encounter small groups of Razorbills, duck-sized black-and-white relatives of the Great Auk, a giant, flightless species now extinct. The Razorbills, too, are elusive and we get only distant glimpses of them. With the up-and-down movement of the boat and the constant motion of the wave crests, birds typically are visible only momentarily before disappearing behind a wave.

There is no question that winter pelagic birding is the most rigorous birding there is. Today is no exception. For long periods, there is nothing of interest to see, but one cannot not afford to go inside the cabin, because there is always the chance something rare will pass by and then disappear over the horizon. Late in the trip, several robin-sized, small pied auks, called Dovekies, appear by the boat, bobbing atop the olive waves. These are the first Dovekies we see well, so everybody shifts to the rail that provides the best view of these little birds. Several of us are pointing our long lenses at the closest bird when a Great Black-backed Gull, much larger than the Dovekie, swoops into our field of view and grabs the little auk by the back of its neck and carries it off. The Dovekie becomes lunch for the big predaceous gull. There are shouts and one or two inadvertent exclamations by the assembled birders, but it is over in the blink of an eye. Paul, our leader, actually gets a series of images of the act of predation, of which he is rightfully proud. This is not something one sees every day.

A winter pelagic trip is a battle against hypothermia and fatigue. The relentless wind chill over a ten-hour period can cause the fingers and toes to tingle. Also, the never-ending pitching of the boat forces the birder to continually use core muscles to brace against some surface of the boat. That is exhausting. We return to port after dark, and for the last hour of the ride most of us jam into the overheated cabin, seated and semiconscious, rocking back and forth against one another, not a seat to spare. After disembarking, it is more than an hour before I stop feeling the sensation of being on a rocking boat. I am feeling queasy just writing this passage.

So why do we weather the seasickness and the tossing boat to join a pelagic trip? This is the only way to gain glimpses of many of these seabirds, which rarely come to land except to nest. And these birds nest mainly on inaccessible islands in northeastern Canada or the Arctic, far from home. So we bite the bullet, and see what we can see. It is not for the faint of heart.

End of February. It is twenty-five degrees. Snow and sleet have fallen the morning before. I hear Downy and Pileated Woodpeckers doing their territorial drumming. They're drumming up spring! Today I bike to work on the sidewalk to avoid the dark icy patches on the Capital Crescent Trail. Along the route I see a large female Sharp-shinned Hawk soaring. I encounter a flock of Red-winged Blackbirds on the ground with starlings at Gravelly Point. More than two hundred Fish Crows come over in a huge flock giving their soft call. A pair of Horned Grebes are out on the river. Although February is the shortest month, it can seem to last forever. Naturalists are eager for the arrival of March.

NINE

March—First of Spring

> Looking across the River, I see the sun rise brilliantly between the Monument and Capitol dome, and feel its warm rays flash across the land at the same moment that the countryside about me is transformed into light and shadow.
>
> —LOUIS HALLE, *Spring in Washington*

Spring comes in stages here in the nation's capital, interspersed with pulses of winter, which weaken after each thrust of spring. The tilting of the earth toward the sun is gradual and relentless, but the climate's response to this steady astronomical trend is herky-jerky and unpredictable. This first stage of spring is dominated by cold, gloom, wind, and the occasional dollop of snow. In spite of these meteorological setbacks, nature marches onward toward full spring, led by the bright rays of the sun, ever higher and more northerly in the sky.

First of March. Today is cold and clear, but the male cardinals are singing their spring songs and lots of birds are on the move. A male Red-winged Blackbird, on its newly claimed territory at Roaches Run, is singing *konk-ka-lee!* Forsythia is blooming. House Finches are singing in downtown Crystal City. Male robins are chasing each other. There are lots of Ring-billed Gulls on the verges of the river.

Northern Cardinal

The very next day, I am homebound because a snowstorm hit Washington the previous night. I witness a desperate rush of birds to the backyard feeder. The snow transitions to rain and sleet. It is dreary and damp, with an east wind blowing.

Early March. A boldly patterned adult Peregrine Falcon circles over the towers of Georgetown University in the early morning. Black and Turkey Vultures soar over Brookmont in the afternoon. There are robins singing their spring song and grackles in abundance in the neighborhood. A Yellow-rumped Warbler gives its repeated *chek!* call note in a mixed flock—the first warbler of spring.

The next day, the Fish Crows are making a huge racket in the neighborhood. Wood Ducks are on the move—I encounter three parties of them on the C&O Canal—and a Pied-billed Grebe bobs about on the Virginia side of the Potomac. A Killdeer cries out on the ball field at Gravelly Point. Lots of birds are in song. Finally, at dusk, a Barred Owl hoots from the woods just east of our house. At dinner my wife, Carol, reports seeing her first Osprey of spring soaring over Key Bridge.

Second week of March. A drake Common Merganser looks like a sleek submarine on the Potomac. This is the mergansers' season on the river in the DC area. An adult Bald Eagle perches beside the Humpback Bridge, a guardian spirit of the morning commuters. There are eleven night-herons in their shrubbery roost beside the river above Gravelly Point. Even though it is near freezing at sunrise, the temperature reaches sixty degrees by early afternoon. Crocuses bloom on the neighborhood green. Five Red-winged Blackbird males vie for high song perches in the small row of pines at Gravelly Point; male Common Grackles glisten in the sun. Biking home from work, I see more than a hundred Bonaparte's Gulls scattered on the river above Key Bridge.

The White-breasted Nuthatch and Mourning Dove are in song this morning. Grackles, blackbirds, and cowbirds still flood into the backyard feeders. Feeding the birds is one of those issues fraught with differences of opinion and practice. Especially when fifty blackbirds are swarming over the feeding station, there can be doubts about the efficacy of this practice. My wife and I feed the birds for one reason: we love to have birds in our backyard. We do it for our own pleasure. We think that is reason enough to feed the birds. Another good reason is to see how many kinds of birds can be attracted into the yard. For instance, the first time a wily Pileated Woodpecker feeds on suet is for most people a reason for celebration—and one of those surprise bonuses of feeding the birds. Neighbors seeing a Pileated Woodpecker the very first time are bowled over by its size and striking black-white-and-red pattern. Those who know a little bit about birds often think, "Ivory-billed Woodpecker!"

Of course, there are downsides to feeding the birds. Squirrels, for instance. The best way to address the downsides of bird feeding is to think of the whole enterprise as a challenge involving intellect and engineering. One must tinker and experiment until a system has been devised that generates the most pleasure for the person doing the feeding. For me, that is having lots of birds I like a lot (goldfinches, cardinals, woodpeckers, juncos, White-throated Sparrows) and fewer of the pesky foragers (squirrels, House Sparrows, starlings). Every year I try different things to maximize my bird-feeding pleasure, and the experimenting is a fun pastime.

But think about it a bit more. Hundreds of millions of pounds of birdseed is grown and sold and used up feeding the backyard birds each year in the United States. It is, as scientific wags say, the largest uncontrolled and unmanaged experiment on seed-eating bird populations in the history of the world. It *has* to have a huge impact on our nation's birdlife, but nobody thinks about it, because it is a backyard activity without any government involved. Many birds that might otherwise migrate south can now stay put and subsist off the largesse of the bird feeders. What sort of unintended consequences might this have?

Here is one scenario to consider. Feeding the birds leads to the expansion of the East Coast populations of Blue Jays, Virginia Opossums, and Raccoons, all of which can benefit from winter feeding of seed and suet and other backyard treats offered by homeowners. The larger populations of these three mesopredators that feed on eggs and nestlings of songbirds might lead directly to higher rates of nest loss in locally vulnerable species, such as Wood Thrushes. Suburban woodlots that once were enlivened by the cadenced and pleasure-inducing thrush songs are now silent. It is something to consider.

Early mid-March. It is cloudy and cool. A vocal flock of Cedar Waxwings passes over the house. I lost an hour of sleep last night because of the arrival of Daylight Savings Time. Imposed on us by a bossy government, Daylight Savings is one of those seasonal constructs that people love to complain about. The spring arrival of Daylight Savings is particularly annoying because we all lose an hour of sleep on a Sunday morning. And on the following Monday, we then must deal with darkness extending an hour later into the morning hours, in a Faustian bargain that provides a bonus hour of illuminated life at day's end. For the objective naturalist, the spring time change should be welcome, because the all-important arrival of first light is not so god-awful early.

When I go outside (before first light) to pick up the paper at 6:20 a.m., I hear the roar of the river at Little Falls Dam—a remarkably loud sound that hints at the Potomac's immense raw power. The Potomac is the big show here in my Brookmont neighborhood. It is here that this great river has to squeeze through its narrow rocky gorge between Great Falls and Little Falls. When the river is up, the noise it produces is an impressive low background rumble. Hearing the river while standing on the front porch reminds me that we are living next to a changeable and living force of nature. When events conspire to produce a flood, as happens every decade or so, the river spills its banks and covers parts of the canal and towpath as well as much of the lowest parts of

Georgetown. And flooding is only one of the river's many moods. It brings so much of nature to our doorstep.

Because of the advent of Daylight Savings, I get to see sunrise on the way to work once again for a few days. That is an often-forgotten bonus to local naturalists. The wonder of a new day is always worth savoring.

Today I hear spring song by our Big Five: Carolina Wren, American Robin, Northern Cardinal, Tufted Titmouse, and Carolina Chickadee. I also hear a Winter Wren singing this morning along the towpath—hearing the song of this species in the DC area is a rare and welcome event. Two adult Bald Eagles perch close together atop the great oak behind the Humpback Bridge. And robins are doing heavy territorial chasing at Gravelly Point.

Mid-March. A spring snowstorm dumps eight inches of fluffy snow and creates an early spring–late winter wonderland. The blackbirds are pouring in to the backyard feeder, and the nuthatches and Fish Crows are vocalizing in spite of the snow. Carol and I walk down to the canal and find a calling Eastern Phoebe, a Winter Wren, a pair of Common Mergansers, and several Great Blue Herons. The mergansers are very fine—the hen perched demurely on the bank by the riffle, next to the gorgeously patterned drake. The tiny wren is adorable with snow as a backdrop. The phoebe is a surprise. Is this a spring arrival? The herons look miserable, standing in the cold, murky water. In addition, we hear Fish Crows calling throughout, as well as a singing cardinal. Finally, a Red-bellied Woodpecker is doing his spring drumming in spite of the snow.

A woodpecker does three important things with its powerful chisel-bill: it excavates an elongated cavity with a neatly rounded exit hole in a trunk for a nest; it drills deadwood in search of hidden arthropod prey; and it drums. A woodpecker drums to send out a territorial signal, much like a human beating on a drum. Each species of woodpecker has its own pattern of drumming, which undoubtedly are recognized by the other woodpeckers in the neighborhood. In the same manner, knowledgeable birders can identify the species by the pattern and intensity of the bird's drumming. Hearing and identifying a woodpecker's drum from a distance always gives the listener pleasure. It speaks to the occasional orderliness of nature.

I regularly hear complaints about woodpeckers from neighbors who are not bird watchers. These birds sometimes drum on a resonating surface of a house and at other times will actually drill into a wood facing. The first activity is simply annoying; the second is damaging. Drumming on part of a house is presumably attractive to a woodpecker because of the resonance of the sound created. It is common for woodpeckers to drum on metal flashing because of the brilliant sound it produces. Excavating into the wood of a house is more troubling, implying the presence of tunneling insects or termites in the wood itself, which of course is a bad sign about the house's condition. In this latter instance, the woodpecker is inadvertently doing the homeowner a favor by highlighting a possible pest infestation that should be addressed.

Latter half of March. It's cold. Snow is piled up on street corners, but the Fish Crows are noisy and swirling around our neighborhood shopping center. Spring presses forward—even though our backyard is blanketed with snow.

On March 19, I see an Osprey, a pair of Common Mergansers, a Horned Grebe, two Eastern Phoebes, and a sapsucker. I bike home through a clear and crisp evening with the temperature in the fifties; lots of joggers are running the local trails. Spring Peepers are out in force in certain favored wet bottoms along the Potomac. Tomorrow is the first day of celestial spring.

The evening chorus of Spring Peepers is an iconic sound of spring. These tiny chorus frogs gather in springtime near ephemeral wetlands in low-country woods and woodland edges. Although hard to see, these little creatures cannot be overlooked because of the high-pitched, musical, and up-slurred and interrogative *pea??* note they deliver once every few seconds. When scores of these little frogs deliver this note in chorus, the sound generated is continuous and transcendent—it is, simply, *the* sound of the Mid-Atlantic spring. Some damp woods along the Potomac literally ring with this chorus in the dusk of warm evenings in March and April. As an antidote to the depression of winter, one might consider spending some time within earshot of a peeper chorus.

March 20—the first day of astronomical spring! Before my departure for work, I find a Spring Azure butterfly in the backyard. One of the nesting Red-shouldered Hawks is vocalizing in the neighborhood as I depart. More Double-crested Cormorants are settling in on the Potomac. Horned Grebes are also present in small numbers. The Japanese Cherry blossoms are in full show at the Dalecarlia Water Treatment Plant on MacArthur Boulevard at the DC line. Biking home, I see the first bat of the spring above the canal.

The blooming of the cherry blossoms down at the Tidal Basin on the south side of the National Mall announces the formal arrival of spring to urban Washington. Office workers take a break at lunch and stroll over to see them and to photograph them with their smartphones. Tourists visit in busloads in the afternoon and early evening. At that time one must be sure to avoid driving anywhere near Independence Avenue west

Mourning Cloak

of the Smithsonian Castle because of the traffic mayhem. Best to do what Louis Halle did, and visit at dawn, while there is still a chill in the air, the sun is low for wonderful light, and no one is about. At that time there are photo opportunities galore and parking spaces in abundance. One final thing. Let's not forget that this is the single most artificial nature event of the year—the flowering of an urban planting of a big cluster of imported trees. It cannot compete with the real spring, which is bursting forth in the parks and green spaces all around.

It is late March. I hear the pleasant percussive notes of a Chipping Sparrow at the water treatment plant and see a Mourning Cloak butterfly fluttering erratically at the edge of the woods below Fletcher's Cove. An Eastern Phoebe calls near its traditional nest site under a bridge, and a Rough-winged Swallow is hawking over the canal. On the evening ride home I encounter Bonaparte's Gulls on the river above and below Key Bridge—one exhibits the striking black hood of its breeding plumage. The river's surface is broken in many places by a fish run where the river is wide and lakelike, above Key Bridge.

Typically, the Mourning Cloak is the first butterfly I see in spring, though this year it was topped by the Spring Azure. Still, the Mourning Cloak traditionally holds pride of place. Solitary and fast-flying, this large anglewing is one of the most affecting of the region's butterflies. When perched with its wings closed, the butterfly is quite cryptic, but when it opens its wings, one is struck by the rich colors of the upper wings—mainly dark brown with maroon highlights, and a distinctive pale yellow border to the wings, offset by a curving row of small blue spots set in the dark brown adjacent to the yellow fringe. Beautiful, but in an understated way. As a boy, in my butterfly-collecting days, I always found the Mourning Cloak an elusive and highly desirable quarry, its dashing and irregular flight making capture with a waved net nearly impossible. This is typically the first butterfly of the year because the adults overwinter in protected niches, from which they emerge on warm and sunny days in early spring. One often finds them flying in late February or early March, well before any leaves have emerged. The caterpillars feed mainly on willows but also occasionally on elms and poplars. The butterflies themselves rarely visit flowers, instead harvesting tree sap.

It is the last days of March, and I initiate my daily spring bird count. On the way to work I hear twelve Cardinals in song. The Spicebush is starting to bud out bright yellow. I count six Horned Grebes on the River, and two Ospreys circle each other over Roaches Run. Down behind our house a pair of Red-shouldered Hawks have built a nest and are apparently sitting on eggs. The day's highlight is a singing male Yellow-throated Warbler that I hear from the towpath.

Louis Halle devoted several pages of *Spring in Washington* to the return of the Yellow-throated Warbler from its winter quarters in the Deep South. An uncommon breeder in the DC area, this songbird is most reliably located in sycamores that border the Potomac in DC and Maryland. Discounting the commonplace Yellow-rumped and Palm Warblers, which often winter in the region, the Yellow-throated is the first long-distance migrant breeder to arrive back, hence Halle's paean to this golden-throated harbinger of spring. There's plenty to love about this bird. It is gorgeous to see, elegantly patterned in black, white, deep yellow, and dove-gray. Its song is sweet and syrupy and slow, as if it has a southern accent. And its affection for sycamores makes it a habitat specialist with an affinity for the Potomac and the C&O Canal. Of the three warblers breeding along the canal, this is certainly my favorite, even though I also admire both the diminutive Parula as well as the fantastic orange-washed Prothonotary. The Yellow-throated is special because it makes itself scarce. The Prothonotary is gorgeous but in a slightly garish way. It is not at all clear to me why this golden bird is named for a "chief clerk" or "notary"—did those bureaucrats formerly wear a cloak of gold?

On my morning ride to work, a lone Horned Grebe bobs on the river at Gravelly Point, a Pileated Woodpecker drums on a big dead stub of a sycamore, buds of the Spicebush in the floodplain are glowing yellow, and the Canada Geese are all in pairs now. Biking home, I see an Osprey, a flock of forty cormorants, and many decent-sized fish breaking the surface on the Potomac—the spring run of shad and herring is on.

Each day brings more spring activity. Robins chorus big in the early morning. Many flocks of grackles and other blackbirds are on the move. White-throated Sparrows are joining up in big flocks. Big Vs of cormorants are going overhead. I see an Osprey languorously circling over the river, headed to its northern nesting site. This evening, Comet Hale-Bopp is in full view after dark; it is the only thing visible in the northwest sky, fuzzy and pale—but in the binoculars it is a real-live comet with a visible tail! And Spring Peepers are in full voice.

On the following day, I hear the "Old Sam Peabody" song of the White-throat in the morning. The Double-crested Cormorants are now starting to roost in numbers in the riverside sycamores above the Three Sisters rocks. I get a big thrill when I find twenty-two Horned Grebes in a tight cluster by the eastern bank of the Potomac in DC. I encounter the group first in the morning, and they are still there in the evening when I bike home. Some are in breeding plumage. They are preparing to return to their breeding habitat in the prairie potholes of central Canada.

On March 28, I observe a pair of adult Bald Eagles perched in the tallest tree of the Lyndon Baines Johnson Memorial Grove across the parkway from the bike path. I also see a juvenile eagle about a quarter mile south of there. Then I encounter an adult Red-tailed Hawk in the big Red Oak by Humpback Bridge, where the eagles normally settle. I pass a pair of Tree Swallows investigating a nest hole in the dead tree at Gravelly Point where more pale green is showing in the woods. At the end of my day, I hear a few Spring Peepers sounding off in our little swamp behind the house.

On the very last day of March, biking in to work, I see a Zebra Swallowtail zipping around a sunny spot along the towpath. Buds are breaking on the Red Maples. I encounter an American Kestrel and an Osprey over Roaches Run. Lots of White-throats are on the ground beside the bike path, collecting grit. Noisy flocks of the American Goldfinches are starting to do their spring songfest. At Crystal City, the House Finches are singing like crazy. As the days of March run out, more and more of spring arrives at our doorstep. We are being swept up in the rush. . . .

April—Awakenings

Today the singing of birds was continuous and uninterrupted; where before
today the orchestra had simply been tuning up, the individual instruments
sounding separately.

—LOUIS HALLE, *Spring in Washington*

By April 1, the DC area is solidly locked in on spring. There is a long
way to go regarding the leafing out of the woodland canopy and the
major movement of migratory songbirds, but a lot of spring phenomena
are already in play, enough for most of us to have bought in to the idea
of spring's arrival. The wildflowers are starting to peak, the fish are running in the Potomac, the Ospreys are settling in locally, and the goldfinches are noisy in the elms. We may have some mud and cold to deal
with, but winter is gone, and it only gets better from here.

Having suffered through the long and brutish winter, I am thinking
it would be nice to glimpse how spring is developing sixty miles to the
south, so I take a day trip to the Northern Neck of Virginia to visit three
lovely natural areas, Wakefield Plantation, Westmoreland State Park, and
Stratford Hall estate. The three are lined up in a row along the southern
shore of the lower Potomac, where the river is about five miles across—

essentially a wide, salty arm of the Chesapeake. There is something for everyone down here on the Northern Neck, which is the uppermost of three fingers of land that jut into the southern Chesapeake, sandwiched between the Potomac, Rappahannock, James, and York Rivers.

My first stop is Wakefield, the birthplace of George Washington and the ancestral home of the Washington family. Now a national monument, Wakefield combines colonial and natural history. It features frontage on the Potomac, the mouth of Popes Creek, and a mix of fields, marshland, and low-country forest dominated by Loblolly Pine with an understory of American Holly. Four generations of Washingtons lived on this rural property. The original house burned in 1779, and its foundation was rediscovered only in 1936. Today there is a full recon-struction of a colonial-era working tobacco plantation as well as a visitor center.

Spring is not in abundant evidence the morning of my visit. It is cool and clear, and there is just a hint of green in the deciduous forest canopy. Only the holly and pine stand out as arboreal greenery. On the sandy shore of the Potomac, a Bonaparte's Gull plays about with sev-eral Ring-billed Gulls. A Forster's Tern glides past. Pairs of Buffleheads bob about farther offshore. Cormorants cruise high over the great river.

I retreat to the interior of the great pine forest that dominates the western sector of the preserve. Here Tufted Titmice sing and Northern Cricket Frogs give their musical snapping call from a wet grassy swale at the forest's edge. I wait a bit, listening, and am treated to another sound of early spring—the sweet, languid trill of the Pine Warbler. The song signals spring, but both the titmouse and this particular warbler are year-round residents on the Northern Neck, so their presence in earliest April is no surprise.

I move on to Westmoreland State Park, just a few miles down the shore. Established in 1933, at the height of the Great Depression, the park was crafted by a battalion of FDR's Civilian Conservation Corps, who built cabins and bulldozed access roads. The physiography at Westmoreland is distinct from that at Wakefield. Here a substantial upland meets the river, and what is produced is a stunning high cliff of Miocene sediments, which is the park's most remarkable feature. Atop the cliff lies a broad, open field enlivened by singing Chipping Sparrows and a Northern Flicker with its prominent white rump. Both are foraging on the ground in the short grass. The clifftop views look across the wide expanse of Potomac to the wooded coastline of Saint Mary's County, Maryland.

I hike the half-mile down through the grand deciduous woods to the beach. A Pileated Woodpecker, signaling its territory, drums its iconic slow and resonant beat from a distant hilltop. Otherwise the woods are silent. The trail leads down to the foot of the hill into a cattail swamp raucous with Spring Peepers. The river is dotted with water birds. Common Loons dive for fish right offshore. Most sport their gray-and-white winter plumage, but one shows the velvety black head and elegant white neck-banding of breeding plumage. Farther from shore, small rafts of Surf Scoters bob on the water's surface, sleeping. These black sea ducks can be identified by the patches of white on the forehead and nape along with the orange bill. Tiny winter-plumaged Horned Grebes and more of the handsomely pied male Buffleheads are scattered across the calm surface of the river.

After a brief and unsuccessful search for fossil shark teeth in the swash zone of the beach, I return up the back side of Horsehead Cliff, through the upland hardwood forest. Towering Tulip Trees, American

Beech, Chestnut Oak, and Black Gum cloak the hilly terrain behind the cliffs. I search the leaf litter for signs of life and find a single wildflower, a Cut-leaved Toothwort, scattered under the oaks. It has a fragile beauty, with its jagged leaf and slim stalk of white-and-pink four-petaled flowers.

From above me comes a high, whining note, repeated with tremolo. An Osprey, in full spring mode, hovers over the canopy, announcing to the world and his mate that he is ready to nest—right here, in fact. A cliffside forest looking over a vast river is ideal Osprey nesting habitat, and several pairs make their presence known this day across Westmoreland State Park.

My final stop is Stratford Hall, the ancestral home of the Lees of Virginia and the birthplace of Robert E. Lee. The estate, now owned by a private historical association, encompasses 1,900 acres of riverfront much like that at Westmoreland but with a strong historical flavor. The two properties are abutting, and high cliffs are also a feature of Stratford Hall. Here the original 1730s Georgian mansion is the centerpiece of the property, which is a combination of gardens, agricultural fields, and mature upland woods. Of the three sites, this one sets the gold standard.

The high cliffs of Stratford Hall have produced superb Miocene marine fossils much like those found at Calvert Cliffs in Maryland. For safety reasons, the cliffs are off-limits to all but professional paleontologists. This day a team from the Calvert Marine Museum is at the cliff to exhume the skeleton of a long-extinct whale. I can see them working at the base of a cliff through my telescope. I myself scour the small beach open to fossil collecting at the Old Landing and find a single mako shark tooth. From a small leafless branch protruding from the cliff face, a pair of Rough-winged Swallows sally out in search of insects. These swallows are typically among the earliest spring migrants to arrive from their wintering ground in Central America. I am happy to see this pair, the vanguard of a wave of land birds about to flood into the Mid-Atlantic region over the next month.

Driving back up through the grounds, I first come upon an iconic spring sight across a fallow field. Three turkey gobblers display to a flock of eight hens at the edge of the woods. The males fan their erect tails and expand their chests in a manly effort to impress the ladies. This is a sight that has become more and more common in the East in the twenty-first century. Wild Turkeys were extirpated from this region by the end of the nineteenth century. Only through an energetic program of reintroduction has the turkey been brought back. As a testament to the bird's former rarity, I saw my first turkey in 1982, though I had been looking in earnest since 1961. Now I see them several times a year. What a remarkable story of recovery—perhaps more remarkable than that of the Bald Eagle.

Speaking of Bald Eagles, as I drive to the entrance gate of Stratford, I see an adult eagle fly into a tall row of trees bordering a plowed field. Across the road there is activity on the ground. Three Black Vultures tear at the carcass of a White-tailed Deer. I stop to photograph the grisly scene, and when I look to my left, I note six eagles perched patiently together in the tall trees at the edge of the field, presumably waiting their turn with the deer. A Black Vulture is probably a third the punching weight of a Bald Eagle, but that species is the junkyard dog of carrion-eaters, and apparently eagles know that it's better to be patient.

It's April 7, and an Eastern Phoebe is singing up a storm down on the canal. The cherry blossoms in DC have peaked and are mainly finished. Biking home from work in the dark, I am greeted by Comet Hale-Bopp—with no moon to wash out the effect. The comet blazes in the dark sky high above the bike path.

As a youngster I became interested in astronomy and joined the astronomy club in high school. At my most extreme astronomy phase, I had a four-and-a-half-inch reflecting telescope, through which I gazed at planets and other celestial objects. In those years, I read about the wonders of Halley's Comet, which had put on a show in 1911, and which was scheduled to return to view in the year 1986. Before that time, other lesser comets (such as Ikeya-Seki) came and went, producing disappointments for me as an observer. What we saw was often nothing more than a tiny pale smudge. On other occasions, we failed altogether to locate the comet. For me, Halley's Comet produced the same disappointment in 1986. Thank heavens for Comet Hale-Bopp in April 1997—finally a comet that did not disappoint. Bicycling up the Capital Crescent Trail, headed westward, I can glance up and see this wonderful tailed sparkler in the dark sky. It is the astronomical highlight of my life. There is something almost magical about it—perhaps mainly brought about by my long wait to see a comet worth its salt.

In the early days of April, the mornings start chilly, but by afternoon the temperature reaches the seventies. The first Chimney Swifts of spring are racing through the sky high over our house today, and grackles, blackbirds, starlings, and goldfinches are all active. The song of the Carolina Chickadee is now much in evidence—the two-note *hii-hoo*. Boxelders are flowering, and some are also starting to leaf out. The next few days will see a lot of botanical activity. Down at the Potomac's edge,

Pawpaw with flower

I see a cormorant dive and then surface gripping a shiny silver-sided eel about eight inches long, and I hear Spring Peepers singing tonight below Brookmont.

At this time the car's windshield and roof are coated with a fine dusting of tree pollen. The woodlands around us are busy reproducing! Spring is all about plants of all sorts sending out pollen into the breezes to meet up with the reproductive parts of plants of their own kind. These days, the weather person on the local TV station reports the pollen count, so that affected people can prepare their defense against allergies. This is one of the downsides of spring for humankind.

A cold front blows in late overnight, bringing rain and gloom. What a change from the balmy sunshine we've been getting. The big beds of daffodils along the George Washington Memorial Parkway, which have been flowering for days, are fading. White-throated Sparrows are singing to beat the band. I see a Bonaparte's Gull in its breeding plumage as well as a Caspian Tern over the river; I hear a Brown Thrasher singing behind the water treatment plant. In Brookmont, the Redbud is in peak blossom. Along the C&O Canal I find Lesser Celandine and Spring Beauty in flower. The May Apples are leafing out, and pawpaw is in bloom. Also the forest undergrowth along the river is greening now.

Along the bottomland of the Potomac, the Common Pawpaw is one of the abundant understory treelets, along with Spicebush and sapling Boxelder. A member of the tropical custard-apple family, pawpaw is an important part of the local flora. At this time of year, it produces purple hanging blossoms on its outer twigs, coming at the same time as its new leaves push out. It is mainly a southern species, ranging not much farther north than Maryland and Ohio. It produces an edible fruit that ripens in autumn. I grew up with Burl Ives's song in my brain: "Pickin' up pawpaws, Put 'em in your pocket."

As we get deeper into April, I see more and more signs of unfolding life. One morning it is a mother Mallard with a crèche of small ducklings. On another day it is a Common Loon in breeding plumage out on the river. One early morning, in downtown DC, I encounter a Virginia Rail on the sidewalk on Twentieth Street across from my office. It is flopping and scurrying about in panic. Presumably this bird was migrating at night, became disoriented by the urban night lighting, and hit a window of our building predawn. It is a shock to see this reclusive marsh bird on the sidewalk next to my office building. I gently grab hold of the frightened and disoriented bird and place it in a corner shrub planting, hoping it might recover from its concussion.

During spring migration, when low cloud and rain befuddle nocturnally migrating birds, the bright external lighting of tall city buildings, with their abundant reflective glass, can lead to bird strikes. The nocturnal migrants, descending from on high during the predawn hours, fly straight into windows, viewing the reflection as a safe passage through the urban jungle. The impact leads to a concussion, and falling to the pavement below can cause a fatal impact. Surveys indicate that as many as a billion birds are killed each year from striking buildings, towers, and windows. The Virginia Rail I encountered at the base of my office building in downtown DC probably recovered and survived its impact with reflective glass. It is one of the few. Conservation organizations are working on the problem and seeking to make cities more bird-friendly.

There are two fossil-collecting areas in the DC area, each about a seventy-five-minute drive from downtown. Both are popular with young and old alike because of the colorful fossil shark teeth to be found there. In an earlier chapter, I described a visit to Calvert Cliffs on the western shore of the Chesapeake Bay. The other site is on the eastern shore of the Potomac. Douglas Point Special Recreation Management Area, just north of Purse State Park, in Charles County, Maryland, is about forty miles due west of the more famous Calvert Cliffs. Both host rich marine sediments featuring the fossilized remnants of sharks and rays and various shells. But the fossils at Calvert Cliffs are twelve million years old, whereas those from Douglas Point are fifty-five million years old.

When we collect at Calvert Cliffs we find lots of whale and porpoise bone. The Douglas Point site has no evidence of cetaceans—this major lineage of marine mammals had not yet evolved from earlier mammal lineages at the time the Douglas Point fossils were laid down. In fact, the time captured at Douglas Point—the Paleocene—was only shortly after the extinction of the dinosaurs (sixty-six million years ago). Perhaps most remarkable of all, the teeth one picks up on the beach or pulls out of the small cliff at Douglas Point are fresh and sharp and beautiful after more than fifty million years. It's all about the preservation.

Walking the eastern shore of the Potomac is not much different from walking the western shore of the Chesapeake. In Charles County, the Potomac is vast and baylike. But the cliff is smaller, and the fossil-bearing sediments are a dull blue-green.

This mid-April fossil-hunting trip to Douglas Point Special Recreation Management Area is another field trip in which I seek out spring in the rural territory south of Washington. The reserve is a large tract of mature woods bordering the low but fossil-rich cliffs overlooking the broad Potomac. The main access trail leads me from the parking lot west through rich mesic woods of White and Chestnut Oak, American Beech, and an understory of American Holly. The canopy still shows little leafing, though looking across to the Virginia side of the river brings views of a pale green haze of the canopies of Tulip Trees that are starting to leaf out.

The butterflies are more encouraging. I encounter four species in my walk to the river: Mourning Cloak, Question Mark, Spring Azure, and what I think was a Red-banded Hairstreak. The woods are very quiet for much of the walk. Then I hear the cheerful and upbeat buzzy trill of a Northern Parula in the forest canopy, and I walk up on a big

Wild Turkey gobbler. As I approach the cliff, I can hear a Yellow-throated Warbler singing high in the canopy. A quick playback with my iPhone brings the curious male down to eye level and six feet from me. Binoculars are not needed to ogle this gorgeously patterned yellow, gray, black, and white bird.

As I start looking for fossils on the beach, I encounter mixed bird flocks that include both permanent residents (titmice, woodpeckers) and migrants (Northern Parula and Yellow-throated Warbler). In the far distance I hear the slow drum of a Pileated Woodpecker. Bald Eagles are cruising up and down the beachline in the cool morning. The shark-tooth collecting is productive, and I find a "personal best" *Otodus obliquus* tooth and many shiny *Striatolamia striata* teeth. I also stumble upon the find of the year—a three-inch-long crocodile tooth fresh from the cliff. The access trail has placed me just south of the best fossil-bearing cliffs of Liverpool Point. That is why this stretch of beach is so rich for collectors.

It is very pleasant to walk the beach here in early spring because the cliff creates a warm microclimate that is protected from the wind. On a weekday like this, it is common to have the whole reserve to myself. Walking the beach in the sunshine, with songbirds singing, eagles overhead, and Paleocene fossils in the sand at one's feet is a good way to spend a spring day in nature. Alone on the beach, I have this little corner of the natural world all to myself. Picking up fifty-five-million-year-old shark teeth makes me think about the eternal aspects of nature. Gazing at the glossy blue-gray tooth lying in the center of my palm creates a sense of awe regarding how long species have been interacting on the planet and just how short a time humans have been dominating the landscape.

Fossil shark teeth collected on the Potomac

We humans seem so confident of our position atop the pyramid of life. But how long can we maintain this position of dominance, especially in light of our mismanagement of the biosphere? The *Striatolamia striata* tooth in my hand is a reminder that all species, after their moment in the sun, get sucked down the vortex of extinction, to be replaced by newer forms, in a never-ending cycle. In light of that great pageant of life and death, standing here on the lonely beach, I feel happily insignificant: an observer of a great and unstoppable game that plays across the continents and seas of planet earth. I am but one individual of a single species among earth's fifty million species. Our relative weakness and insignificance can be seen in our inability to even catalog and name the species on our planet. Will we accomplish that before our name is called? It probably does not matter, really. Dismissing the eternal, I recognize how happy I am to be here, by myself, on this little-known beach on the

Potomac River in woodsy Charles County. The song of the Yellow-throated Warbler reminds me how fortunate I am.

It's mid-April, and I am out and about. Raking the front yard, I look up to see a flock of chittering Chimney Swifts high above, recently arrived with spring from a winter spent in the rainforests of Amazonia. I hear the note of a Yellow-bellied Sapsucker from some trees in the park behind our house, reminding me of winter, recently past.

On Sunday, while attending a local horse show with my wife in Rock Creek Park, I hear a Louisiana Waterthrush singing from a swamp of Skunk Cabbage not far from the show ring. The waterthrush is a Neotropical migrant warbler that must have recently made its migratory flight across the Gulf of Mexico and then northward in several stages to arrive in this patch of woods on the verge of Rock Creek. There's plenty of nature to be found in Rock Creek Park. It is DC's answer to New York's Central Park. In fact, Washington's park is more than twice the size of the more famous one in New York City. It is a big swath of woods that follows the catchment of Rock Creek from its mouth at the Watergate Hotel right on the tidal Potomac north into the piedmont of Montgomery County. There are miles of woodsy trails and various recreational and sports facilities. There are even two stables where one can rent a horse for a trail ride.

I like to visit two birding hotspots in Rock Creek when the songbirds are migrating in April and May. Both locations are south of Military Road. The first is the clearing behind the Maintenance Yard, which is a short distance southeast of the Nature Center. The second is the set of woodland clearings about half a mile south of the Nature Center on

Ridge Road. Both sites are fine places to hunt for warblers and other migrants if a good southwest wind has been blowing the preceding evening. Even if you arrive early, savvy birders will already be there and will surely make the bird-finding more productive. An advantage of visiting a local birding hotspot is the knowledgeable and friendly birders who will gladly point out interesting species. This is one of the pleasures of social birding. It does not have to be a solitary pursuit.

In Georgetown are three abutting properties that can be great for spring migrant songbirds—Dumbarton Oaks, Montrose Park, and Oak Hill Cemetery. Aside from beautiful formal gardens and ancient oaks, the Dumbarton property offers a superb museum featuring Byzantine and Pre-Columbian art.

Eastern North Carolina is a wonderful getaway destination for a naturalist in early spring. I first explored the region by myself on a spring break when the rest of the family was not available to travel. The second time I took my daughter Cary during her spring break. And on this third trip, I take my wife, Carol, in mid-April.

We drive from DC to North Carolina via the rural back route to avoid the terrible traffic on Interstate 95 in Virginia. Of course, there is also more of interest to see when off the interstate. We stop for lunch in Tappahannock, Virginia, which sits on the west bank of the Rappahannock River. Tappahannock was founded in 1682 and is in the heart of colonial plantation country that was settled early because of its ready access to England via sailing ship. After delicious crab bisque at Java Jacks, we tour the historic district before getting back on the road.

We then drive the two-lane back roads to Columbia, North Carolina, set in low country on the Scuppernong River, thick with tall cypress trees festooned with Spanish Moss. Stopping at the national wildlife refuge visitor center on the Scuppernong, we are surprised to find a booth where we can sample the tasty local wine made with Scuppernong grapes, and we locate a flock of Rusty Blackbirds in a small wet spot next to the center.

Of immediate interest to us that afternoon is the unbroken line of massive thunderstorms that is building to the west of us and racing eastward toward Columbia. We check into our bed and breakfast, the Brickhouse Inn, and turn on the TV to scrutinize the weather radar, which features the lurid colors allied with supercells. I have always wanted to see a twister, so I convince Carol that we should drive out west of town to a flat expanse of fields where we can scan the skyline for funnel clouds. We do that in the late afternoon while the light is still good, but we are premature. The storm line, which stretches across the breadth of North Carolina, is taking longer than expected to reach us, so we bide our time by dining at a small café in Columbia and then retiring to our cozy room to wait for the arrival of the big storm. A bit before midnight we are awoken by lightning, thunder, and wind-driven rain, but the sturdy inn stands firm, and we are not forced to retreat to the root cellar.

But the damage is done elsewhere. Thirty twisters touch down that night in eastern North Carolina, killing twenty-four people—the worst tornado cluster in a century. One twister strikes nine miles west of us in Creswell, and another about four miles east of us in the hamlet of Dillons Ridge. The next morning, we by chance drive through Dillons Ridge and see, firsthand, where dozens of tall pines have had their trunks snapped off fifteen feet up, a trailer home has been heavily damaged, and the adjacent small church has had its roof pulled off and a wing virtually demolished. A small twister had briefly touched down here. Why is it that twisters are so strongly attracted to trailer homes and rural churches?

Later that morning we visit a restored 1830 plantation named Somerset Place and the adjacent Pettigrew State Park on the northern shores of Lake Phelps, one of the large natural lakes here in the pocosin country back from the Pamlico Sound and the Outer Banks. Here we find spring warblers in song—Yellow-rumped, Prairie, Prothonotary, and Parula—as well as White-eyed Vireo. The state park was formerly famous for a stand of ancient trees on the lake's northern shore, but most of these old-growth giants were blown down in a windstorm several years before our visit.

There are three large pocosin lakes in this region—Phelps, Pungo, and Alligator—among the very few natural lakes in the southeastern United States. *Pocosin* is a term for a type of marshy-boggy wetland of acidic, sandy, peat soil. The mucky soil is saturated except during droughts, is nutrient deficient, and is found mainly in eastern North Carolina. This fire-adapted vegetation is sometimes called a shrub bog, mainly because the vegetation is low. One finds impenetrable thickets of bays and pines (mainly Pond, Loblolly, and Longleaf). This large expanse of pocosin is most famous as the current home of the only free-ranging population of Red Wolves on earth. It is also home to a good-size population of Black Bears. So mainland eastern North Carolina is a bit gnarly—wild and swampy and little known, and worthy of exploration for its natural wonders.

Before we head east to our next destination, we stop at the Palmetto-Peartree Preserve on the south shore of Albemarle Sound—just a bit west and north of Columbia. This swampy-piney corner of the peninsula between the Albemarle and Pamlico Rivers is home to Brown-headed Nuthatches and Red-cockaded Woodpeckers. We wander the narrow, sandy back roads in search of these two piney-woods birds. We stop at a decaying signboard that highlights the preserve, and here we hear the squeaky calls of a nuthatch flock and then the high sneezed notes of the little pied woodpecker. We burn twenty minutes admiring these two denizens of the southern piney woods. For me, spending time with these two is a bit like going back in time. I had last seen these two specialty birds together on the Florida-Georgia border in the Okefenokee Swamp in March 1972.

From the preserve, we head east toward the town of Manteo, situated on Roanoke Island, which is set in the sound waters between the North Carolina mainland and the Outer Banks. But on the way, we pass through Alligator River National Wildlife Refuge, where we spend some time checking out the swamps. The butterflies are beginning to emerge. We tally Zebra and Black Swallowtails and a Red Admiral. Buffalo Slough is chockablock with turtles. We see a single lonely alligator in a small creek. The forest understory is loaded with Jack-in-the-Pulpit.

Roanoke Island was the site of the first, feeble attempt at English settlement in North America. Elizabeth I commissioned Sir Walter Raleigh to establish the colony, which was formed in 1585. Over the next five years, the colony suffered various difficulties with the Native Americans, and many settlers called it quits and returned to England. In 1590, a resupply ship returned to the colony to find it dismantled and all the settlers gone. They found the word "Croatoan" carved into one of the remaining fence posts. The story behind whatever happened to the people of the Lost Colony remains a mystery to this day. Now there is a national park memorializing this settlement, with a restored fort and a collection of archaeological findings. The park also features a beautiful formal garden and an expansive forest tract with Longleaf Pine and Live Oaks, very pleasant for wandering and for birding.

Roanoke Island today is a bucolic vacation and retirement destination, and perfect for a low-key spring vacation. It is flat as a pancake, so it is possible to bike everywhere. We had brought our own bikes for that purpose. An eastern causeway links Roanoke to the Outer Banks, intersecting that sandy barrier island just a bit south of Nags Head. Thus, from Roanoke one can wander both east and west to an abundance of natural destinations. Having already worked the mainland, we set our sights on Oregon Inlet, Pea Island, and Cape Hatteras, all on the Outer Banks. Oregon Inlet is a break in the barrier island created by a hurricane in 1846. The inlet itself is great for fishing and birding, and the vast expanse of sandy beach and dunes south of the inlet is wonderful for shell collecting and naturizing. We spend several hours out on the sand as flocks of Double-crested Cormorants and Brown Pelicans pass overhead, part of a major local spring migration movement. Northern Gannets sail out beyond the breakers. Carol collects shells, and I photograph the aggregations of seabirds passing to and fro as the sun sets.

The next morning, we return to the Outer Banks to visit Pea Island National Wildlife Refuge, where we find lots of shorebirds and plenty of mosquitoes as well. We bike the four-mile circumference of the North Pond and have to race the mosquitoes back to the car. The payoff is a good view of a flock of breeding-plumaged American Avocets in the shallow impoundment. These black, white, and tan waders with up-turned bills are quite a sight when assembled in a big flock. Later in the morning we move a further twenty-five miles down the barrier island to the sandy parking lot for Cape Point. The first thing we do there is bog my four-wheel-drive SUV in the fluffy dry sand. I'm stuck! By lowering the tire pressure to twenty pounds, and with the help of four cheerful college boys who have also bogged their car, we escape unharmed back to more solid ground. Thus chastened, we take off our sandals and walk the mile south to the very tip of Cape Hatteras, which is worth the effort. This vast expanse of sea and sand we have entirely to ourselves, shared only with large pre-breeding flocks of Royal, Sandwich, Least, and Common Terns. The Royal and Sandwich Terns are doing their spring courtship. The Royals put on a show for us—calling, displaying their wide-opened deep-orange beaks, and flailing their long white wings in the bright sun. I fill my viewfinder with these superb birds in their pristine breeding plumage. Busy with thoughts of love, the birds pay us little mind. The shell collecting is even better here than at Oregon Inlet, so Carol is in shell heaven. At one point I glance up to see an adult Parasitic Jaeger pass overhead, chasing a Royal Tern. The jaeger is a sea-dwelling pirate that gets most of its food by stealing it from other birds—mainly terns and gulls. Our time out here in the cape's solitude is the highlight of the trip. It has the feel of an uninhabited sandy tropical desert isle—something we had experienced only in faraway New Guinea in decades past. That's always a special feeling.

The next day, we rise before dawn and drive down to Wanchese, at the southwest end of Roanoke Island, to photograph the sunrise over the piney marshes. Then we drive back to the Outer Banks and bike around the Wright Brothers National Memorial at Kitty Hawk, laboring on our bikes up the slope of high grass-covered artificial dune in order to visit the huge granite plinth that rises from the summit. Boat-tailed Grackles dot the grassy expanse and perch atop the visitor center. Next,

Yellow-throated Warbler

we drive a few miles farther north to hike about the gigantic natural dunes at Jockey's Ridge. This is a place best done without shoes. We watch groups of small children joyfully tumbling down the face of the tallest dune. Last, we raid the shopping outlets for great buys on things we do not really need. That silly stop always seems to be a part of any vacation at a beach resort.

On our last day, we rise early and depart Roanoke Island, heading for the Great Dismal Swamp, in northeastern North Carolina. We decide to check out Dismal Swamp State Park, on the eastern side of this large natural feature, just south of the Virginia line. The state park is a little-known gem. There are several miles of packed-sand roads that we bike on, encountering nobody along the way. It is a mix of piney woods and cypress swamp. Our highlights are Wild Turkey and singing

Yellow-throated Warblers in the pines. The elusive Swainson's Warbler was recorded here a week earlier, but we never locate it.

The worst part of spring vacation is the dreary drive home, northward into degrading weather conditions. We arrive back in Bethesda to a cold rain and lowering cloud.

After the bout of cold and rain recedes, things perk up. The Yellow-throated Vireo returns from its winter home in Central America to the tall trees behind our yard, as do both oriole species. A Northern Waterthrush sings in the woods that encompass Little Falls; the Flowering Dogwood and Eastern Redbud are at peak now in Brookmont. Also the canopy is starting to green up nicely. The grass is glowing—and growing by the hour. Tonight I go down to the tiny swamp behind our house in search of Spring Peepers. I find one four feet up in a thorny shrub. The little guy is 1.3 inches long, with a mottled gray-brown back, and he blows up his throat sac like a pale gray bubble-gum bubble.

A Fish Crow is calling this morning from the White Ash in the front yard. Garlic Mustard is flowering in full force along the canal verges now. Walkers along the towpath are pulling up this noxious weed adventitiously—one finds handfuls of it laid out drying on the towpath gravel. I see eight Caspian Terns on the sandbar at the Three Sisters, along with four Forster's Terns. I hear a Northern Waterthrush, Prothonotary Warbler, and Northern Parula. Fluffy yellow goslings of the local Canada Geese are out with their parents this morning. Biking home in the evening, I witness a massive fish run in the river above Key Bridge, with scores of fish breaking the surface every minute.

In Louis Halle's day, the Potomac was probably filled with all sorts of toxic substances from the urban runoff of DC and the smaller towns upstream. His *Spring in Washington* says nothing about the fish runs that this river, a century earlier, was famous for. These days, some of the runs have started to revive, as environmental efforts continue to clean up the river's water quality. Of course, they will never return to the bounty of the runs of the 1700s and early 1800s, but there is hope that, with the reduction of the nutrient overload from upstream agriculture, these famous fish runs will continue to rebound.

The four most famous river-running species in the Potomac are American Shad, Hickory Shad, Alewife Herring, and Blueback Herring. All four are placed in the genus *Alosa*, and thus these four are all true herrings. These fishes are anadromous, which means they spend their adult lives in the ocean and return to freshwater to spawn where they were born. Their runs span from March to May each year. They are joined by many other fish, including Atlantic Sturgeon, Atlantic Menhaden, and Striped Bass, that call the Potomac home for part of the year. All are much reduced in population from their earlier heyday, when they fed the people of Washington each spring. In the 1830s, thousands of sturgeon and tens of millions of shad were caught each season and sold to cities throughout the East. We will never see those days again. The sturgeon is essentially gone from the Potomac, but the others continue to run, albeit in relatively low numbers. I enjoy seeing them breaking the surface of the calm river above Key Bridge on spring evenings.

In the latter half of April, I make a herpetological field trip to the Bull Run Mountains of Virginia with Marty Martin, the rattlesnake man. Rattlers! I have always been fascinated by rattlesnakes. They were featured in the Saturday morning TV westerns like *Sky King:* riders on horseback would come to grief when a coiled rattler threatened and then struck out at the horse; the horse invariably threw its unwitting rider. To a young TV-watching boy, desert country was real rattler territory. That may have been the case long ago, but these days much of the United States has been cleared of its rattlers by annual roundups in which all rattlers (and any other snakes) are gathered up and put in bags and, in many instances, killed and cooked or sold for their snakeskin.

In fact, there are rattlers living peacefully not more than forty minutes' drive from my backyard, and there are no roundups in Maryland or Virginia, thankfully. On this spring day I join Martin, the world expert on the Timber Rattlesnake. This day trip is part of his annual spring Timber Rattlesnake survey. We hike up onto a ridge in the Bull Run Mountains west of Haymarket, Virginia, to check a series of traditional rock dens he has surveyed in years past. Martin, a Vietnam Vet and master snake-handler, is a colorful character, and we discuss all the world's problems while hiking in the woods. I am along to learn about the life history of Timber Rattlers and photograph the snakes in their native habitat.

First, a bit about rattlers. Timber Rattlesnakes hibernate in a traditional rocky hideaway, usually in an underground den that is both dry and not subject to severe cold. Rocky outcrops facing southwest are particularly popular with the snakes, because of the warming powers of the afternoon sun. The rattlers often share their hibernaculum with Copperheads and Black Rat Snakes. In spring the snakes emerge and head out into the forest to begin hunting for the year. In July, the female rattlers return to prominent rocky openings to bask in the sun and give birth to their young, which are born live (most snakes hatch from eggs). In the autumn, when the temperatures drop, the snakes return to their rocky den to hibernate.

Because of these annual traditions, Timber Rattlers are quite easy to locate, and thus are susceptible to poaching and overharvest. That said, actually locating a snake at a den is not terribly easy for the novice. This is because, first, the snakes hide themselves, and, second, they blend in with the dried leaves that typically cover the ground in their favored habitats. Rattlers have evolved to be cryptic, and if a rattler is not moving, it can be exceedingly difficult to notice even when a colleague is pointing right at it from a few feet away.

These snakes can live a long time. As a result, their annual reproductive capacity is low. Thus local populations can be snuffed out with relative ease. Marty told me that an older snake might be more than thirty years old and that females do not reproduce until they are six years old. The number-one threat to rattlers is the combination of woodland roads and cars. Snakes dispersing in the spring and returning to den in autumn cross roads and are run over and killed by passing cars.

On this day, we find six rattlers, two Copperheads, and one Black Rat Snake. I photograph them all, of course. Finding the rattlers is a chore, because many of the rocky areas are encumbered by tangles of greenbrier, which is wicked and spiny. Luckily, I am wearing heavy trousers and leather gloves. Finding the snakes requires a developed search image, which, of course, Marty has but I do not. All the snakes we encounter are docile and allow close approach and close-up photography.

The woodland jaunt is productive for other wildlife as well. Hiking up the hill we encounter both Pileated and Red-headed Woodpeckers. Up on the ridge we find a male Scarlet Tanager singing his burry song. One of the rock piles includes an active nest of a Black Vulture, which hisses at us and comes flapping out of the cave noisily, giving us a start. It poses with its wings spread, just like in a cartoon. The forest is filled with singing Red-eyed Vireos. A rocky overhang includes a fresh nest of an Eastern Phoebe with three eggs. We come upon two Eastern Box Turtles on the move. New for me is an Eastern Fence Lizard, which I photograph clambering about on a rock face. The most beautiful creature we encounter today is a Luna Moth freshly emerged from its cocoon. The colors of a newly emerged Luna are beyond belief—pale green with maroon trim and four lifelike false eyes, two on the forewing and two on the hindwing, and of course its two long swallowtails.

When I get home, I find I have not prepared adequately for the depredations of one other wildlife group—the ticks. By the time I shower in the late afternoon there are four Deer Ticks and two Wood Ticks sucking my blood from soft corners of my anatomy. Other ticks I find clambering over my discarded clothing. My wife removes the ticks as best as she can, and then I take no chances and start a course of doxycycline. It does not pay to play around with borreliosis (Lyme disease) or ehrlichiosis, babesiosis, or anaplasmosis. The lesson learned is that I should have (1) tucked my pants into my socks, (2) sprayed my clothing liberally with a good insect repellent before entering the woods, and (3) sprayed my clothing again once I had returned to the car at the end of our field jaunt. Another lesson learned—hunting for Timber Rattlesnakes in spring guarantees multiple encounters with the dreaded Deer Tick. Take notice!

Early one Sunday morning, I bike the Mount Vernon bicycle path from Belle Haven Marina, just south of Alexandria, southward to the Mount Vernon historic site—sixteen miles round-trip. I have chosen Sunday morning because this is when the car traffic will be minimal, allowing me to hear the birdsong. Magnificent ancient oaks and Tulip Trees surround much of the Mount Vernon grounds. I hear Great

Crested Flycatcher, Gray Catbird, Wood Thrush, Hermit Thrush, and House Wren. Yellow-rumped Warblers are on the move in the big White Oaks, and Red-eyed Vireos are everywhere in tall forest; the ornamental azaleas are blooming now at Mount Vernon, as are the Dandelions. I then finish the morning on the woodland bike path at Mason Neck State Park. Spring Beauty is in flower everywhere at Mason Neck, and a small similar lilac-blue flower is present in dense beds. Jack-in-the-Pulpit, Pawpaw, Eastern Redbud, and Flowering Dogwood are flowering in abundance; also a wild pink azalea is in flower in a swampy section of the trail. I see four Ospreys circling together on the river at Mason Neck.

Louis Halle spends several pages in his *Spring* book celebrating the song of the Wood Thrush. During much of my bike ride through Mason Neck State Park, I am serenaded by this woodland vocalist. Hearing this bird's song carries me back to the late spring of the mid-1960s, to Dohme's Woods in north Baltimore. This ancient patch of forest stood just upstream from my grandparents' house, where I spent many a happy weekend. Because of the presence of this substantial forest tract, Wood Thrushes abounded in this neighborhood. My grandparents took their evening cocktails on a flagstone patio and were entertained each night by the ethereal song of the Wood Thrush, drifting down from Dohme's Woods. They loved this peaceful interlude in their day, and I fell in love with the bird and its song on those spring evenings.

The Wood Thrush is, indeed, one of the beloved songbirds of the eastern forests. It is handsome but not flashy, with a crisply spotted white breast and red-brown upperparts. Because of its retiring nature and its preference for the understory interior of woodlands, this species is heard more often than seen. But, oh, what a voice! It surpasses its European counterpart, the Nightingale, in vocal beauty, with fluted musical phrases and flourishes that carry through the woods.

Sadly, the Wood Thrush has declined throughout much of its range, and it can be heard singing only rarely in Dohme's Woods in Baltimore or in Glover-Archbold Park in Washington, or from so many other urban woodlands where it once serenaded lucky residents in the 1960s. Its decline can be blamed on several causes. White-tailed Deer have decimated the vegetation of forest understories. Increasingly abundant mesopredators like Raccoons and Opossums raid the thrush nests. Also, the now-abundant Brown-headed Cowbirds lay their eggs in thrush nests. I rarely hear the Wood Thrush anymore, and that makes me sad.

On April 25, I bike the towpath out to Widewater, just downstream from Great Falls, and then loop back to my neighborhood. This fifteen-mile circuit is a great way to encounter migrant songbirds at this time of the year. Highlights of the circuit are Golden-winged Warbler, Yellow-throated Warbler, Northern Waterthrush, Yellow-rumped Warbler, Black-and-white Warbler, and Yellow-throated Vireo, plus lots of singing White-throated Sparrows. Lesser Celandine is blanketing the forest floor next to the towpath. Spring Beauty and Bluebells are blooming like mad now in the woods. At this point, there is a lot of leafing out, the fresh green moving from the understory upward into the canopy. I spy five tiny hatchling Wood Ducks bobbing in the canal.

As Halle noted in his book, spring is a time of departures as well as arrivals. We tend to focus on the arrivals because of their novelty, but the departures are significant, too. The flocks of White-throated Sparrows have spent the winter here and now are putting on fat to be able to migrate back up to the North Woods. They have been our constant companions for five months; now they are singing their last for us, and to see them in June or July we will need to head to the Adirondacks or northern New England.

The Northeast Kingdom of Vermont has everything a wilderness-loving naturalist appreciates, mountains, forests, rivers, and bogs—yes, bogs. This northeastern section of Vermont is little developed, with few people and a border shared with Quebec. At the end of April, when there is still snow on the ground in the hidden and shaded nooks, a rare and elusive boreal resident bird—the Spruce Grouse—makes itself visible to humankind because of its courtship display. I take a few days off in late April to head up to Moose Bog in northern Vermont, a site famous for this boreal grouse. The spring season at the top of Vermont is about a month behind that of the Washington, DC, area. By driving north, I head back into early spring.

The Spruce Grouse ranges from Alaska and the Yukon southeastward to northernmost New England. In the eastern United States, its remnant populations are small and declining. Behaviorally, the species makes itself scarce. It spends most of its time foraging silently on the needles of spruce and fir trees in the Great North Woods. Over six decades, having spent summers in prime Spruce Grouse habitat in the Adirondacks and elsewhere in the Northeast, I have seen the species a handful of times. Now I am headed up to photograph the species doing its nuptial display. I visited Moose Bog the preceding year and did not see the grouse: I am headed back for another try.

Moose Bog is just east of Island Pond, Vermont, and a few miles west of the Connecticut River, which forms the state border with New

Hampshire. The only campground open at this time of the year is in North Stratford, New Hampshire, nine miles east of Moose Bog. It takes me fourteen hours to drive from DC north to my campground, with a few stops along the way. I set up camp at 9:30 at night, and I camp there three nights, shuttling back and forth to the bog each day. In my three days of visiting the bog, I never encounter another birder or naturalist. I am clearly here early in the season. I pass patches of snow on my walk in to the main bog access trail.

Moose Bog is perhaps the most popular bog in New England for birders wishing to see such boreal birds as Spruce Grouse, Black-backed Woodpecker, Boreal Chickadee, Red Crossbill, and various wood warblers that breed there in season. Most birders visit in May and June, when conditions are warmer and drier (and buggier). On my first morning of this trip, I find heavy frost glazing the marsh grasses of the bog itself. It is cold up here! I have to use my little space heater in my tent each night to keep warm. None of the deciduous trees have leafed out at this point. The hillsides have the look of full winter, bare except for the conifers, which stand out as dark green among the pale branches of the maples, aspens, and birches. That said, I hear Spring Peepers calling in one of the ponds, and three migrant wood warblers have already arrived and are singing on territory—Yellow-rumped and Palm Warblers, plus Northern Waterthrush. I also encounter both species of kinglets and the Hermit Thrush. One advantage of visiting in this early season is that the biting insects (black flies, mosquitoes, deer flies, horse flies, and no-see-ums) have not yet emerged. The disadvantage to the naturalist is that many of the migrant birds have not yet arrived from the tropics— they time their arrival to coincide with the leafing out of the deciduous trees that produces the flush of caterpillars for daily consumption.

Of course, I am here for one thing—Spruce Grouse. And it is not easy. The first morning I walk the main bog trail three times. These three back-and-forth walks (more than six miles) produce no grouse. Aside from the various smaller birds mentioned above, it is pretty quiet in the forest. That said, the forest is the finest mature lowland spruce-fir forest I have ever visited in the East. The Red Spruce stand more than seventy-five feet tall, their trunks more than a foot in diameter. The forest along the main trail is strongly dominated by conifers—spruce, fir, and tamarack—with a thick cushion of spongy moss covering the forest floor. It is unusual to find terra firma lowland forests in New England that remain dominated by conifers: the conifer forests were all cut over by the beginning of the twentieth century, and what regenerated were deciduous stands dominated by birch, maple, and aspen. So this flat conifer forest is a superb remnant of an earlier time.

The associated bog is also very beautiful, with a lovely lake at its heart. It is a classic Black Spruce bog with the concentric rings of increasingly taller vegetation as one moves from the verge of the lake to the surrounding uplands. The state has put in a boardwalk out onto the open bog mat to allow visitors to get a good look at the bog's heart. From the benches at the tip of the boardwalk, one can see how the surrounding forested hills hem in the depression where the bog lies, and just a few feet of elevation creates substantial changes in dominant arboreal vegetation.

As I sit with my camera at the end of this boardwalk, the quiet is broken by repeated tapping. This sound comes from a stand of long-dead Black Spruce, presumably killed by persistent inundation by the bog waters. Low on one of the dead trunks, a female Black-backed Woodpecker is carefully chipping bark to gain access to hidden beetles and beetle larvae. Through my binoculars I take note of the glossy black upperparts, the black face and white cheek stripe, and the long black chisel-beak. This species is just rare enough to give me a bit of the shivers every time I encounter it. I sit and admire this handsome bird doing its work out in this glorious patch of wilderness.

Late in the morning, I decide to do one final walk of the main Moose Bog trail, which transects the heart of this strip of spruce forest on dry ground just north of the boglands. It is nearing noon and things are very quiet. Then I hear the low-pitched *thrrrrrrrdddd!*—the sound produced by the wings of a male Spruce Grouse when he does his brief vertical display flight from the ground up to a spruce bough in the shaded forest interior. The bird I hear is about thirty yards from me and about ten paces off the trail. After some strained searching, I manage to pick him out in the forest gloom—he is perched about head-high on a branch. Now it is a matter of making my way toward this bird without disturbing his display activities.

A deep yellow-green bed of soft sphagnum moss covers the ground and cushions my footsteps. But the many conifer branches that choke the understory make picking a clear route slow going. I also have my heavy zoom lens around my neck and a small pack on my back, making my progress even more difficult. Still, I feel confident that I can sneak up on this randy male. Spruce Grouse are famous for their absolute lack of wariness during the display season. In retrospect, probably nothing I did on my way to the bird would have disturbed his sex-focused activities. It is obvious that I cannot approach the bird closely without it seeing me.

So, I approach, stop, approach, stop, and keep at it. When I get within twenty-five feet, I start shooting images, and I keep shooting as I creep closer and closer, to a point where I have no need to be any closer. I am literally *with* the bird at this point, and his display activities are as much for me as anybody—as I see no female in the area on this late morning.

The male drops off his branch to the ground and runs up onto a low mound of moss, where he plumps himself up, pushes his breast feathers out, spreads his tail feathers, splays out his white-tipped undertail coverts, and makes himself gorgeous. And gorgeous he is! Perhaps understated in his beauty, he still is stunning to behold—feathered with a mix of bold and complex patterns. Overall, the male is black and white with a rich red eyebrow spot. He sports a black breast and throat fringed by large white spots. His erect tail is black with chestnut tipping. His undertail coverts are black with white tips. His back and flanks are finely barred gray, black, and white. His throat and cheek are jet black, and his crown and nape are finely barred gray and white; his expandable eyebrow is deep red. What a bird!

He signals to females by the loud thrum of his wings when he powers from the ground up to a nearby branch. This is what drew *me* to the bird. Otherwise he poses, cocks his tail, enlarges himself by fluffing out all his feathers, and even makes his red eyebrows larger. I shoot scores of images as he moves back and forth from the ground up into the trees and back, all while I stand or sit within fifteen feet of him. At one point, as I stand stock still, he runs up to within two feet of my motionless boots. Perhaps he is displaying to *me*.

After decades of disappointment with hunting this species, it is satisfying to walk slowly back to the car all the while reviewing in my mind my close encounter with the elusive Spruce Grouse. Yet I am in for one additional treat on this afternoon. As I move down the trail, I hear quiet squeaking notes of a Red-breasted Nuthatch. The bird is calling to me, believe it or not. I stop and put out my empty hand, and the little buff-breasted nuthatch alights right on my fingers and begins rapping my hand with its bill, as if to show its displeasure at the absence of sunflower seeds (it is clear that this bird has been hand-fed by generous bird lovers in the recent past). These two very close encounters with wild birds make my day.

At dusk, I return to the Moose Bog area and drive down Route 105, which is famous for its Moose. Right at the bend where a wetland of alders lies on the north side of the road, a calf Moose saunters out into the middle of the pavement. I brake to avoid hitting it. This young creature is all legs—it totters along like the gangling youngster that it is. As Bill Bryson has written, it's as if "its legs have not been introduced to each other." A few miles farther west on 105, I stop at the railway crossing because there is a stand of mature Quaking Aspens, where I have hopes of luring out a nesting Northern Saw-whet Owl. As I emerge from the car I hear the high keening of a raptor. I have stumbled upon the site of a Merlin nest high in a thick stand of old conifers. The male cries incessantly and circles high above, warning me off his territory. That caps my short early spring visit to Moose Bog.

On the very last day of April, I am back in my neighborhood. It is cool but bright, and a light northwest wind is blowing. And lots of migrant songbirds are around: Northern Parula, Yellow Warbler, Northern Waterthrush, Ovenbird, Eastern Kingbird, Swainson's Thrush, and Red-eyed Vireo. I hear a Purple Finch singing in a tall oak. The canopy vegetation is really filling in. Now we prepare to head into the main event—full spring in Washington, DC.

ELEVEN

May—Fulsome Spring, the Warbler Rush

> The appreciation of birds, indeed the appreciation of all the phenomena of
> spring, cannot be dissociated from the accumulations of memory. The
> appearance of a familiar bird immediately awakens a train of forgotten
> associations, and this makes each spring transcend its predecessor. The
> interest accumulates and is compounded.
>
> —LOUIS HALLE, *Spring in Washington*

For naturalists in Washington, the first of May is much like the first day
of the fishing or hunting season—a time of great anticipation. The binoculars are out, and many head to their favorite birding spots around
DC, with the hope that the preceding evening's southerly winds have
carried in migratory thrushes, vireos, warblers, and flycatchers. At first
light, these eager birders strain their ears to hear the first song of the
Wood Thrush, Black-and-white Warbler, or Blue-headed Vireo.

It is May Day, and I have to work. No day off for me. On my bike
ride to the office, I hear the songs of seven species of warblers: Prothonotary, Yellow-rumped, Blue-winged, Yellow-throated, and Yellow
Warbler, Northern Parula, and Ovenbird. Also three vireos: Red-eyed,
Warbling, and Yellow-throated. New for the year is a singing Indigo

Barred Owl

Bunting. Most exciting, I observe two male Bobolinks in tall grass at the head of the National Airport runway at Gravelly Point. On my ride home in the afternoon I see an Osprey carrying a big fish over Roaches Run. In addition, I witness a herring run on the Potomac this evening at dusk, with thousands jumping and breaking the surface. Anglers cluster in rowboats off Fletcher's Cove upstream from Key Bridge. Finally, above Fletcher's I hear two Barred Owls hooting back and forth to each other. It is a good day to be a naturalist on a bike outside for a couple of hours.

On May 2, it is cloudy, and a southeast wind is blowing. The sun breaks out during my ride to work. I see a hen Wood Duck with nine little fluffball ducklings in the canal. I hear the songs of five warblers: Yellow-rumped, Parula, Yellow-throated, Chestnut-sided, and Prothonotary. I count eight Orchard Orioles in song along the towpath. Bobolinks are very active in that patch of tall grass at Gravelly Point—at least five individuals, chasing each other, and the males are giving their bubbling song that evokes spring pastures in New England.

On May 3, I tally the songs of nine species of warblers. I see two Common Loons high overhead, migrating northward. The single-species high-count for the day is twenty-one Yellow-rumped Warblers.

On May 4, I bird Glover-Archbold Park, in the city. My morning highlights are eight warbler species: Black-and-white, Black-throated Green, Black-throated Blue, Northern Redstart, Chestnut-sided, Magnolia, Kentucky, and Worm-eating; I also hear the songs of a Veery and a Wood Thrush. Glover-Archbold Park is the second largest contiguous greenspace in Northwest Washington. Early in my career I lived just a block away from this lovely bottomland park that extends from the Potomac River north to Tenleytown. In the 1980s I would wander the park on weekend mornings in spring, searching for birdlife. It was great for warblers, thrushes, flycatchers, and tanagers. It remains a greenway and is still a good migrant trap, but as the decades pass, many of the migrants that nested there no longer do so. Acadian Flycatcher, Wood Thrush, and Red-eyed Vireo presumably still breed there today in small numbers, but among the migrant breeders common there in the 1960s and 1970s, we have certainly lost nesting American Redstart, Scarlet Tanager, Kentucky Warbler, and probably more. As discussed in an earlier section, the probable causes for their declines are the same as I described for the Wood Thrush.

On May 5, I bike the towpath to work and encounter a beaver and a pair of Mandarin Ducks in the canal. The Mandarin is the East Asian counterpart to our beloved Wood Duck, so this pair of Mandarins almost certainly escaped from a collection of captive waterfowl. Other highlights of the morning include Veery, Yellow-billed Cuckoo, and Rose-breasted Grosbeak. Biking home this evening I see a Red-shouldered Hawk toting a squirrel back to its nest in the tall sycamore in woods above Fletcher's Cove.

On May 6, I am startled and pleased to hear a Cerulean Warbler singing in our neighborhood. This is another species that formerly bred along the Potomac in the DC area but no longer does so. Below Brookmont on the towpath I encounter two Canada Goose pairs with their gosling hordes—a species that formerly did not breed along the Potomac and now does so in big numbers. Two more examples of the ebb and flow of species geographies over time.

For weeks I have been thinking about a field trip to Magee Marsh in northern Ohio. I will make my final choice of days for the trip to coincide with the southwest winds that bring in large numbers of Neotropical migrant songbirds. For this, I depend on meteorological intelligence gathered from various weather websites, plus the weekly blog from Ohio-based birding guru Kenn Kaufman, who is based at Magee Marsh, where his wife, Kimberly Kaufman, directs the Black Swamp Bird Observatory. For productive visits to migrant traps, it is all about the weather, as we know from our visits to Cape May, New Jersey.

When Louis Halle wanted to plan an outdoor field trip back in 1946, he either looked out the window at the sky conditions or he looked for weather information in a little text box near the masthead of the

Washington Post. And the information provided by the paper was probably not very reliable—entirely uninformed by a weather satellite or global circulation model being run on some distant supercomputer. In contrast, each day before I bike to work, I go online and check weather .com, looking at the hourly forecast for DC. I am looking to see if any storms are headed my way, and I also check the expected daily low and high temperatures, data that inform what I shall wear on my morning and afternoon bike rides. If I need additional information, I look at the National Weather Service enhanced radar loop for the Northeast Sector of the United States (which shows the movement of weather systems) and the map of winds for the United States. Having access to these data sets allows me to refine my daily travel plans. The ten-day forecast on weather.com guides my planning for timing a future nature field trip.

On May 5, Kenn Kaufman's Ohio birding blog targets the morning of May 8 as the first big day of songbird migration across the region. After checking the weather forecast, I decide on my dates for travel: May 7 to 12. Though I normally prefer to travel to Magee Marsh later in May, I decide to jump because I have some free days on my calendar.

Magee Marsh is situated on the south shore of Lake Erie, nestled between Toledo and Cleveland. It is America's answer to the spring songbird migration hotspot of Point Pelee in southern Ontario, which has been famous for much longer. In fact, the two birding sites are mirror images of each other—Pelee lies on the north shore of Lake Erie, just across the water from Magee Marsh. In spring, both sites feature stunning concentrations of land bird migrants under ideal (often eye-level) viewing conditions. When resting and feeding at these lakeside refuges, the birds essentially ignore humankind and go about the business of refueling for the next stage of migration. That makes for great close-up observations of birds that under typical circumstances can be very difficult to see.

Why are these two places so special? When a southwest wind blows out of the Mississippi Valley, vast numbers of migrating warblers, vireos, thrushes, flycatchers, and others are carried up to the south shore of Lake Erie. The lake constitutes an existential threat to these little wandering waifs. The broad expanse of cold water presents itself to the birds in the late predawn hours, and each migrating bird must then make a decision: drop down into the narrow band of woods on the south side of the lake (Magee Marsh) or follow the chain of islands across the big lake to the wooded peninsula that beckons on the lake's northern shore (Point Pelee). Probably half make the flight across and drop into the vegetation at Point Pelee, whereas the remainder quit their flight before sunrise and drop into the strip of cottonwoods south of the lake at Magee Marsh. When the birding is great at Magee, it is also great at Pelee.

I depart home in the early morning and drive northwestward, gaining altitude as I head up and over the Alleghenies. Washington at this time is in the full dress of spring, with the canopy trees fully leaved except for the most recalcitrant oaks. As I cross the Laurel Highlands, southwest of Pittsburgh, the landscape has the look of late winter, with only a few hardy shrubs beginning to green. I have, in two and a half hours, turned the clock back several weeks. This quickly reminds me that northern Ohio will offer not the lush greens of the DC area in early May but climatic conditions more like those I experienced in late March.

The drive to Magee Marsh takes seven and a half hours. On arrival, the first thing I do is check in at my motel in Port Clinton, "Walleye Capital of the World." The name of the motel—White Caps—is truth in advertising, for even this afternoon the lake is dotted with whitecaps; the northwest wind is blowing, as it has been for much of the preceding three weeks. The motel manager laments that her business has been dead because the rough lake waters have kept the Walleye anglers onshore.

This awful northwest wind also keeps the songbirds from migrating. They get bottled up in the valleys of the Ohio and Mississippi, waiting for winds that will carry them efficiently across the Great Lakes to the Canadian North Woods. When there are days and days of northwesterlies, then vast numbers of birds build up in the south, waiting. . . . The release of that buildup is what creates the wonderful birding experience at Magee Marsh and Point Pelee.

After checking in, I eat lunch and then head to the Magee Marsh boardwalk. The parking lot is crowded, and there are a lot of birders milling around. I start at the east end of the boardwalk and immediately encounter individual warblers feeding low in the willows and Red Osier Dogwoods. Clearly, there has been a flight earlier in the week, and these birds are waiting for the next southerly wind to allow them to move north across the lake. Here is a Black-throated Green Warbler. Over there is a Palm Warbler. Up above there are several Yellow-rumped Warblers flicking their tails and giving their *chek* notes that are so commonplace early in the season. Then a friendly fellow birder points down onto the verge of the wooden walkway to a Winter Wren—a deep brown, nearly tailless mite of a bird, foraging for spiders on the boardwalk itself. The bird is entirely oblivious of me, nearly passing across the top of my shoe. It is too close for me to photograph with my telephoto lens.

So, within minutes, I am immersed in the glory of up-close migrant birding at Magee Marsh. I watch and photograph birds for two hours

Baltimore Oriole

that afternoon, recording fifteen species of warblers, as well as several uncommon birds of interest—Philadelphia Vireo, Gray-cheeked Thrush, and Lincoln's Sparrow—birds that practically define the best of spring migration.

Let me explain a bit more about the spring migration of songbirds. The featured groups that make this interesting include thrushes, flycatchers, orioles, tanagers, wood warblers, vireos, and sparrows. The phenomenon varies a great deal. For instance, the American Robins that nest out my back door may winter no more than a hundred miles south of here. By contrast, the Baltimore Oriole that nests in the park behind my house migrates across the Gulf of Mexico and may winter in Panama. The paragon of songbird migration is the family of wood warblers—about fifty species of small and colorful land birds, many of which spend the summer in the conifer woods of Canada and New England and winter in Central and South America and the Caribbean. These birds migrate at night and rest and forage during the day. They weigh only a few ounces and make a remarkable circuit each year from the tropics to the North Woods and then back to the tropics. They apparently do this because the North Woods is a great place to raise a family in June and July but a tough place to spend the winter for those that subsist mainly on insects—hence the winter sojourn in the tropics.

Those of us who live in the United States get to see these little migrants twice a year, in spring and fall. Spring, however, is better for two reasons. First, the birds are wearing their colorful breeding plumage. These birds, exemplified by the male Blackburnian Warbler with its tiger stripes and flame-orange throat, are among the most intricately patterned and colorful birds in North America. Second, spring, not fall, is when the males sing their complex songs. The song makes it easier to find them in the treetops, where they spend much of their time. In the autumn, these birds are dull plumaged and almost silent. It is fun to watch warblers in fall, but not nearly the treat it is in the spring, when the whole natural world is exploding with life and color.

Magee Marsh is a wildlife area associated with Crane Creek State Park and Ottawa National Wildlife Refuge. Its most important feature is a mile-long strip of woodland that parallels the south shore of Lake Erie. To the north of the woodland strip is the water, and to the south is an open grassy marshland. The only wooded habitat for miles around for the migrant songbirds is this narrow strip of woods dominated by tall Eastern Cottonwoods. An elevated boardwalk has been constructed the length of this woodland for bird lovers. Here they can commune with the migrating birds and other denizens of the woodland understory. But there's more. The adjacent marshlands are very productive for herons, blackbirds, rails, and many migrating waterfowl species. Adjacent Ottawa National Wildlife Refuge, Howard Marsh, and Metzger Marsh also feature a diverse array of wetlands that fill with birds in spring and fall. Simply put, the Magee Marsh environs are rockin' with birds and birdsong in mid-May when the weather is favorable.

On Thursday morning, I am the first to arrive in the Magee parking lot, at 5:45 a.m., before the sun has risen. I do not want to miss a thing. The migrant warblers generally do not become active until after 7:00, so I am early for them. Driving in through the marshes, I see Muskrats swimming low in the water, I hear two Sandhill Cranes giving their far-carrying musical bugling call, and I see dozens of Great Egrets and Great Blue Herons standing out in the still water. Male Red-winged Blackbirds display from every patch of cattails. Tree Swallows hawk for insects over the marsh. The sound of all the birds before dawn is overwhelming. The sky is coloring in the east. This is exactly the place I want to be at this moment—in the bosom of nature.

Before heading to the boardwalk, I walk the narrow strip of trees on the West Beach. Three years earlier, I had seen a Kirtland's Warbler here, and the year after I had found a singing Connecticut Warbler here. These are two Holy Grail species for birders at Magee. So I am hoping I can turn up something cool. It is not to be. I mainly find Red-winged Blackbirds, Eastern Kingbirds, Gray Catbirds, American Robins, some other flycatchers, thrushes, and a few warblers. The weak showing during this first hour does not instill hope.

Heading over to the boardwalk, I find it is all a matter of time of day. The migrants needed to rest after having fallen out of the sky, and they also need light to find the little gnats they are mainly feeding upon. By

7:30 things are popping, and clots of birders are streaming onto the boardwalk. I always start at the east end because that is less crowded. The west end is the official entrance so invariably is jammed with slow-moving birders. I am happy to share the warblers and vireos and thrushes with a smaller number of birders brave enough to start at the back of the boardwalk. Five Nashville Warblers forage in this tree, three Redstarts feed in that thicket, and several Black-throated Green Warblers are right by the boardwalk. A Northern Waterthrush is singing from a swampy tangle, as is an Ovenbird. Yellow Warblers, which are local breeders, are zipping about everywhere, making a nuisance of themselves. Nobody comes to Magee Marsh to look for Yellow Warblers, which are hyperabundant and ever-present in spring here. They get in the way of the rarer and more beautiful species—the Bay-breasteds and Cape Mays—the passage migrants that breed far to the north.

Here's one thing: for those naturalists who shy away from crowds, Magee is not the place to be. On a big day, there may be five hundred people on the boardwalk at 10:00 a.m. The west end gets so backed up that it looks like a crush of shoppers waiting to get into a sale at Wal-Mart on Black Friday. One has to push one's way through politely but firmly to get to a quieter location—not so easy with all the bodies encumbered with tripods and long lenses and backpacks filled with gear.

On the other hand, there is a clear birding advantage to the congested boardwalk—crowd-sourced information. If a Mourning Warbler is discovered, the word quickly is uploaded to Twitter, and word of mouth also passes this news along. I spend much of the morning simply asking perfect strangers, "What do you have?" That's the way to get sightings of Golden-winged Warbler and Philadelphia Vireo and American Woodcock and the like. Some individuals of a particularly rare species might be observed by hundreds of birders in a morning. The word goes out that there is a Mourning Warbler at stop 16. I hoof it down to the section of the boardwalk where a "16" has been etched onto the railing, and there are thirty-plus birders waiting patiently for the Mourning to show itself yet again. I gain a brief glimpse over somebody's shoulder of that handsome large warbler, sporting a gray hood, black throat, yellow belly, and olive back as it clambers through low ground vegetation.

Let me share how my main day (Thursday, May 8) went at Magee Marsh. I got up at 5:00 a.m. Had a quick breakfast by microwave. Drove twenty minutes west down Route 2 to Magee. Birded the morning until about 11:45, at which point I was hot and dehydrated. I zipped back to my motel room and ate lunch and then took a ninety-minute nap. I showered, freshened up, and organized my gear and was back at Magee by 4:30 p.m. I worked the boardwalk, mainly doing close-up bird photography, until 7:30 p.m. and then headed back to the motel to shed my gear. After another quick and very hot shower to restore myself, I headed into downtown Port Clinton to a local pub, where I got a basket of deep-fried Walleye and a draft beer. I had a table to myself to spread out my field diary and big Sibley bird guide, and I made a day list of my observations and checked the weather forecast on my tiny laptop (the restaurant had Wi-Fi). I finished up there by 9:30 p.m. and headed back to the motel and lights out, with the thought of rising again at 5 in the morning on Friday, for a good half-day of migrant watching on the boardwalk before driving home to Maryland.

During my two mornings and two afternoons at Magee Marsh, I recorded 111 species of birds, including 27 species of my favorite migrant group, the wood warblers. I loaded my camera's memory card with frame-filling images of all sorts of birds. I also birded with a half-dozen friends and colleagues. This was unalloyed, wall-to-wall fun. A perfect field trip, in spite of the required fifteen hours of highway driving.

May 15. Warbler Big Day. I team up with David Wilcove, Chuck Burg, John Anderton, and John Symington to hunt warblers for the day in the countryside northwest of Washington. Our route is bracketed by the Patuxent and Potomac Rivers in Montgomery, Frederick, and Howard Counties, Maryland.

A warbler big day is a late-spring event spent with a small party of like-minded birders intent on seeing as many species of wood warblers as possible in a single day. Over the years, we have carried out our warbler big days mainly northwest of DC, but we have also targeted western Maryland and southern Illinois. No matter where it is done, there is nothing quite like it for intensity and excitement.

In the DC area it should be conducted on a likely day between May 10 and 15. A likely day is one with expected fair weather and with southwest winds blowing the previous night. To us, the very best weather for a warbler day is a misty dawn followed by a cloudy and cool day, with no wind. Bluebird days, with bright sun, heat, and substantial wind, are the worst days for such a count. On this particular May 15 we hit it just right. The five of us get a dreary, damp day to count warblers and, in spite of setbacks, break the thirty-species barrier.

Considerable advance planning for the big day is required—not only regarding the weather but also with respect to the itinerary, for the chief enemy of the warbler-big-day team is time. The morning hours are precious, and the afternoon hours can be deadly dull. One must visit the best birding spots while minimizing transit times between sites. Moreover, one must make sure no time is wasted in the morning hours. In the preceding days and weeks, effort is invested reviewing the results of previous big days and tinkering with possible routes and priority stops. The travel agenda is finalized well before the day in question. Preceding weekends are used to scout locations for the more elusive breeding species. One needs to balance sites targeted for local breeders versus sites that produce passage migrant species. Without both, the goal of thirty species is not possible.

This big day, we focus on an area northwest of DC because it provides a wealth of warbler habitat, two river catchments (Potomac and Patuxent), and not too much in-transit driving. The longest leg—from Brookmont up to the Patuxent River bottomland woods at Hipsley Mill Road—is driven before first light by departing the house at 4:45 a.m. Thus we make our longest drive of the day before the sun rises. John Symington generously offers to drive us in his Honda Accord. The first challenge of the day comes when John's car skids when exiting off Interstate 270 at too great a speed under slippery, wet conditions. We hydroplane up over a traffic island, trashing the car's front undercarriage. Rather than put our day's count at risk, John decides to press on to our first stop on the Patuxent. The car is difficult to drive and evidently badly damaged, but first things first! The Hipsley Mill stop, for the predawn chorus, is a bit uncertain for all of us, still shaken from the driving mishap. We hear a predawn Northern Yellowthroat from a wet meadow on the way down to the river bottom (warbler species no. 1). Low cloud and a Scottish mist greet us as we gingerly exit the wounded car. We hear the bright song of a Louisiana Waterthrush, typically an early riser. This bottomland is prime breeding habitat for that species. Next, an American Redstart chimes in, another breeder here. Northern Parula buzzes in a sycamore by the bridge—another breeder and warbler species no. 4. On the oak hillside we manage to pull in Black-throated Blue, Ovenbird, Black-and-white, and—bonus bird—a Canada Warbler. Our first stop produces a fair number: eight warbler species. The year before this site had given us fourteen species, so we are not upbeat, especially with our car possibly in terminal condition. We drive up out of the bottomland and work the northern uplands above the Patuxent for about an hour. The agricultural fields and hedgerows give us Yellow-breasted Chat and Prairie Warbler—two locally breeding habitat specialists (recently, molecular systematists have removed the chat from the warbler family). Some rich oak woods produce both Hooded and Kentucky Warbler as well as Worm-eating Warbler. These three are difficult-to-find local breeders. We are back on track. Farther on, we find an old overgrown orchard that has a singing Blue-winged Warbler, bingo! Another goodie. It shares the orchard with a brightly singing Yellow Warbler (warbler no. 15). Another tract of rich oaks produces a big swag of warblers in the fresh leaves of the canopy—Black-throated Green, Yellow-rumped, Blackburnian, and Chestnut-sided. After our second stop, we are at nineteen species.

But the car seems to be in its death throes. As a group, we agree it is necessary to stop in nearby Damascus and try to trade in our wreck for a rental car. Amazingly, there is an Enterprise Rent-A-Car office right on Main Street. Within thirty-five minutes we are on the road in a fresh vehicle (and John has dropped his car at the fix-it shop next to the rental car office). Before Damascus, we all believed that our big day was over. After Damascus, we have a new lease on life.

Headed along a back road toward Little Bennett Regional Park, we glimpse a luscious grove of oaks and decide to stop and check for warblers. Oh yeah! We nab thirteen species there, including three new ones—Tennessee Warbler, Nashville Warbler, and Northern Waterthrush. One of the frustrations of a warbler big day is that after each stop, the list of "seen" species grows and the list of "needed" species diminishes. It becomes harder and harder to find new species, and the seen species get in the way, as you have to sort through all the birds in the tree to find the novel ones. This day, it is the pesky Yellow-rumped Warbler (sixty individuals) that litters our view. Time and time again, we see clots of warblers in an oak canopy and then find that every single bird is a Yellow-rumped Warbler. Still, we have reached no. 22. And lunchtime is still not upon us.

Next stop is the Kingsley Trail section of Little Bennett Regional Park. This place can be deadsville, and there is a lot of walking involved. As a result, this place can be the graveyard of warbler big days. This day, not so! There must have been a warbler fallout at dawn in this spot, because Little Bennett itself produces twenty-one warbler species. Never in our twenty-year history of warbler big days has a single site produced so many species. But, amazingly, this list of twenty-one includes only two newbies—a Pine Warbler singing right in the planted plot of pines by the parking lot and a Magnolia Warbler in the low vegetation not far from the parking lot. We then spend almost two more hours here traipsing about but add not a single species in this wonderful though frustrating stop. We have now reached twenty-four species.

The prime location for passage migrants is always Sugarloaf Mountain because it is a big wooded target jutting up out of the plain, begging passing birds to stop there. How can they resist? In fact, eighteen species cannot resist, so this is another productive warbler stop. But of those eighteen species, only two are new—a single Cape May, one of the toughest passage migrants to get, and two Bay-breasteds, another uncommon species and a favorite of warbler watchers. Sugarloaf gets us to twenty-six. It would be sweet to spend some more quality time in this big upland woods, but time is short.

Next, we visit two stops along the Potomac River—Nolands Ferry and Monocacy Aqueduct. These are two beautiful locations where the river and canal mix with swampy maple forest. Today these two spots are very productive, giving us twenty species of warblers. We hear the swamp-loving Prothonotary Warbler singing when we get out of the car at the first stop. Prothonotaries breed in numbers all along the canal in Maryland. The Prothonotary is a given, but the surprise is a silent adult male Mourning Warbler, which David Wilcove locates in a Spicebush right along the towpath. It's always nice to have a great pair of birding eyes at work on a big day. We all stop dead and *oo* and *ah* at this wonderful and rare bird. Most of us do not see a Mourning Warbler every spring in migration. They are heard far more often than seen. This sighting was perhaps the best of the day. We have reached twenty-eight.

We now have a short list of birds that we might be able to add to our total. At this point in the day, we start our loop back toward town, and our next-to-last stop is Great Falls Park, Maryland. It is a cloudy afternoon, and cool, and we are hoping that some warblers will be in song. We drive to the far upstream edge of the park's parking lot and get out to strain our ears. *Veedl-veedl-veedl-Vee!*—over there is a singing male Cerulean Warbler. Number 29. This is the only place in the area where we knew we could get a Cerulean, and here he is, singing in the afternoon for us. Then we get out our little Radio Shack tape deck and play the song of the Yellow-throated Warbler. There are loads of sycamores across the canal by the river, and we are hoping against hope. After five minutes, John Symington, our sharpest-eared team member, points his finger. There is the male's response to the tape. Number 30! High fives all around.

Twenty minutes later, at 4:00 p.m., we are back in Brookmont. And we still have not recorded one of the most common passage migrants of mid-May—the Blackpoll Warbler. We decide to do a circuit of the neighborhood because there are some nice White Oaks over by the palisade overlooking the Potomac. After three stops we get two males singing high in the oak canopy. We now have logged thirty-one species of warbler for the day, with daylight to spare.

We decide to create a name for the achievement of seeing thirty species of warblers in a day. We call it a "Zusi," in honor of Richard Zusi, then a curator of birds at the Smithsonian's Natural History Museum, a great warbler watcher who every spring would go with another sharp government ornithologist, Marshall Howe, and watch warblers in and around Sugarloaf Mountain. His casual statement at coffee hour one day, that "seeing thirty species of warblers in a day is no challenge," led us to find out for ourselves.

Of late, a combination of compromised hearing and a rarified migration passage of birds has led to much reduced expectations for our warbler big days. In the years 1995–99, we hit thirty species three times and twenty-nine species once. Over the subsequent ten years, we reached twenty-nine species only once, and now it is difficult to record twenty-five species. The passage of migrant warblers in the DC area is no longer what is was even twenty years ago. I have given up the hope of reaching a Zusi here.

May 16. Biking to work this morning, I count (by ear) seventy-two Blackpoll Warblers along the C&O Canal towpath. This is an all-time high count for me of a single warbler species. I also encounter a big and scary-looking Common Snapping Turtle encrusted with green algae crossing the gravel of the towpath.

Snapping turtles are a part of spring. Most of the year, one sees few of these antediluvian creatures, which remain hidden below the surface of fishing ponds, lakes, and freshwater swamps. But in the spring, these perfectly hideous creatures are on the move, and it is possible to see them on a road or bike path or playing field. Females move about in search of a patch of sandy soil to lay their eggs. Young males are out looking for new habitat. These creatures are long-lived and require more than a decade to reach sexual maturity. It is not uncommon for an older individual to weigh more than thirty pounds. The record for the species is seventy-five pounds.

May 17. Central Park, New York. The preceding afternoon I took the Amtrak train up to New York City to bird the urban park with Roger Pasquier. The city of Washington is famous for its abundant green space. That is nice for residents of the city but is problematic for birders looking for urban migrant traps to see concentrations of spring warblers and other songbirds. There simply is too much habitat for the birds, what with the Potomac greenway and Rock Creek Park. What is good for the birds is challenging for eager birders wanting to see concentrations of migrants. It is best for eager birders to get on the bus or train and head to New York. Few places in the East can compete with the concentrating powers of Central Park when it comes to spring migration. I try to schedule a few days' work at the Natural History Museum there, so I can crash at the apartment of my friend Roger, who happens to be the dean of Central Park birders. Roger visits the park every morning during spring migration and also for much of the fall transit as well. It is the spring show that is worth seeing for anyone who loves warbler migration.

Why Central Park? It's simple. For nocturnal spring migrants, the greater New York City area offers a vast and nearly uninterrupted expanse of gray—roads, sidewalks, buildings, and playgrounds—and only a few patches of green: parkland. Central Park is the patch of green in the center of all the gray, and all those migrants passing overhead make a beeline in the predawn hours for the green refuge offered by the lush vegetation of Central Park. Southwesterly winds bring in large concentrations of migrants, and this offers riches to birders out early the next morning. The numbers can be mind-boggling. For common species such as Black-throated Blue or Magnolia Warblers, there can be dozens and dozens of individuals singing and foraging in spots where oaks and other favored trees dominate. When I go to the park with Roger, all of these places must be visited once or perhaps twice in a morning—the Ramble, Belvedere Castle, the Turtle Pond, and Strawberry Fields, among others.

Part of the wonder of birding Central Park is that the birds are accessible and predictable. A Cape May Warbler feeding at eye level in a small flowering tree on Tuesday will often be foraging there in the same small tree the next morning. One can perch on the stone patio of Belvedere Castle and be at eye level with five or six species of warblers in the canopy of several adjacent trees. The birds are singing and feeding and putting on a show for the birders smart enough to know where to be on a good morning in mid-May. Also, savvy birders share the latest sightings. Thus, a rarity, such as a Kentucky Warbler in the Ramble, gets seen by many birding parties. The final benefit is that after several hours in pursuit of migrants, one can walk a few minutes within the park to a place that serves a full breakfast with a generous portion of savory bacon and a hot coffee. One can celebrate the day's sightings and continue to hear the songs of four or five warblers, singing from the tall trees around the restaurant. Not a bad way to wrap up a great morning of birding in the Big Apple.

The secret we naturalists keep to ourselves is that the glory of the natural world is the heaven that the world's religions seek through prayer, meditation, and self-denial. As children we are taught to see heaven as a distant place above the clouds—not dark and brooding clouds, but puffy white clouds that have the sun's rays shining down through them. At least our teachers got a small part of it right. The morning sun shining on a green-canopied woodland with birds in song is the only heaven a naturalist needs to see the light.

May 27. Blair's Valley, Maryland. In 1984, Carol and I joined my mother—a birder—in attending a weekend outing to Clear Spring, hosted by the Maryland Ornithological Society. Clear Spring is situated west of Hagerstown in Washington County, where the neck of western Maryland begins to narrow, with the Potomac impinging from the south and the Mason-Dixon Line situated just to the north. It was on this outing that I was introduced to Blair's Valley, one of my favorite secret places in all of Maryland. It is a small agricultural valley entirely closed in by forested mountains. Much of the valley floor is now designated a state wildlife management area, which also is home to a man-made lake. It is one of the most beautiful places in Maryland. Because of its mix of agricultural, old field, shrubland, and woodland-edge habitats on the valley floor, it is also an excellent birding location. Moreover, it was the site of the last outlying breeding population of Golden-winged Warblers east of the Alleghenies.

We only got a taste of Blair's Valley in 1984, but Carol and I returned there in late May of 1985, on a Memorial Day weekend. Hiking up through the old fields and hedgerows dominated by Black Locust, we heard and saw a number of territorial male Golden-winged Warblers. One perched and sang on a telephone wire in the top corner of the highest field, sharing the wire with a male Ruby-throated Hummingbird. On that day, we encountered not a single Blue-winged Warbler, the sister species that has been gobbling up breeding habitat of the Golden-wing for decades at the eastern and southern verges of the Golden-wing's range.

Between 1985 and 2002, I returned to Blair's Valley in late May to monitor the status of this isolated population of Golden-winged Warblers. In 1988, Blue-wings started showing up in my counts. By 1996, I started seeing mainly Blue-winged and hybrid individuals and the occasional Golden-wing. It's been quite a few years since I have recorded a Golden-wing there, and now the hybrids are rare. The Blue-wings have taken over.

Blair's Valley is now a great place to see Blue-winged Warblers. The slow shift in breeding ranges of these two species is well documented in the detailed range maps of the Peterson field guide of 1980 versus the Sibley guide of 2014. Over that thirty-four-year period, the Golden-wing disappeared from Connecticut and Massachusetts and expanded westward and northward into Saskatchewan. The breeding range of the Blue-wing has expanded in Pennsylvania, New York, and western Maryland, as well as along the northernmost fringing of its traditional range in New England and the Great Lakes. It's not clear what factors are driving the shifting ranges of these two species, but climate change may be one influence, given the way that the birds' ranges are shifting north and west into the cold interior.

In spite of the sad disappearance of the Golden-wing, Blair's Valley remains a wonderful spring birding site. I have camped here with the children in the late spring, when we hear the staccato trilling of the Whip-poor-will, as well as the evocative nighttime sounds of the American Woodcock and Barred Owl. For most visitors, it is a fishing destination, but it should also be high on the list for birders and nature lovers.

End of May. A morning trip to Great Falls Park, Virginia, offers a nice walk in the riverside woods, a close-up look at the great rocky falls, and the songs of Worm-eating and Kentucky Warbler, Louisiana Waterthrush, and Yellow-throated Vireo—all local resident breeding songbirds. We also hear a few high-pitched songs of the Blackpoll Warbler, a passage migrant heading to the Great North Woods. The end of May spells the end of the spring migration of songbirds and the beginning of the end of the spring season. Bittersweet.

TWELVE

June—Chasing the Last of Spring

I found the delicate bird [a Veery] at the head of the ravine, singing in the forest mist, amid the long rays of golden light. He was moving from branch to branch, raising his head at intervals and opening his bill to release that lovely series of intertwining and falling phrases.

—LOUIS HALLE, *Spring in Washington*

June is still a favored month for naturalists in spite of the completion of the passage of the songbird migration. This is a time I can focus on the local resident wildlife. This morning, before departing on my bicycle for the office, I hear a Baltimore Oriole singing behind the house. It is probably building a nest in the tall American Sycamore next to the tennis court. On my return in the evening, I hear an American Toad trilling in the wetland below our backyard, not far from the big sycamore.

In late spring and early summer, it is not unusual to hear the high musical trilling of the American Toad coming from that swampy low spot in the neighborhood park out back. We see toads infrequently, but they do make their way into the yard from time to time. To me, they seem harmless and are easily overlooked, like so much of nature. The evening serenade of the male toad singing for a mate reassures us that spring is progressing and that nature's cycle of reproduction continues in our local environs. Although many people find toads repellant and think touching their wrinkly dorsal skin causes warts, no one has ever complained about the gentle background sound produced by this species in early June. This, along with the sound of Spring Peepers and the evening song of the Northern Mockingbird, is the night music that sends us to a peaceful evening's sleep, if we keep our window open to let in nature's night sounds.

A few days later, while biking to work on the towpath, I hear a singing Yellow-throated Warbler just above Fletcher's Cove, with a Yellow-throated Vireo in song there as well. These are two more sycamore lovers that breed along the Potomac. Also, I find that the pair of nestling Red-shouldered Hawks are getting ready to depart their nest in one of the big sycamores beside the bike path. Lots of sycamore action today!

American Sycamores, with their flaky white bark, are one of the dominant forest canopy trees down along the Potomac bottomlands. It seems that this distinctive species prospers where floodwaters scour the ground every now and then. The tiny windborne seeds must readily germinate in the black alluvial soil that is deposited after each flood. Early successional pioneers, sycamore seedlings presumably quickly sprout up in the sunny opening caused by the rushing floodwaters—rising waters caused by heavy rainfalls in the Potomac's headwaters. On this particular day, however, the rainclouds I see on the horizon during my afternoon bike ride home warn of a storm that will be a decidedly local phenomenon.

June, July, and August are the thunderstorm months in the DC area. Thunderstorms are local and patchy in time and space, and it is, at times, difficult for bikers such as myself to dodge a passing afternoon storm.

American Toad

Most of Washington's thunderstorms rumble right down the Potomac, from northwest to southeast. My bike ride from the office in Crystal City takes me upstream, right into the jaws of any storm traveling down the river. Usually, by leaving a few minutes early or by delaying departure for fifteen minutes or so, it is possible to slip around the worst of any storm. But not always.

One afternoon in early June I bike right into the middle of a whopper of a storm. As I leave Crystal City and head north on the Mount Vernon Trail, on the west bank of the Potomac River, I can see stacks of dark cumulonimbus clouds upriver to the northwest. Southeastward, it is all fair skies. I figure that I will travel as far as possible along my route and then take refuge some place when the worst of the storm breaks. I see flashes of lightning to the northwest, followed by rumbles of thunder. As I continue on my way, I initially encounter brief bouts of large raindrops. Then some rough gusts of wind. The tree leaves flip over to show their pale lower surfaces. Next, I suffer some light but steady rain under darkening skies overhead. I stop and pull on my raincoat. The volume of rain picks up. I keep on. As I cross Key Bridge, the wind and rain really start in a big way. Several times, a strong gust nearly blows me off my bike. I hasten down under Key Bridge and to the ancient low granite underpass just north of Key Bridge, near the start of the Capital Crescent Trail. The rain is coming down so hard that there is no question of continuing up the bike path. I share the dark, tunnel-like underpass with several other wet bikers taking refuge. This is the stone base of an old rail trestle that once crossed the Potomac, parallel to Key Bridge. We watch as the heart of the storm arrives. Big gusts of wind blow rain sideways into our cavelike shelter. Then we hear the sound of hail. Visibility is nil—a whiteout.

Hail falls for no more than a minute, and then the storm reverts to heavy rain. Rivers of water stream into our refuge. We wait. There is a big flash and immediately a terrifying crash as lightning strikes nearby. Five minutes pass. We wait. The rain declines to a steady shower. At that point, our impatience gets the better of us and we all head back out into it. We know we will be soaked to the skin anyway by the time we get home. Several large limbs are down in the bike path, but we are able to lift our bikes over the annoying encumbrances. Storms are one of the periodic challenges facing a summer biker.

On the following morning, it is sunny and cool. On my bike ride to work I am serenaded by Northern Parula as well as Prothonotary, Yellow-throated, and Yellow Warblers. Biking home in the evening I see several Little Brown Bats foraging over the C&O Canal.

The Little Brown Bat (or Little Brown Myotis) is the best-known species of bat in the Mid-Atlantic region. It has long been a regular

Little Brown Myotis

summer resident in our neighborhood, fluttering about during the evenings. I most often have seen them when I have been down at our neighborhood park at dusk. One or two individuals would pass back and forth, enlivening the evening with their silent presence. For my whole life I have taken these gentle little bats for granted—to be there as part of the neighborhood environment. Just knowing that they are there, doing their job chasing winged arthropods, is a source of comfort. They roost and reproduce in eaves of buildings and attics, and migrate south to hibernate in caves. Thoughtful nature lovers set up bat houses in backyards to provide safe roost sites for these and other local bat friends for the summer.

Now things have changed for the Little Brown Bat because of white-nose syndrome, which has decimated this and other species that spend their winters roosting colonially in caves. The syndrome, which was discovered in the winter of 2007, is a virulent fungus that has killed at least six million bats of several species. Some populations have declined as much as 80 percent. These bats subsist on flying insects and thus are important in controlling a wide range of insect pests, providing a substantial ecological benefit. It is too early to say how the loss of our bats will influence the region's ecosystem. It is yet one more example of environmental change in an uncertain world.

On June 6 and 7, my wife and I travel to central Connecticut to attend a wedding. Could there be any more iconic late-spring event than an outdoor wedding in New England in early June? The flowers, the fresh green vegetation, and perfect weather combine with the beauty of youth and a hushed, traditional ceremony. The ancient institution's deployment of the best of nature produces a deeply incised memory for young and old alike.

After the event, my wife and I head toward home, with a plan to overnight in a bed and breakfast in Shawnee on Delaware, at the bottom of the Delaware Water Gap. At this time of year the natural area is at its peak, and the hamlet is verdant and welcoming, nestled down in the gap where the river cuts between the mountain ridges. This old-fashioned community is the very place where one would wish to retreat during the heat of summer in those decades before the advent of air conditioning. It is protected on all sides by green mountain ridges and cooled by the presence of the cold Delaware flowing by.

After a comfortable night and a home-made breakfast at the quaint inn, Carol and I rent a canoe and paddle down the Delaware from

Smithfield Beach National Recreation Area (in Pennsylvania, on the west bank of the Delaware) to Dunnfield Creek in the gap itself (on the New Jersey side). This was all cheerfully facilitated by a local canoe rental operation based nearby. Our paddle down the river takes about two hours and is relaxing and picturesque. We float by various hen Common Mergansers; one is leading a group of seven hatchlings—little chestnut-gray-and-white babies, each only slightly larger than a golf ball. Also, many American Shad are running up the river—we see their fins slicing the surface as they push their way upstream through the rocky shallows. At close range, the silver-sided fish are readily visible in the clear water, and many of them are more than a foot long.

From our perfect vantage point, the rich brown of the rocky river, the green of the two ridges, the blue of the sky, and the white of the puffy cumulus clouds create outdoor perfection. This is a route worth paddling on any sunny day in early June. Along the way, we hear the songs of Baltimore Orioles, Warbling and Yellow-throated Vireos, Yellow and Hooded Warblers, and Gray Catbirds. The patch of rapids just above the gap is fun and substantial enough to get our full attention. Before long we are back on the road and heading across Pennsylvania on the way back to Maryland, refreshed from a morning on a broad and beautiful river filled with migrating fish.

This time of year is, really, "early summer," characterized by the lush vegetation, the ever-growing lawn grass, and the songs of local breeding birds. Migration is done. We are settling in, waiting for the arrival of the big-time heat and humidity and thinking as well about a northern escape. I am thinking of northern New England, where I will trade tropical conditions for a suite of biting insects—mosquitoes, no-see-ums, black flies, deer flies, and horse flies. Of course, where the

American Shad

arthropod diversity is high, one hopes to find equally rich plant and vertebrate diversity.

It is always an adventure traveling to some place entirely new. I used to travel to new places in distant realms such as western New Guinea or northeastern India. Now it is to novel nooks and crannies in the United States and Canada. This is no less exciting, believe it or not. It's just a matter of adjusting one's point of view.

My last trip of the late spring and early summer is to the Connecticut Lakes of far northern New Hampshire. This destination is truly a hidden nook of our Northeast. I discovered it one winter evening while passing the time looking at the satellite imagery of northern New England offered by Google Maps. I was hunting for boreal boglands, and I found a seductive-looking site to the southwest of Baxter State Park, just across the western boundary of Maine.

The location I glimpsed via satellite imagery was a place I wanted to visit during the height of the songbird breeding season—the very headwaters of the Connecticut River, one of New England's iconic streams. What I found on the map is that the Connecticut ends in a series of four lakes, sequestered in a small salient of New Hampshire that pokes into Quebec. Northernmost Vermont lies to the southwest, Quebec to the east and north, and Maine to the west. To me, this looked like the land that time forgot. I *had* to go there. And, better yet, online, I found a small state campground set right on the main flow of the Connecticut, right next door to a large tract of boggy conifer forest that I could explore for boreal birds and mammals. After spending some time studying the distribution of boreal bird species on eBird, I knew I had stumbled on a birding hotspot.

Once in New England, much of my long drive up to the Connecticut Lakes follows the historic course of the great river northward across Connecticut, through Massachusetts, up the length of Vermont, and then across Vermont and into the very top of New Hampshire. This took me from the summerlike warmth in the Mid-Atlantic to the chill and damp of a typical northern New England spring. The combination of elevation and latitude produces this pronounced climatological retreat— cold, wet, and cloudy.

I invest a week exploring the top of New Hampshire. Here I am in a world apart. Few people. Lots of trails and gravel back roads, and birds galore. I have my bicycle and do most of my birding by bike.

I set up camp among the tall spruces of Deer Mountain Campground, right on the east bank of the rocky and tumbling waters of the

Connecticut, where the river is no more than thirty feet across—a small but fine trout stream. This northern corner of New Hampshire is trout-fishing country. Little Route 3 crookedly leads northward to the mountainous border with Quebec, along the way passing by First, Second, and Third Connecticut Lakes. Tiny Fourth Connecticut Lake nestles high up on the international boundary, serving as the river's headwaters.

Although it is June, I am not prepared for the cold and damp. The conditions are a shock. I have not packed sufficient cold-weather and wet-weather gear. This is a brutal New England early spring, and I am forced to raid the small general stores of Pittsburg and the Glen to find long underwear, a woolen undershirt, a watch cap, and gloves. A new addition to my camp setup is a twenty-by-twenty-foot green nylon tarpaulin. This shields my whole campsite—tent, picnic table, and all the way to my car parked in the gravel campsite entrance. The tarp keeps everything dry, in spite of the daily rain showers and low cloud that persists, day after day. Even with my new weather gear, I suffer chills.

I spend most of my time hiking, biking, or driving the little gravel roads around Moose Falls Flow, Scott Bog, and East Inlet Flow. Each lake, with its boggy wetlands, offers productive openings in the boreal forest that are good for birding and naturizing. This cold and damp season is when all the boreal breeding songbirds set up shop and begin the business of reproduction. That is why I am here.

Early the first morning as I negotiate a gravel road in the boggy low country, I come around a corner and surprise a cow Moose that is crossing from one wetland to another. She stares mutely at me for a few seconds, then trots out of sight. This is big-time Moose country, and during my stay here I come across Moose tracks just about everywhere. I encounter Moose on three occasions. Otherwise, I encounter mammals in small numbers—a few White-tailed Deer, a Muskrat, a Northern Short-tailed Shrew, and a few Red Squirrels. A Red Fox, in his scruffy spring pelage, visits my campsite daily in search of scraps. The only Porcupines I see on the trip are roadkills in Vermont. I see no sign of Black Bear or Coyote.

Of course, I am here for the birds, so the shortage of mammals is a minor inconvenience. The big conifer stands in the low country hold small parties of Boreal Chickadees, Blue-headed Vireos, and the occasional vocalizing Olive-sided Flycatcher. Nearby aspen groves are the hiding place of the Philadelphia Vireo. Vocal Red-eyed Vireos are everywhere. Alder Flycatchers sing from the low deciduous swamp vegetation choked with alders, and Yellow-bellied Flycatchers call from the thickets of young Balsam Fir. Black-backed Woodpeckers are present in the conifer stands in small numbers. Naturally, the wood warblers are the main feature of this avian show. I manage to locate fourteen species of these little songsters. The most abundant and vocal are Northern Waterthrush, American Redstart, and Magnolia, Black-throated Green, Black-throated Blue, and Yellow-rumped Warbler. The conifer forests and mixed forests are alive with warbler song. That gives me the most satisfaction for weathering the cold and damp.

In early mornings and at the dark at the end of the day, I am treated to the voices of Common Loon, American Bittern, and American Woodcock, as well as the drumming of Ruffed Grouse. These birds give the north country its wilderness sounds. The loons vocalize while floating about on the lakes—wild yodeling with vibrato. The bittern makes its weird *pump-lunk* notes from thick lakeside wetlands, sounding a bit like a malfunctioning piece of mechanical equipment. The woodcock twitters and chatters in the gloaming while soaring high overhead in a courtship song flight. The Ruffed Grouse, standing atop a hollow fallen log in the woods, creates a low and rapid drumming that from a distance has the sound of a heartbeat. These wonderful and strange sounds remind me that I am surrounded by wild nature.

Widespread and commonplace species are strangely absent—Song Sparrow, American Goldfinch, Common Grackle, and Red-winged Blackbird. Perhaps the weather and habitat are too severe for them.

A few people do share the campground with me. I try to be friendly with everybody. One day, biking back into the campground, I see a couple of grizzled folks who look my age. I stop to chat. Both are Episcopalian priests. One, dressed head-to-tail for fly-fishing, mentions that my car has a Colby College sticker on the back. Turns out that he, too, is the father of a Colby student. As we speak, we suddenly realize that we are long-lost friends. Although I have not seen him for nearly three decades, I am chatting with Mark Robinson, who baptized my elder daughter, Grace, in 1989. He and his wife, Eleanor, moved to Connecticut shortly after that, and we had kept in touch only through the occasional email. Mark was here in the field organizing a spiritual pilgrimage down the Connecticut River for his parish and was awaiting their arrival. Yes, it was a surprise meeting him in this little-known and faraway corner of New England.

The highlight of this late-spring adventure is my own pilgrimage to the Fourth Connecticut Lake, the headwaters of the Connecticut. To get there, I drive up to the international border crossing and park in the lot there. I then follow the marked path that traces the US-Canada boundary. I walk this rocky ridgetop border trail, marked by USGS boundary benchmarks in the granite. This is the first occasion I walk along an international boundary, and it feels both a bit threatening and strangely empowering. I can peer down into Quebec to my right and then back to my left into the United States. After about twenty minutes of hiking, the trail makes a left turn down the slope through boreal forest toward the little woodland lake. I can glimpse the water and its marshy verges through the spruces and firs. Once there, I walk a complete circuit around the lake, listening for two songbird specialties—Blackpoll Warbler and Bicknell's Thrush. These two breed in boreal uplands of New England and Canada. It is the end of the day, and things are quiet up here at the headwaters. I eventually hear call notes of several Bicknell's and the rapid staccato song of the Blackpoll. They are joined by a drumming Ruffed Grouse and voices of the Ovenbird, Dark-eyed Junco, and Swainson's Thrush. Bicknell's Thrush, after some searching, I find up close. This is perhaps the most rarely glimpsed songbird in the eastern United States. I savor the moment, as the light begins to die in the sky. This is a remarkably solitary and wild spot. I have the entire lake and its environs to myself, at the very edge of northernmost New Hampshire.

As dusk approaches, the chorus of the Spring Peepers at the Fourth Connecticut Lake swells. I have never heard such a chorus. And all around me in the upper Connecticut valley spring is in full flower. At the ground level, two species of trillium are blossoming. Shadbush and Hobblebush show off their white flowers. Pin Cherry is in bloom. I am experiencing a second spring. What pleasure in solitude!

Afterword

But in the endless repetitions of nature—in the recurrence of spring, in the
lush new growths that replace the old, in the comings of new birds to sing
ancient songs, in the continuity of life and the web of the living—here we find
the solid foundation that, on this Earth, underlies at once the past, the
present, and future.

—EDWIN WAY TEALE, *Circle of the Seasons*

I return from northern New England and my sentimental journey to
belated spring in the North Woods. Back in Bethesda, I am enjoying a
warm and humid evening on the C&O Canal towpath as I bike home
from work on the summer solstice, the first day of astronomical summer
and the end of our year in nature. Pop-up showers are headed my way.
The summer doldrums are fast approaching.

As I bicycle up the gravel path, I reflect on the wonder of the seasons
along the East Coast and the privilege of being able to bike through
nature year-round. All those sights, sounds, scents, and species! All those
valued deposits to the memory banks. For isn't it all about the creation
and storage of welcome memories?

I smile inwardly at the thought of a June evening many years ago, in a rural outdoor setting when the fragrance of honeysuckle overwhelmed the senses making the nightfall glow with the possibilities. Wouldn't we all want to return to that very moment in the distant past, if only briefly? Well, we can, through treasured memories—made rich by nature and our appreciation of nature—our gathering up nature in our hearts and the interweaving of nature with the living of the special moments of our lives.

Memory of an encounter with nature can take us to a place of calm and peace. For instance, this morning, along the canal, I watched a big American Beaver make a silent wake across the dark canal waters, its paddle tail trailing on the surface. The experience was but a few moments but now remains timeless in my memory of it. Just recollecting that encounter lowers my heart rate and puts me at ease. By actively seeking out these natural experiences, we give ourselves reserves of tranquillity that we can return to from time to time.

Sharing nature with our loved ones and closest colleagues brings us together and gives us rich memories to share. Even though it took place thirteen years ago, I can assure you that David and I will never stop thinking about that day in late October at Higbee Beach in Cape May, New Jersey, when we stood in that sheltered sandy clearing below the dike and watched those thousands of warblers blow by us. That very spot is forever inscribed as an image on a virtual wall in our brains, binding us through shared memory. Those special places in our memory are what make up a life.

As we add years and slip closer to our unknown fate, the annual promise of a returning spring, with all its attendant pleasures and future memories, provides the motivation to plan new adventures, to seek new sights, and to experience natural wonders both new and old. To my dying day, I will look forward to hearing, yet again, the distinctive, affecting, and ethereal notes of the Hermit Thrush in a cool and shady hemlock glen, the musical reeling of Bicknell's Thrush high in some fir-clad mountain forest, or the slow and cadenced notes of the Wood Thrush in an expanse of Mid-Atlantic bottomland deciduous forest. These are our songs of eternal nature.

Acknowledgments

I wish to thank my mentors, teachers, family, and fellow naturalists. Both my parents (now deceased) loved nature and encouraged my love of nature in the sixties and seventies, living in north Baltimore. My brother Bill hunted with me for fossils, birds, and butterflies in our earliest boyhood years. The late Chandler S. Robbins inspired me at junior nature camp and on birding adventures in the Pocomoke Swamp, Cape Henlopen, and Camp Woodbine. At summer camp in the Adirondacks, director Elliott Verner encouraged me to follow my muse—my love of birds and nature. Fellow naturalists David Wilcove, Roger Pasquier, Eric Dinerstein, John Lamoreux, Chuck Burg, John Symington, John Anderton, Jim Savia, and Stacey Maggard shared cars, motel rooms, and diners good and bad while searching for wild nature at DC's doorstep, along the Potomac, and elsewhere up and down the East Coast. Critical reading of earlier drafts was provided by Roger Pasquier, Lucie Lehmann, and Patsy and Tom Inglet.

I thank Jean Thomson Black, Michael Deneen, and Margaret Otzel of Yale University Press for guiding this project to fruition. Laura Jones Dooley copyedited the manuscript with care, and Sonia Shannon created the handsome book design and the lovely cover. Finally, Lela Stanley critically reviewed the proofs.

My children, Grace, Andrew, and Cary, joined me in all sorts of outdoor adventures and seem none the worse for wear. I thank them for their joyful companionship. And finally, my darling wife, Carol, has been my steadfast partner on nature rambles near and far while from time to time allowing me to head off on my own into the wilds. She proved her mettle on our honeymoon, spent on the banks of the Sii River, in the lowland rainforest of New Guinea. To Carol and everyone else mentioned, as well as those I have forgotten to mention, I salute your valuable guidance as well as your appreciation of nature.

References

Borland, Hal. 1957. *This Hill, This Valley*. J. B. Lippincott, Philadelphia.

Borland, Hal. 1964. *Sundial of the Seasons*. J. B. Lippincott, Philadelphia.

Cramer, Deborah. 2015. *The Narrow Edge—A Tiny Bird, an Ancient Crab, and an Epic Journey*. Yale University Press, New Haven, Connecticut.

Garland, Mark S. 1997. *Watching Nature*. Smithsonian Institution Press, Washington, DC.

Halle, Louis. 1947. *Spring in Washington*. William Sloane Associates, New York, New York.

Harwood, Michael, and Mary Durant. 1974. *A Country Journal*. Dodd, Mead and Company, New York, New York.

Haskell, David George. 2012. *The Forest Unseen*. Viking, New York, New York.

Horton, Tom. 1987. *Bay Country*. Johns Hopkins University Press, Baltimore, Maryland.

Teale, Edwin Way. 1951. *North with the Spring*. Dodd, Mead and Company, New York, New York.

Teale, Edwin Way. 1956. *Autumn Across America*. Dodd, Mead and Company, New York, New York.

Teale, Edwin Way. 1953. *Circle of the Seasons*. Dodd, Mead and Company, New York, New York.

Teale, Edwin Way. 1978. *A Walk Through the Year*. Dodd, Mead and Company, New York, New York.

Vogt, William. 1948. *Road to Survival*. William Sloane Associates, New York, New York.

Other Books by the Author

North on the Wing: Travels with the Songbird Migration of Spring (2018)

Birds of New Guinea: Distribution, Taxonomy, and Systematics (with Thane K. Pratt, 2016)

Birds of New Guinea, 2nd edition, Princeton Field Guides (with Thane K. Pratt, 2015)

Lost Worlds: Adventures in the Tropical Rainforest (2008)

Ecology of Papua (with Andrew J. Marshall, 2007)

A Naturalist in New Guinea (1998)

Birds of New Guinea (with Thane K. Pratt and Dale A. Zimmerman, 1986)

Birdlife of the Adirondack Park (1978)

Upland Birds of Northeastern New Guinea (1978)

Index

Pages in *italics* indicate illustrations.

oaks, 30, 140
October, 85–104; American Robin, 89–90; biking at night, 96–98; Cape May birding, 90–95; Eastern Mole, 86–88, 87; Greenbrier State Park camping trip, 95–96; pumpkin patch outing, 100; Ring-billed Gull, 85–86; Sugarloaf Mountain day trip, 88–89; Superstorm Sandy, 100–103; Yellow-bellied Sapsucker, 98–100, 99
Ohio: Crane Creek State Park, 235; Magee Marsh, 230–239
Ohio River, 10
Ontario, Canada, 168–173, 231–232
Oriole, Baltimore, 234, 250
Osprey, 65, 159, 161, 197
Ottawa National Wildlife Refuge, 235, 236
Otter, River, 133
Our Lady of the Pines church, 25
Outer Banks, North Carolina, 211–213
overpopulation, 176–177
Owl: Barred, 16, 108, 136, 142, 228, 228; Eastern Screech, 149; Snowy, 163–164

Palmetto-Peartree Preserve, North Carolina, 209–210
Parker River National Wildlife Refuge, Massachusetts, 61–63
Pasquier, Roger, 245–246
Patuxent River bottomland woods, 240–241
Pawpaw, Common, 200, 201
Pea Island National Wildlife Refuge, North Carolina, 211
pelagic seabirds, 51–52, 103, 178–181
Pelican: Brown, 159; White, 161

Pennsylvania: Shawnee on Delaware, 255; Waggoner's Gap and Hawk Mountain, 84, 128–132
pesticides, 65, 140
Peterson, Roger Tory, 12, 117, 248
Pettigrew State Park, North Carolina, 209
pewee, 35
Phoebe, Eastern, 35
Plum Island, Massachusetts, 61–63
pocosin lakes, 209
Point Pelee, Ontario, 231–232
Poison Ivy, 46–47, 48
pollen and pollen counts, 200
Porcupine, North American, 57–58
Potomac River: as defining feature of Washington, DC, 9, 10–11; Fairfax Stone (headwaters), 26; fish and fish runs, 214–215; floods, 163, 186–187; ice on, 154, 156; Monocacy Aqueduct, 243; Nolands Ferry, 243; waterfowl populations, 123–125
predation, 113–114
predator-swamping effect, 30–31
presidents as birders, 148
pumpkin patch outing, 100

Race Point Beach, Massachusetts, 68–69
Rail, Virginia, 201–202
Randle Cliff Beach, Maryland, 119–122
raptor migration, 82–84, 93, 128–132
Rattlesnake, Timber, 71, 88, 215–217
Raven, Common, 59–60
Ray, Cownose, 50
Razorbill, 179
rewilding. See urban wilding
road-killed wild animals, 78, 81

Ward, Andrew, 73–77
Washington, DC: arrival of migratory birds in, 227–230; Capital Crescent Trail, 38–39; climate and weather, 150; design and features, 11–12; Glover-Archbold Park, 229; National Mall fireworks, 28–29; physiographic and natural setting, 8–10; Rock Creek Park, 9, 12, 206–207; September birding walk, 73–77; weather and climate, 3–7, 10, 154–158
Washington, George, 11–12, 83, 195
Waterthrush, Louisiana, 206
Waxwing, Cedar, 134
weather and bird migration, 230–231, 233
Westmoreland State Park, Virginia, 196–197
West Virginia: black bears, 27; Canaan Valley, 152–154; Dolly Sods (Monongahela National Forest), 27–28; Fairfax Stone (Potomac headwaters), 26; July photography weekend to Allegheny Plateau, 21–25; Silver Lake church and post office, 25
whales and whale watching, 66–68
White House Christmas Bird Count, 147–148
White Mountains, New Hampshire, 54

white-nose syndrome, 254–255
Wilcove, David, 94, 103, 149, 239–244, 264
wilding. *See* urban wilding
wildlife recovery: American Beaver, 137–138; Bald Eagle, 140; Canada Goose, 18–19, 154–156, 164–165, 230; forests, 9, 135–136; raptors, 82; White-tailed Deer, 134–136
Winchester, Virginia, 28
wind farms, 26
windows and bird deaths, 201–202
winds, regional, 141
winter (overview), 5. *See also specific months*
witch hazel, 117
Wolf, Eastern, 172
Woodcock, American, 260–261
Woodpecker, 187–188; Black-backed, 223–224; Pileated, 125, 184–185; Red-bellied, 15; Red-cockaded, 210
Wood-Pewee, Eastern, 35
Wood Ticks, 218
Woolly Bear caterpillars, 108
Wren, Winter, 104, 187, 233

yard listing, 149–150
Youghiogheny River, 25

Zusi, Richard, 244

Index | 283